On My Own Two Feet

On My Own Two Feet
The life of a mountaineer

NORMAN HARDIE

Norman Hardie [signature]

CANTERBURY UNIVERSITY PRESS

UNIVERSITY OF CANTERBURY
Te Whare Wānanga o Waitaha
CHRISTCHURCH NEW ZEALAND

First published in 2006 by
CANTERBURY UNIVERSITY PRESS
University of Canterbury
Private Bag 4800
Christchurch
NEW ZEALAND

www.cup.canterbury.ac.nz

Copyright © 2006 Norman Hardie

The moral rights of the author have been asserted.

ISBN 1-877257-47-8

A catalogue record for this book is available from
the National Library of New Zealand.

This book is copyright. Except for the purpose of fair review, no part may be stored or transmitted in any form or by any means, electronic or mechanical, including recording or storage in any information retrieval system, without permission in writing from the publishers.
No reproduction may be made, whether by photocopying or by any other means, unless a licence has been obtained from the publisher or its agent.

Editing and pre-press production by Rachel Scott

Printed through Bookbuilders, China

Canterbury University Press acknowledges generous grants
in aid of publication from
FEDERATED MOUNTAIN CLUBS OF NEW ZEALAND
and
NEW ZEALAND ALPINE CLUB

Cover photographs of Mt Sefton and of the author in Antarctica
by Colin Monteath

CONTENTS

Foreword by Sir Edmund Hillary	7
Preface	9
1. Birth of a Mountaineer	11
2. Higher Education	32
3. The La Perouse Rescue	48
4. Work by the Mountains	61
5. Passage to London	71
6. Working in London	82
7. Barun Himalayan Expedition	101
8. Private Expedition	118
9. Preparing for Kangchenjunga	128
10. Kangchenjunga	135
11. West to the Khumbu	161
12. Mapping New Ground	178
13. Back in New Zealand	183
14. The Silver Hut Expedition	192
15. Instructing in Antarctica	218
16. The Mt Rolleston Rescue	228
17. The Himalayan Trust	236
18. Mt Herschel, Antarctica	252
19. Back at Home Base	264
20. Scott Base Season	273
21. Reunions	293
Bibliography	313
Index	315

FOREWORD

Norman Hardie, a skilled mountaineer and a formidable explorer, with a small group of very competent friends, battled their way over difficult New Zealand glaciers and passes – many of which had never been traversed before. They built a reputation for surmounting challenging and remote routes.

He then moved on to the Himalayas with considerable success. His outstanding effort was the first ascent of Kangchenjunga, the third-highest mountain in the world. He is renowned for his considerable determination and refusal to accept defeat on any problem on the mountain.

He was a remarkable companion to have on a mighty climb.

Ed Hillary

Sir Edmund Hillary

PREFACE

This book arose initially from a desire to rectify omissions in the recording of some aspects of mountain exploration in the 1950s. With the encouragement of my family and my many mountaineering friends, it soon developed into an autobiography.

I give special thanks to my wife, Enid, who accompanied me on some journeys and made numerous constructive comments on the draft of my work. Colin Monteath was helpful in Antarctica, as well as in launching me back into the writing of a book after a 50-year gap. He, Jim Wilson and Ian Gardiner each checked a relevant chapter of the draft. Bill Beaven has been a regular companion in the mountains and in the business world. I discussed with him some of our earlier exploits before committing them to paper. I am grateful to Linda Harvey for some checking and much encouragement.

To Ian Gardiner again and to Peter Squires I owe 40-plus years of my life. They dragged me out unconscious from an avalanche during a tragic search operation.

Many friends have provided photographs, which are a vital part of the book. Photographs that do not carry credits are my own.

I acknowledge generous financial assistance towards publication from the New Zealand Alpine Club and the Federated Mountain Clubs of New Zealand Inc.

I am most grateful to Richard King and the staff of Canterbury University Press, to editor Rachel Scott and cartographer Tim Nolan for their professional input and support.

Birth of a Mountaineer

It had not been my intention to write about my childhood in this account of where I have been in a long life. However, so many people have asked me, 'What made you get involved with big mountaineering?' or 'Did your parents support the directions you took?' Therefore I give this summary of my background, as I see it, after the passage of 60 and more years.

My parents had farmed a small property in Otago in the South Island of New Zealand during the early 1900s. Because of their earlier isolation neither had received any secondary education – not unusual in those days. In rather depressed times they, with five small children, moved to Timaru, buying a four-acre property on the outskirts of that town. Usually my father just had part-time work, with a small income supplemented from his beehives and milk from cows on the mini-farm. Much of what we ate was grown on that land.

I was born in Timaru at the end of 1924. The complete family had five girls and three boys. Before the age of two I had double pneumonia and for some days, I've been told, I drifted in and out of consciousness. Several times a day I had hot packs of antiphlogistene placed on my chest inside a tight wrapper. This is apparently a type of heat-retaining muck not now used. It was meant to be able to draw out congestion from the lungs. On one occasion, when the wrappings were removed, large areas of burnt skin also lifted. The resulting extensive scars are still with me, now partly hidden by a thin coating of hair, but in childhood they were a source of great embarrassment and stares from my peers. During my early years I hated taking off my shirt in sight of others.

When I was eight my brother Jim, aged 17, died of rheumatic fever, allegedly brought on by an earlier chilling at a badly organised scout camp. One of the results of the shock to the family was that I became the one to protect. If I coughed or wheezed I was kept away from school. At the beginning of high school my mother encouraged our doctor to certify that I was not strong enough to play rugby or cricket. For years I accepted that I must be a weakling. My older sisters took major parts in my upbringing, until two of them, in their late teens, left to undertake nursing training. I became very close to the three remaining sisters.

My parents were from strict Presbyterian stock, with my mother in particular believing in the literal truth of everything in the Bible. For us, Sunday attendance at church and Bible classes was compulsory and at various stages most of us sang in the church choir. Mother inflicted on us a weekly written biblical quiz, published in the Presbyterian magazine *The Outlook*. They were known as the OKPs – the 'Outlook Knots and Puzzles'. These were meant to instil an in-depth knowledge of the Bible, and to our mother they took priority over school homework. Liquor was banned from our house, and by the age of 12 most of us had signed The Pledge. I did have some sympathy for my mother. She had a hard struggle bringing up a large family during the Depression.

In spite of my 'weakness' I was milking the cows and assisting my father with the bees by the age of 13. From these unpaid tasks I learned a lot, and I still have one beehive. My father and brother Jack were very good rifle shots and I was frequently away with them, shooting rabbits and sometimes wallabies. Our garage would often have scores of rabbit skins drying for the next skin sale. We saw much of the delightful South Canterbury foothills and I, too, soon became proficient with rifle and skinning knife. My father was also accomplished at fishing with a line and sinker. We spent hundreds of hours in various family combinations, on the furthest wharves and breakwaters of Timaru Harbour. Our efforts were usually highly successful. My father's parents had come from a long line of seafarers in Scotland and he inherited an

Birth of a Mountaineer

affinity for the large oceans. His ability to fix almost anything, with a limited range of tools, always amazed me. I tried hard to follow his example.

During my third year at Timaru Boys' High School I grew several inches taller and found the internal motivation to do homework. I did manage to shake off the dreaded burden of OKPs, assisted by my close association with a neighbour, whose son was brilliant at all aspects of school life. This disappointed my mother, but gradually she accepted my wishes.

As I had been away from school sports for three years I was reluctant to join the established teams and their coaches. Instead I adopted isolated outdoor entertainment, particularly long-distance solo bicycle riding. At the end of my third school year I rode to Otekaieke, Moa Creek via Danseys Pass, near Alexandra, in Central Otago, next lap to Tuapeka, then Dunedin and home to Timaru, some 800 kilometres. The bike had no gears and the only bitumen road was the Dunedin main highway. There were many other big rides, one of the more significant being one to the Hermitage, Mt Cook, and a one-hour walk up one of the tracks. This made a great impression and I was determined to return.

I received a good grounding in classical music. My brother Jack and sister Gladys had singing lessons from a former operatic soprano, Mrs Tait. They sang by the piano in the room where I persevered with homework. From their practising I gained wonderful introductions to Handel oratorios, Schubert songs, Donizetti, Puccini and, most of all, Mozart. I can still quote more of the Bible from oratorios than I ever absorbed from the compulsory OKPs.

I played a cornet in the high-quality school band, but not particularly well, as I seldom practised. The instrument made such a noise that it could be heard by neighbours as well as by my family. Their comments, meant to be friendly, were generally a source of mortification to me. However, two benefits were that I learned sight reading of music and the feeling of working in a well-disciplined team.

In the late 1930s my parents became involved with the British Israel organisation (BI), which claims that Americans and British (with Jews a close second) are the chosen people of God. With the beginning of the Second World War, BI had a great boost – among the British, anyway. Books and magazines on that subject were always in the house and I was pressed to read them. New interpretations of various parts of the Bible – the Prophets and Revelations – were distorted into the twentieth century. To the believers, the second coming of Christ and Armageddon were just around the corner. During the war at least, my mother thought the world would soon end. To me, this very odd stuff was most disturbing at that impressionable age. However, I must record that 10 and more years later, when we had all spread out and blossomed, she never mentioned the BI organisation and generally rejoiced in the progress each of us had made. But she never understood my love of mountaineering. My youngest sister, Carol, alone in the family nest for five years, did not have to sustain as many religious pressures as were applied to her older siblings. I was very close to Carol.

Very little of this attempted indoctrination from home made a permanent impression on me. The staff at Timaru Boys' High were an excellent straightforward team who were keeping their pupils as far as possible in touch with the developing scientific world. However, the religious background I received has resulted in one of my favourite modern reading topics being the origins of religions in relation to recent archaeological discoveries in the Mediterranean.

Soon after war started my brother Jack applied for aircrew in the Royal New Zealand Air Force. As training facilities and aircraft were scarce, he was told there would be nearly a year of waiting. For a while he worked on a farm and then he spent some six months as a deer culler in South Westland, mainly in the remote Landsborough Valley. He was highly successful at this work and brought back great tales of the country and his experiences. Thus began a fascination with this valley, which drew me to it 10 times, and I still have some contact with projects in that area.

Birth of a Mountaineer

On 7 December 1941 Japan entered the war. University Entrance examinations began two days later. On the day they concluded I went by bus from Christchurch to the Boyle base camp beside the new Lewis Pass highway, travelling past vast braided riverbeds and steep bush-clad mountain slopes, far beyond signs of habitation. This Lewis link to Westland had been completed in 1937. I had with me my brother's pack, rifle and sleeping bag, heavy new boots and very few other items.

The 'camp', a single-room hut still standing in 2006, was securely locked when I arrived. Soon two short, elderly ruffians and a spaniel bitch emerged from the beech forest, looked me over, grunted and opened the door. Their mail had arrived in a bag that had disgorged with me from the weekly bus. There were two items in the mail. The first was a racing paper with lists of horse performances for the previous month and details of the next month's races. After they filled in betting forms they put them in the mailbag for the bus driver to collect on his return journey next day.

Then they looked at the second item. It was a short note from the Internal Affairs Department advising that a new man would be arriving on the bus – no name, age nor instructions. This was me. Jack McNair was one of the pair. He had shot for the department from 1930 when 'culling' operations began. I later worked out his age – 59 that year. In the 1970s, each time I saw the grizzly BBC Steptoe character I thought of Jack McNair. I soon found that his bandy legs had long since stopped him going any distance uphill. He shot around the river flats on days when the sun shone.

The other man was Vic Keen, who had been shooting for about three years, in mostly fairly easy country. In age, stature and interests he was very like Jack. He was not a brilliant shooter, frequently hitting a deer in the lungs or belly. The reason for his dog soon became apparent. It was an expert at silently following bloody trails at Vic's pace, allowing him the chance to apply a second shot.

They looked over my gear, which was quite good. My brother had shot in harder country than this Boyle block. I had his best wishes and the benefit of his advice. By now he was at the Wigram air base, training to be a pilot. Vic put up a target about a hundred metres away and asked me to fire three shots. I had frequently used a .22 rifle but never a .303. The kick and noise of my first effort put me in the corner of the target, but the next two were reasonably central. There was a grunt and, 'You'll come right.'

Several species of deer had been released in New Zealand between 1851 and 1922. They spread rapidly in this land of good feed and no predators. For much of this time they were protected and the few overseas hunters who pursued them were looking for male trophies only, so the breeding numbers were not reduced. Eventually, after years of reports and discussions, it was decided to remove the restrictions on shooting deer. Some numbers were being reduced adjacent to farms and easy-access roads but in the remote high country the situation was rapidly reaching a crisis situation. Most inland forests, where animals tended to gather during the winter, were losing their young undergrowth. The higher tussock slopes and many of the edible alpine species were being eaten down to the state where they no longer provided erosion protection. Both tahr and chamois had also been introduced to New Zealand as trophy hunting animals. Goats and pigs had escaped from farms. They all added to the erosion problems higher up the mountains.

The government 'cullers' were meant to thin out the big numbers in the immense expanse of forested mountain country. Culling infers selected shooting of perhaps old, injured or even breeding animals, but from the outset there was no type of selection. The policy was to shoot every possible animal, and the payment was the same for any animal killed.

Each man was paid a basic minimal wage and had to provide his own clothing, sleeping bag and rifle. Bonus payments were one shilling for each tail, with 2s 3d for each skin. Tails had to include a one-foot-long strip of skin up the backbone to ruin the skin, preventing shooters claiming two payments for one animal. For each animal killed the shooter would be entitled to three bullets. If he used more than three the cost of the surplus was deducted from bonuses.

The department provided food, which, because of the remote

situations, included no fresh vegetables and little meat. There would be occasional tins of corned beef, but generally the men ate venison. Canned peas and beans were the only vegetables, besides occasional potatoes and ageing onions. There was also a very hard biscuit, one type of cheese, plus flour, baking powder, yeast, milk powder and tins of jam. New Zealanders were rationed then for sugar, tea and butter, and we had to conform.

About once a month a packman would arrive with four big horses, bringing food supplies, ammunition and mail. He would count all the tails, record them on pay sheets, and then burn the tails. Skins would likewise be counted, then put into big bundles and strapped to the horses' pack saddles.

I had to learn to skin a deer. I had seen sheep skinned, suspended from a gallows behind a farmer's woolshed, where both the skin and the carcass were to be used. But for the cullers there were no gallows and rarely would the meat be used, apart from one or two choice cuts from a young beast. Jack McNair demonstrated on a stag. The opening knife-cuts dodged all the hard and smelly bits around its belly, and excluded half the neck and most of the legs. Then, with a boot applied firmly to any bare part, he dragged off the rather cut and grossly shortened skin.

The whole operation was accompanied by strings of oaths and almost feverish haste, the way most sheep shearers operate when picking up a blade. They perform flat out as if they always want to beat some sort of record. My bulging eyes must have expressed surprise and criticism for the speed and the waste of a quality skin. It was explained to me that we were paid by the numbers of skins, not by weight or quality. Why fill a pack with five big stinking coats? Do it this way and one can carry out seven skins for the same amount of work. Normally they would not bother to skin a stag unless it was near the path of an incoming field officer. The hinds and yearlings are easier to skin and lighter to carry.

Another stag was on the ground and now it was my turn. I attacked it with vigour but took twice as long as Jack, and I also made a few unnecessary knife-cuts. The naked beasts with great hunks of skin on them looked ghastly on the floor of the bush. I hoped the forces of nature would soon remove them.

'Don't worry about that,' I was told. 'There are a few wild pigs about. They and the blowflies will have it all tidy again next week.'

The St Andrews hut, up the river from the Boyle base where we three were living, was made from corrugated iron rescued from the burnt-out remains of the house allegedly used by a French group during the previous century. They were supposed to have grazed cows and goats on the river flats. Much of the cheese they made was carried through to Kiwi Saddle and the Hurunui for the miners walking to the West Coast. This was what I was told, but there is now some doubt about this 'legend'.

The hut had few windows, no reading material and at night was lit by candles. We were not supplied with insect repellent or flyspray, so we were plagued by hordes of blowflies and sandflies. Skins and tails were dried under a large tent fly just 20 metres from the hut and these attracted clouds of eager bluebottle flies. Food scraps, tins and bones littered the ground and no attempts had been made to bury them. My comments brought the statement that the dog would uncover them if buried, so why bother. As there was no shortage of firewood, a fire was kept going all the time we were in residence, and the smoke helped to keep the sandflies back three or four metres. In the hut there was no plumbing of any variety, but there was a small stream nearby where one could wash the body and from time to time attempt to remove the smoke smells and deer blood from one's long-suffering clothing.

On the third day we were walking cautiously around the bush edge when Vic said, 'Those flappers will be nearly right.'

'I could do with a meat change,' said Jack.

Around the next corner they suddenly dropped firearms and packs and rushed across the tussocks to a group of nearly full-grown paradise ducklings. The parents flew off a few metres and put up a noisy display of pretending they had broken wings, to divert us away, while their young scattered towards the nearest water or protecting tussock. Vic caught one, but bandy Jack was too slow. He yelled at me to get into action. On legs alone the ducklings could not run fast, but with wildly flapping wings they made considerable zigzag progress. I did run one down and that

Birth of a Mountaineer

afternoon I was required to pluck and clean them. I confess they were delicious.

My mates were very dull cooks on the whole. Although they had yeast, they never made interesting bread. Instead they stirred big scone mixtures of flour and baking powder and cooked them in a circular cast-iron camp oven over the wood fire to make an uninteresting loaf. Venison and onions were always fried. From the limited ingredients I did introduce stews.

With the aid of Vic's binoculars I had seen that there were small groups of deer above the top bushline. Upon my suggestion that we should try shooting up there, Jack said his legs were not capable of climbing but Vic could go with me. Next morning Vic and I started up in the bush, which was not hard going, the deer having cleared most of the undergrowth years ago. Within 10 minutes Vic said he would stop for a smoke and would try stalking at the level he had reached. His only advice was: 'Don't try skinning a deer on the loose scree slopes.'

I went on for an hour and emerged into beautiful open country, with a panorama that extended for about 50 kilometres in two directions. The vegetation was suddenly completely different – flax, snowgrass, dracophyllum, daisies and tussocks, all severely nibbled. I stopped for a long time before thinking about deer. It was my first introduction to the delights of travel above forest level, which I have been able subsequently to achieve in some 10 countries.

In this more open territory it was difficult to get within range of one's prey. At the first shot all deer in the big basins would run for the bush or vanish over the next spur, and they would take two or three hours to settle down again. During the heat of the day most of them were lying in the shade near the top edge of the bush.

I had some successes and was soon bringing in more tails than the other two were getting down on the flats. Jack's advice about skin size and numbers was immediately confirmed, particularly when working in the steep country far from the skin-drying shelter. It soon struck me how much better it would be to have a friend of similar fitness who could be walking along the shelter of the bush edge while I went from ridge to ridge above him. The daily tallies would be much higher and the situation would be improved for our mutual safety.

Rainy days were depressing. Cold and clouds on the tops would make the climb through the bush not worth the effort. In the hut, with nothing to read, the conversation from the other two was mainly about their exploits in Christchurch, where they could blow away three months' earnings in a week, on beer and race meetings. They expressed no interest in the state of the war, nor my views on anything that concerned me. After a lengthy sleep I would repair clothes, get washing up to date and walk off for an hour or two in the dripping forest.

The bus went past the Boyle base every Friday. On the third Friday of my stay Jack went out for the day to meet the bus. He brought back the racing page of the *Press*, three letters for me and one for him. The latter was from Jack Mead, the Internal Affairs field officer for the Canterbury area.

He read out: 'If Hardie is OK as a shooter he is to join a man in the Lake Sumner area. Tell him to be at the Boyle next Wednesday morning with his gear. I will drive him through to his new position.'

Jack, with his normal sneer, said, 'You're off to live with Dirty Dick.'

Both roared with laughter.

I sought enlightenment but obtained little more than that the man was Dick Morris, aged early forties, with a great shooting block and good huts, but no one would stay with him for more than a week. I did not know how much to believe, but I would at least like to be away from these two. However, I might find myself shooting the tops alone again if Dick was too disagreeable.

The field officer, with a modern Ford light truck, met me at the appointed place. Soon I began enquiries about Dick, and I told Jack Mead the little I had heard.

'You'll have one night at his base and then you go on to the South Hurunui. Dick is all right. He just likes being alone. You're to join Jock Findlater, who is a really fine man. It would be good to have some co-operation with Dick, on the next block. Find out when he will shoot the tops on his south boundary, so you and Jock work the range on your side at the same time, catching those that try to cross the passes.' He added that Dick had been allocated a mate for the season, but as there were three huts in the area, they had chosen to operate separately. This other was Lance Boyd, who became a field officer in the department two years later.

We collected supplies at Hawarden and drove through the enchanting, winding route to Lake Station, and then on to the large, comfortable hut beyond the head of Lake Sumner. I have been there many times in recent years. The country is just as beautiful as it was in 1941, but the road is now worse. The landowners are doing their utmost to make it difficult for uninvited visitors to enter the area, and I have some sympathy for them.

Jack Mead gave me a copy of a new instruction sheet for his shooters. From memory, most of it was related to safety matters, particularly avoiding the shooting of one's mate. There were strict statements about when one could have a bullet in the barrel, the use of the safety catch, and how one was never to cock the trigger until the target was identified. Never point a rifle towards a person, even if you are just cleaning it, or performing for a photographer. These basic rules still seem to be broken each year, but they very rarely were by government shooters.

Late in the afternoon I met Dick Morris. He was short, with dark curly hair, and wiry in stature. The hut was a public one, available for trampers, but his gear was spread all over table, bunks and benches. He and Jack both went to the river with rods, and I followed, empty-handed. Both appeared competent and both caught fine trout, with Dick being more successful, probably through knowing the pools and the food of the local fish. They were using worms or beetles on their hooks. Back at the hut, while Jack cleaned and wrapped his fish for taking to Christchurch next day, Dick and I cooked fish and real vegetables, bought that day in Hawarden.

In the morning Jack gave me lengthy instructions on how to find Jock Findlater's base. As in the Boyle, no one had a map. 'Climb up that hill, veering a little left. See a small lake, called Mason. Go to where its outlet meets the South Hurunui, ford it and walk south-west two miles. The hut is hidden in the bush.'

I have often wondered about his faith in my solo navigation that day, including the river crossing. I was a lad of 16. I did make it. Sixteen years later, in 1958, I climbed up the same slopes to Lake Mason with my wife, Enid, and our friend from Scotland, Liz Sutherland. It was very hot and I carried a fly rod this time. In that year flights to Antarctica had just begun and there were frequent delays of several days, awaiting ideal weather. Hence there were many Americans about in various parts of Canterbury.

We three reached the lovely little lake. Enid asked where I would fish. I chose a place and I headed that way. They went in the opposite direction. The air was still, with perfect reflection across the surface of the water, and no sound except from an occasional bird. Suddenly, from the far side of the lake, about a kilometre away, came an American voice, 'Hank, the girls have got their shirts off.' I knew they would have heard and taken appropriate action.

Then there was the boom of a big rifle, larger than the .303 I by now knew so well. Another boom, a long pause, three more booms. A new voice called: 'Did you get it, Mike?'

'Yep.'

'What was it?'

'I think it's a sparrow.'

I thought more likely a bellbird, as this was far from sparrow country.

※

I did locate Jock and his hut, which was fortunately better than others I had seen. He was a Scotsman who had spent many years in the British Indian army, mainly in the North-west Frontier. He had been alone for a month and was pleased to see me. He had tried shooting with Dick over the hill, but they had had many differences.

The hut had one big room, an open fireplace, one small window, corrugated-iron walls and timber framing from an old house that had been on the site. Nearby was a small stream beside unpruned gooseberry bushes. Rundown sheep yards were not far away, with the usual fly and timber rails for a skin shelter. High above were large beech trees where Jock had installed two pulleys, which made an incredible difference to our lifestyle. One pulley supported a rope and a meat safe for holding butter, small meat pieces and any leftovers worth keeping. On the other was a sack that held venison legs being allowed to mature and soften. They were well above blowfly level and relatively cool inside the forest canopy. These simple innovations made the camp less smelly and the food more varied.

We agreed about shooting methods and generally went out together to the slopes above the bushline. Sometimes we carried up a minimal camp and stayed for a night, thus putting us among the animals as they emerged for their morning grazing. From these high sites I was able to look across to the Mt White country and beyond to the peaks of Arthur's Pass, which involved me so much in later years.

During one of these higher excursions we missed the packman, who had come in an unusual way and had bypassed our mail depot. He left supplies, took our skins but left no mail. Again, we had little to read but at least we had reasonable conversations for a time. We did not bother with ducks and trout, but an occasional wild pig added variety to the menu. In early 1942 we saw no chamois in the South Hurunui, but it seems they arrived in the headwaters just a few years later.

Jock knew a lot about the early European history of the region. At the head of the North Branch is Harper Pass, which was the main route to the Westland goldmines until the Arthur's Pass route was opened in 1864. In the 1930s four good huts were built on the Harper route, to encourage trampers to try that crossing, and Dick Morris occupied one of these huts. Access to the North Hurunui was not difficult from the Lewis Pass road, coming in via the Hope Valley.

At one stage Jock suggested I walk over to see Dirty Dick, as he too called him, to encourage him to work on the slopes near our north boundary, on the Crawford Range. I went to his hut and located him down by the river. He was hospitable and talkative but he was not interested in outside news nor the state of the war. His conversation was mainly about the conservation of birds and bush and the desecration that would follow any attempt to improve the road from Hawarden to his lake hut. He was getting plenty of deer tails near his camp and did not intend climbing above the bush. He seemed to be welcoming the deer we were sending over our mutual passes, but the logistics of climbing up to the Crawford tops at a time that suited us were apparently too complicated.

I stayed one night and we dined on young duck, a subject I did not discuss. We did get on to fishing. Dick's favourite bait was the grub of the young dragonfly, available for about one month of the year, usually under rotting logs near the water's edge. For other months he used earthworms, beetles or a small range of flies. Not far away he had dammed a portion of a tributary stream, which had two beautiful trout in it. If he caught a big fish not far from his base he would run up and, if it was still alive, introduce it to his pond.

I said, 'Fish going upriver can leap over quite high barriers. Why don't these escape?'

'To get up enough speed they need a straight run of about four yards. Here they have just two,' he replied.

'How about predators, farmers' dogs or wild pigs?'

'No troubles so far. My concern is humans of the tramping kind. Fortunately they're rare these days, with the shortage of petrol and the long rough road.'

I departed in the morning, observing, as I passed, a small vegetable patch near the hut. By crossing the range well west of the Mason track I had some shooting successes. Soon I was back with Jock and our fruitful times continued.

᛫❦᛫

At the end of February the packman failed to appear a second time. At long last I was beginning to consider my future career. One day I walked down to Esk Head Station, about four hours each way, to collect mail and obtain news of the world, particularly the state of the war. What a delightful valley it is. Near the

Birth of a Mountaineer

homestead I passed a small hydro-electric installation that supplied lighting for all the buildings. The house, on a terrace high above the noisy river, was a welcome sight. The steep roof was made from thatched local snowgrass and the outer walls of rock and clay were about 60 centimetres thick. The entrance door was just 1.5 metres high.

Esk Head had for many years been managed by members of the Trumper family. Mrs Trumper gave me a welcome lunch and my mail. Among my letters was the notification of a good pass in the matriculation exams for university entrance and a letter from The Levels county civil engineer, who knew me well. He told me I was an idiot to stay shooting deer. Why not have another year at school and then try university and an engineering degree? His son Bob was doing just that. Many years later Bob Callander became a professor of civil engineering at Auckland. I had never considered this course of action. My parents would not be able to help financially. At high school in those days there had been no one who ever made suggestions about career paths.

Over the meal in the Esk Head kitchen I discussed options with my very helpful hostess. The result was that I wrote to my school in Timaru, stating I would probably return for the remainder of the year. So far I had completed a commercial course and in the sixth form I would have to begin studying drawing and physics to meet the engineering course entry requirements.

One of my lasting impressions of that house was its substantial wood-burning stove, an Esse. I was back at Esk Head 57 years later. The house still stands, now with a protection notice from the Historic Places Trust. With the stove removed and no one living in the house, there is now a dampness problem. A new homestead has been built about a hundred metres upstream, and the old Esse stove has pride of place in its giant kitchen. It is kerosene-fired and the mini-hydro scheme has gone. Power comes up from the plains in a cable.

In 2001 I was asked by the new owners of Esk Head to design a bridge on their private road, to cross the North Esk River. It had to be able to support a 'small vehicle'. There are big differences in cost between a structure for a car and one for a multi-wheeled loaded truck. I drew it for a medium-sized truck and it was built later in the year, using steel beams from a demolished Christchurch woolstore. I learned later that the owners and some fishing guides were using the bridge for access to the excellent fishing waters further upstream, providing entertainment for overseas clients. Because the North Esk frequently floods, some clients had in the past missed their vital plane connections at Christchurch airport. The bridge ensures a reliable egress route. Fish caught have to be returned immediately to the river.

Better still, the Department of Conservation staff have been working since 1995 in the South Hurunui on the attempted eradication of stoats, and these people also use the new bridge. Their programme has broadened into the reduction of possums, mice and rats using various poisons and traps. The reduction of pest numbers has been so great that increases have been obvious in the populations of kiwi and several smaller birds, from robins to parakeets.

I walked back up to Jock's camp and we discussed all the issues. With the depressing war news and his experience with the British Army, he considered hostilities would go on for a long time and I would eventually be involved. He advised that I leap into higher education and when my call-up came I would be partly qualified and would get a reasonable army job, rather than being in the trenches. Besides, the politicians were promising bursaries for returned soldiers when all this ended.

I packed up next morning and departed, travelling again past Lake Mason to Dick's hut. To my surprise Jack Mead was there again with his fishing rod. He said he had no one available to take my place as Jock's shooting partner. As he was not going to Christchurch for another day, I acted on Dick's advice and passed the day walking through the bush to Three Mile Stream. He said there was a small open flat that he visited annually and there were often half a dozen deer on it.

After about two hours I glimpsed the flat ahead. I crept to a good location and, sure enough, there were six deer visible. I shot five and struggled back with their heavy wet skins. Near the hut I saw Dick fire a shot in the water and shortly he jumped in downstream and lifted out a large stunned brown trout. They had a lot of fish and we ate well that night. I never saw Jack Mead perform this illegal act, and it was a rare action for Dick, who generally seemed more interested in his fishing rod and in wildlife than the destruction of deer.

Some 45 years later I saw an advertisement in the *Press* saying someone was writing a book about Dick Morris. Anyone who had knowledge of him was invited to contact the writer. I wrote to him and soon a man arrived at my house prepared to take notes. It seems I was one of the first he saw. As I began my narrative I mentioned the nickname 'Dirty Dick'. He bridled somewhat. When I mentioned a little about ducks and shooting fish he said I had the wrong man. He soon vanished.

In 1988 the book appeared. *A Sock in my Stew* by Robin Patterson was indeed about 'my' Dick Morris. It seems that many others had confirmed the shooters' opinions of Dick and the writer had had to acknowledge the nickname. Dick believed that a healthy body had to build up its own protective layer and there was little need for washing. He was not fussy about which camp oven was used for washing socks or making bread. When various deer parts became marketable one would see stag genitals or velvet antlers hanging from the rafters. He made useful possum traps and an unsuccessful deer trap.

Dick was also knowledgeable about the high country – its animals, birds and forests. He was a fluent talker and could go on for hours on these topics. In the long term, however, he preferred his isolation, so callers did not stay long. For some years he gave short radio talks, mainly during *Children's Hour*. On a visit to Christchurch he would record a dozen or so 10-minute sessions and then return to the hills. For a year in the latter part of the war he spread his talent for living in the bush by giving talks to various army units, and escorted recruits into the bush he knew so well. From him they gained information more relevant to jungle warfare than their past training for trenches and deserts. Several museums paid him to collect birds' eggs and skins and he trapped kea for overseas zoos.

It is alleged that Dick virtually farmed deer, perhaps spending more time watching than hunting them, and often seemed to know how many animals would be seen at a particular place. Dick also poisoned possums from time to time. Three of the book's contributors commented on his habit of chopping up his own food with the strychnine knife he used to cut up possum bait. He died at 55 from heart trouble, possibly accelerated by this unwise habit.

Jack Mead, my field officer, was also employed by the army in the latter part of the Pacific war, to train recruits for jungle living. Jack was killed in a tragic car accident, in no way his fault, not far from his home at Hawea.

The return to school in 1942 brought no great joy. Many of the more qualified staff were by then overseas and my brother had gone to England as a bomber pilot. In the May vacation I rode my bicycle to Mesopotamia Station, far up the Rangitata, for some shooting, and a few days later I had further successes at Mt Peel. With petrol rationing permitting just four gallons per month I had no chance of borrowing my parents' little car. I also took my bike from Timaru to the Bealey, in the upper Waimakariri, and shot four deer near the Jordan fan. Being very tired, I decided to go to the Cora Lynn house and ask to sleep in their shed. No one was home and the place was deserted – it looked as if no one had lived there for many years. I opened a loose window and spent a restful night, leaving next morning in a rising nor'wester. I wrote a note and locked the window. Twenty-four years later Enid and I bought that house, and owned it for 22 happy years.

I rode over Porters Pass carrying skins, a set of antlers, rifle and gear – all on a shingle road until the state highway near the Selwyn River bridge. Having a wind behind me I continued on all night, to reach Timaru just before dawn. From Cora Lynn to Timaru is about 260 kilometres.

Birth of a Mountaineer

During the August vacation a series of incidents occurred that influenced my future. I was shooting in the Cass Valley on the west side of Lake Tekapo with another school pupil, Don Webster, who was later a Mt Cook guide for a year. The weather was very cold and much snow fell. We shot a few deer and one chamois. Our base was a tiny hut at the head of the valley.

One afternoon I visited another hut 5 kilometres downstream and I was horrified to find in it two empty breakfast plates and a brief note four days old, written by a pair of mountaineers. I rushed back to Don and we decided to conclude our stay in the valley and go out to report a possible accident. On the way we entered the hut again and nothing had changed. One hour below the hut we met a search party of five coming up, as they had been told in Timaru that the climbers were overdue. The searchers asked us to accompany them back to the hut, to be cooks and general dogsbodies. The new arrivals included a local station owner, and Lyn Murray and Dan Bryant. Murray was the best teacher I ever had at school. He had a sad end some years later. Bryant was on the 1935 Mt Everest expedition, and in recent years I have been involved in researching his exploits for Tony Astill of Southampton, who has written a book on that early expedition. Each of the eight British Everest expeditions between 1924 and 1953 has now been commemorated in a book.

Lyn and Dan told us the missing men were David Jackson and Fred Tozer. Jacko was my sixth-form maths and science master. He had particularly bad eyesight and did much disconcerting blinking during a conversation. In the past he had made several mistakes in mountain route-finding. Tozer was a university student and a friend of my brother's.

We two were forbidden to leave the valley floor, considering the state of the recently fallen snow. I did not mention that I had shot the chamois on the skyline ridge some 900 metres higher than the hut. The others set off and within two hours they saw old footprints that led into a slope covered with avalanche debris. No steps emerged on the other side. They stayed three days to do some digging, and two of them climbed one of the local mountains just in case the missing men had come out of the avalanche lower down. It was a sad party that retreated down the valley.

While waiting at the hut I read a file that Tozer had left on the table. It was the draft of his article for the next *New Zealand Alpine Journal*, describing his journey over the Sierra Range and down the full length of the Landsborough Valley. This was already 'tiger country' to me, as my brother had been shooting there before joining the air force. One of Tozer's companions was Earle Riddiford, who comes into my story on many occasions. The loss of David Jackson was keenly felt at Timaru Boys' High. The two bodies were found three months later when the snow melted at the avalanche site. In later years I made many visits to the Landsborough, three of them with Riddiford.

At the end of the school year I spent the vacation as a porter at the White Star Hotel in Queenstown. This hotel and Eichardt's were then owned by the Mount Cook Company. I had to emerge at 4 a.m., light fires in the giant ovens in the kitchen, then clean up the worst of the night's booze debris, cigarettes, broken glass and vomits. I would then be off until 10 a.m., when I would wheel a barrow down the main street to Eichardt's freezer, butcher a frozen sheep carcass and bring it back, with fish or other food, to the kitchen at the Star, four blocks away. The large White Star Hotel had no freezer in 1942. Later I would be required to meet the two buses and do jobs for the drivers. The regular porter insisted on carrying the guests' bags, as it was his only chance to get tips. My engineering friend Bob Callander had a similar job at Eichardt's.

Much of the time I was at the call of the cook, a kindly, tolerant woman. She usually agreed to my requests to skip breakfast if my clean-up jobs were done and re-appear at 11 a.m. In the meantime I would bike around the lake road, shoot some goats by Moke Lake or climb Ben Lomond before rushing back.

When I left I arranged the freight of my bike to the Eglinton Public Works Department camp. Bob decided to join me. We walked the Rees, Dart, Greenstone and Routeburn Valleys and, mounting our wheels, rode to Milford Sound, which had just two caretakers for much of the war. Although the Homer Tunnel had been pierced, it was not cut to full width all the way and the road surface was broken rock. Then we rode back to Timaru, to receive at my sister Anne's house in Dunedin the horrible news that my brother was missing on operations. Jack's bomber had been shot down over Holland on the way to Düsseldorf. Although injured he was repaired successfully and spent nearly three years in a prison camp. Jack returned to New Zealand at the end of the war in Europe. He farmed in South Canterbury and Westland and is now retired in Motueka. His fascinating story is recorded in his book, *From Timaru to Stalag V111B*.

As I knew more people in Dunedin than in Christchurch I opted to spend my intermediate year at Otago University College before sitting entrance exams for my engineering degree. One could sit the entry exams in any of the four main New Zealand cities.

Student life in wartime was rather quiet and in my case made more restricted as I lived for part of the year with my older sister, Dora, and her husband, Jack Coombs, when they were first married. Another sister, Anne, was well established there, as was Gladys, who was doing nursing training. These three older sisters intended well and I did not get into any mischief. I retain fond memories of enjoying the sight of hundreds of imposing buildings. Another important memory was organ recitals by Dr Galway after church most Sunday nights, although I often skipped the actual service.

On Friday nights students could obtain access, under staff supervision, to the college's large collection of classical records, old 78s. These had been part of a Carnegie endowment. The six or so students present would agree on what was to be played. The supervisor might introduce the piece and would operate the equipment, having to turn over the records about eight times for a Beethoven symphony. This was the best part of my life in Dunedin. Apart from selecting what was to be played, none of us had any conversation. They all seemed to be about as shy as I was. Many years later I was reading a book that included a photo of the author as a student – round face with an abundance of red curly hair. Janet Frame had been one of the occasional students to the musical evenings.

TWO

Higher Education

I spent my first year as an engineering student, 1944, living at College House in Christchurch. At the time CH had about 70 male residents, 15 of whom were theological hopefuls. One was the son of a bishop and another later became a bishop. We all had to wear gowns at certain meals, or when the principal wished to see us, or when we attended the chapel. It was compulsory to appear at three or more chapel services a week. The reverend trainees conducted the services, which were dull repetitions of Anglican standard liturgy, straight out of the Prayer Book. Some attempted singing chants. Two, Philip Baker and Bob Dodgson, were exceptionally good singers. Bob also played the pedal organ very well, so I soon worked out his schedule and regularly attended his performances. He later surfaced as Robert Field-Dodgson, conductor of the highly acclaimed City Choir and a master at Christ's College.

Fees for the year had to be paid in advance, so money was a big problem, particularly as I tasted liquor for the first time and launched gently into some sort of social life.

※

There had been big changes in the deer industry. American factories wanted skins, and payment for them in Christchurch suddenly jumped from near zero to 10 shillings a pound for dry skins of any quality. As a government shooter I had been paid just 2s 3d per skin; now the going rate was about 20 times this sum.

Higher Education

I found later that linings of synthetic rubber and deer skin were being moulded around petrol tanks in military aircraft and tanks. When a non-explosive bullet passed through them the exterior linings would, in a few seconds, become self-sealing with the action of the petrol. This meant the fuel would not pour all over the vehicle motor and catch fire. New Zealand was one of the few countries where skins were available at that time.

I decided to resume shooting as often as I could during weekends. Ammunition could not be bought but I had accumulated quite a store through being given three rounds for each deer shot during the culling work. In addition, I had found two small boxes of .303 ammunition among my brother's toolboxes. It was some years later that he told me that during his pilot training he had had a live-ammunition exercise. He was in the gunner's cockpit in one plane, out over the Pacific Ocean, while another on a parallel course towed a large target. After firing most of his allotted rounds and giving the target a substantial smattering, he put 40 surplus bullets into his small bag, which fortunately fell into my curious orbit.

The rifle, which was also owned by my brother, had been twice called up for Home Guard use but I managed to hold on to it, claiming it was the basis of my livelihood. Transport was a problem, but the old gearless bike was still with me and on the rail line to Greymouth there was a daily passenger train and a slow night goods one, the 'Perishable'. This latter steam train had just one carriage and no real timetable, and it made frequent stops for shunting trucks or taking on water for its boiler. Soon I made friends with some of the drivers and was able to make arrangements to be dropped off in the freezing dark, miles from anywhere. The pick-up next night, with a load of skins, was always a source of doubt, and sometimes a lost day. The drivers received a venison leg or a bottle of beer for their troubles

As skins were paid by weight, I changed from the Jack McNair skinning methods and worked right up the neck, including much of the leg and the smelly part of the stag's belly. On one occasion, away up the Wilberforce, I met two ex-cullers, then shooting privately for the bigger rewards. In their shelter the surfaces of their deer skins felt gritty. They eventually acknowledged that when the skins were still wet they rolled them in riverbed sand to pick up more weight. They had packhorses to carry their produce out to the highway and they lightly brushed the skins down prior to their sale, so that loose sand would not drop on the buyer's scales.

A major problem was drying the skins at a city students' hostel. I erected two wires between two trees at the back of the chapel, exactly where the present entrance exists for the YMCA carpark. There were some failures caused by rain or blowflies, but the skin buyer was sometimes kind and would buy them anyway, less a deduction for the amount of drying they still had to do. The principal never found out about my enterprise but many students were aware of it.

About three months into the university year I was alone at the head of the Edwards River, in Arthur's Pass National Park, with a shooting permit. I shot four deer and wounded another. I struggled down to the Mountaineering Club's tiny shelter and found two men already in it. The building was just like a half barrel, two metres wide and just over a metre high. While struggling through cooking I realised that one of them was in the same course as me, and just as shy. His name, I discovered, was Jim McFarlane. In the morning Jim wanted to come with me to chase the wounded deer, while his father, a world expert on mayflies, searched around in the streams near the shelter. Jim and I went off, found the beast and shot some more. I showed him how to get their skins off and then saw that his carrying capacity was about equal to mine. There began a friendship that lasted until Jim's death in 1999. We became the closest of associates in the engineering profession, and also in the Himalayas. We both, much later, became National Park Board members, at different parks, and together made many new ascents of major New Zealand peaks. Jim began to shoot with me on a regular basis and, even better, he offered to dry the skins at his parents' residence, on St Andrews Hill above Christchurch. It seems the neighbours did not often complain, and Jim also had an income.

In those wartime days men could be called into the forces at the age of 20 and sent overseas at 21. If students were passing most of their examinations, in engineering or medicine, the university would appeal for their military service to be deferred. This was a great incentive to pass. There were, of course, not many male students during those years, nor many student pranks or protests. Because of the shortage of labour, summer vacations were extended by a month and all students had to be employed in some essential work.

One year I was active in the stage crew of a student revue. It ran for four nights at the Theatre Royal, and a group of us built a railcar, which had to go on and off stage during the performance. I also joined the University Tramping Club and, because of my experience, was invited onto the committee in the first term. I soon saw a great deal of Banks Peninsula and some of Arthur's Pass. With the lack of petrol, taking parties to other districts was nearly impossible.

During the first August vacation, five of the Tramping Club committee set off on a climb without inviting the general membership. This was my first venture into mountaineering. A sixth man, Bruce Banfield, was invited to come along. It emerged that he had been awarded his air force wings seven weeks previously. He was then just married and his final leave included a brief honeymoon. However, in the end he was not sent away, but kept back as an instructor for the next intake, having come top of his course. Then came another final leave and he was held back once more. When he was offered a week of further leave, his wife, so upset by all the uncertainties and traumatic farewells, agreed he should go off climbing with his friends.

We walked up the Waimakariri Valley to the Carrington Hut and climbed Mt Isobel in new, uncertain snow and marginal visibility. Then we moved to the head of the main valley and ascended Mt Rolleston in very wintery conditions and without crampons. I was unhappy with these exploits, as I had had no mountaineering tuition, whereas the others had attended formal courses. Bruce taught me a lot on this occasion, having already climbed Mt Cook. Ken Tocker, then a final-year engineering student, was club captain that year. We all discussed the position, and Ken and I decided to leave the others and proceed on more of a tramping journey.

Next day we two crossed White Col, descending in a steep straight line through knee-deep soft snow. We then went up the Wilberforce, crossed the Main Divide and struck the first road two days later at Lake Kaniere. We were mortified to discover, on reading the *Press* in Hokitika, that the others of our party had decided to follow us out one day after our departure, as they, too, had decided conditions were not safe for high climbing. However, as they descended in our footsteps below White Col, the slope avalanched and Bruce Banfield was killed. His body was not found for 16 months.

After the war ended, Bruce's brother Ambrose returned from years with the New Zealand Army. He married Bruce's widow. I saw them on several occasions in later years, at the Court Theatre and Canterbury Opera.

I began to take mountaineering seriously, reading all the instruction documents I could find and studying the 20 or so expedition-type books in the university library. The big names of the main British and German climbers of the 1930s became familiar. Of course I had no idea then that one day I would meet many of them.

⋅∥⋅

Soon the university year was ending. During the exams a small group of us in my study had too much to drink. A well-known cricketer spied my ice axe and asked how to use it. I showed him by cutting four good steps up the vertical plaster wall. On seeing the mess next morning I nailed one of my partly cured deer skins over the damage. I was not surprised, on reaching home in Timaru, to receive a letter from the principal stating that there would not be a place for me at CH the following year. In any case I wanted cheaper digs and less compulsory religion.

I thought I would never darken the steps of CH again. To my amazement I was invited onto the Board of Governors in 1966 and stayed for 22 years. By then it was no longer a theological college, and during my time on the board it admitted female students.

The engineering degree in those days required 18 months of practical work in workshops and in construction, usually not well paid. Apart from another brief government culling session in the Haast and lower Landsborough, I spent the vacations getting on with engineering, happily on the whole. Two long periods were doing surveying for the Ministry of Works on the Rangitata Diversion race. On this large irrigation and hydro-electric scheme I learned a great deal about construction and thought much about the benefits of using water from glacier feeders rather than allowing all of it to discharge to the ocean.

Early in my second year in Christchurch I saw two new students looking at the Tramping Club noticeboard and debating the merits of hockey versus tramping. I interrupted and offered my opinion. One, Enid Hurst, had played hockey at St Margaret's College. At university she continued at hockey and also tramped. Six years later we were married, at Lyminster in Sussex. The other student at the noticeboard played the violin in many orchestras, completed three degrees and her husband became professor of ancient history at Harvard. She had been Nathlie Wimset and later married Dr Ernst Badian.

Jim McFarlane had a close friend, David Hughes, who was progressing on an electrical degree. He was a good walker and skier and lived by open Quaker principles. He was invited to join us and we were together on many later ventures. Jim, David and I took several leaps from tramping into mountaineering during 1946. Early in the year, from the head of the Rakaia, we went most of the way down the bush-clad Hokitika River, where the track had not been cleared since the beginning of the war. Before reaching open country we moved inland to Frew Saddle, the Mathias, Unknown Col and the Wilberforce. Next we climbed to White Col, past where Bruce Banfield's body had been found a few months previously. That col was crossed and the route took us down the Waimakariri and up to the train at Arthur's Pass.

Inspired by that success, at the end of the year we three went up the Rakaia again, to travel south this time. We crossed a series of higher passes, involving glaciers and crevasses in conditions of poor visibility, going through Rangitata tributaries to the Godley, Murchison and Tasman Glaciers and out to the Ball Hut and the Hermitage. Although all the passes had previously been traversed by others, ours was the first linking of all, right through to the Mt Cook road.

We had previously sent some supplies and a rifle to the Hermitage. After a day of rest and organisation we set off again, carrying large packs up the Mueller Glacier and over the rarely used Fyfe Pass, where the steep, smooth rocky slabs can be difficult, particularly if they have an icy glaze. We negotiated the hazards and in the early afternoon reached the tussock gullies at the junction of the Spence and Landsborough Rivers. The Landsborough rises from a glacier near Mt Sefton and flows parallel to the Main Divide until just a few kilometres from Haast Pass. This is most unusual, as most Westland rivers drop steeply and run straight to the sea. There are no easy passes into this valley. In those days it had no huts and just one wire-cage crossing in its entire length. It is now part of a wilderness area and there are still no huts or bridges within the wilderness boundaries.

At the Spence junction we met Earle Riddiford in a party of five men who had just made the first ascent of the nearby Mt Townsend. Earle and two of his companions come regularly into my story. Bill Beaven, another engineering student, was with me on most of my subsequent climbs over many years. We share many interests and have close family contacts. His brother Don was also there. He was later a regular visitor in England, and in 1981 I joined him in a vineyard partnership. He is recognised as a world authority on the prevention and treatment of diabetes – and of many preventative procedures for other problems of the body. This group went on to make the first climb of Mt Brunner, at the beginning of the south ridge of Mt Sefton.

Jim, David and I went up the Gladiator, a magnificent viewpoint for seeing the spectacular ice cliffs of Sefton. The panorama was outstanding in all directions. Great new ridges towered up for a 300-degree view. In the gap to the north-west were the contrasting bush valleys and the far-off Tasman Sea.

Down the Landsborough we walked, following deer tracks and

consuming some of the makers. At Dechen Creek we stopped. While David had a rest day, Jim and I climbed Mt Dechen, a rise of over 2,200 metres, and the first ascent from this side. It was a long exhilarating experience on a giant glacial icecap and recognised as a major mountaineering achievement. Next day the three of us walked further down the river and climbed out over Brodrick Pass to the Huxley and Hopkins Rivers, then to the road at Lake Ohau.

Six weeks later Jim contacted me in Timaru, stating that Bill Beaven wanted to join us on our next project, hoping it would be soon. David Hughes was not available. (David appears later in this book. He was our best man, had one Himalayan visit with me and we shared many fruitful business and social occasions.)

Jim, Bill and I set off for Lake Ohau again. From the summit of Brodrick Pass we achieved a new route on Mt Strauchon. In recent years several parties have repeated that route. We descended to the Landsborough River, crossed it successfully and went up the other bush-covered side for a failure on Mt Hooker, which is the prominent peak so visible now from the Haast road. Our camp was far from our objective. Wet mist, then rain forced a retreat before midday. Camp was moved further up the main valley, aiming at another icecap climb, similar to the Dechen efforts of the previous month.

We made the first ascent of Mt Elliot, but the last 400 metres on the icecap had taken us a good six hours, struggling through a complex array of crevasses in hot, glaring conditions. The thought of descending that way was not attractive, especially considering the fragility of snow bridges late in the day and the avalanches we had heard below us during the late afternoon. Just to the north is Mt Strachan, not to be confused with Mt Strauchon across the valley. Strachan had been climbed only once, by Marie Byles, Marjorie Edgar-Jones and guides Frank Alack and Harry Ayres in 1935. As they had come up from the north, the Mueller Pass side, we felt we could safely traverse the mountain and descend the Byles route. I had read Marie's account of this climb, making it seem reasonably easy. It was not until 1982, when Mike Mahoney's book on Ayres appeared, that I found that Harry had fallen on this ridge and dragged the two women and the other guide with him. Marie Byles had not mentioned that in the *New Zealand Alpine Journal*. I believe this was the first and probably the last big fall Harry had on a mountain.

We reached the summit of Strachan at 6.15 p.m. in the knowledge that we would not get to our camp before dark. The ridge down to Mueller Pass was not too difficult but it was nearly nine o'clock when we arrived there. In a total blackout we struggled on with fading torches for two hours in difficult terrain and finally stopped for the remainder of the night with no protective cover. At the first sign of returning light we pushed on again towards our camp, cold and hungry. This was my first unintended night out on a mountain. The only other one was two years later, with the guide Harry Ayres. More of that will appear in a later chapter.

As we were within range of Mt Fettes we plodded our way up it on a fine afternoon, observing on the way how wrong the maps of the area were in those days. On the summit, under a cairn, was a cigarette tin, placed there in 1935. The tin contained the Fettes hat-band, deposited by one of the first climbers, who was an old boy of Fettes College, in Edinburgh. The second ascent was by the Byles party. Third was Tozer and Menzies. This was the Tozer who died with David Jackson under an avalanche in 1942. We were the fourth party on Fettes.

We departed from the Landsborough via Mueller Pass, and on the way shot several deer. Their wet skins were a burden but their value more than covered the expenses of the journey, in spite of the falling skin prices. However, we were a week late for the beginning of our final year of university studies.

Writing about Mt Strachan reminds me that I stood on its summit 25 years later, to the day. In 1972 Earle Riddiford had been pestering Bill Beaven to organise another enterprising adventure to – somewhere. Bill was now in a managerial position with the family firm, Andrews and Beaven, and it had its troubles. He, like me, was aware that Earle's health had declined and that carrying a big pack up a Westland valley was out of the question for him. But he was persistent, as always, and I decided to arrange a project and use a helicopter for the initial hard part.

Higher Education

I invited Brian Hearfield and Bob Cawley to make up a foursome. Brian had already led an Andes expedition, and Bob an Antarctic one. With nine days' provisions we were landed early one morning on Mueller Pass. We comfortably ascended the long ridge to the top of Strachan and obtained inspirational views from the summit. It was Earle's last substantial climb, although he did later succeed on the lesser Mt Rolleston and Avalanche Peak, near Arthur's Pass.

Our quartet descended to the Landsborough floor and very slowly went up the valley, in fast-recovering beech forest with no tracks. With the availability of helicopters in the last 20 years, deer had been almost eliminated and the young forest seedlings were surviving. We saw kea but not one deer. Initially, animals had been shot on the ground and lifted out for their meat to support a profitable export market. A few years later controlled deer farming took root, out in the foothills. Live animals were caught and lifted to fenced paddocks, and kept for their meat and various by-products, which were sold to overseas buyers.

I located the giant erratic rock that years ago had given us partial shelter near the Spence junction. When the camp was established, Earle walked away behind some bushes carrying the toilet roll. Just after his return Brian shouted: 'Look, a fly-past for the return of the Earl of Landsborough!' A kea flew past our camp with a square of toilet paper caught in its claws. It landed nearby, amid howls of laughter.

In the next few days we crossed Douglas Pass and went out to the Karangarua River and my car on the West Coast road. It had been hard work but rejuvenating, for me anyway. The company had been good and it was an eye-opener to see the changes in the forests after the departure of deer and chamois.

·||·

Jim McFarlane and I were both on the University Tramping Club committee, but we found that by our final university year we were more concerned with bigger mountaineering, and thinking about climbing in the Himalayas. Also, with the end of the war the market for deer skins had collapsed. By then I was hopeful that I would complete my degree and was fortunate in having a generous friend who paid my final year's fees and living costs. These debts took three years to pay back, meaning that when my first chance came to go to the Himalayas, I could make only a minor contribution, which was one of my reasons for declining. Sponsorship for mountain climbing was unknown in those years.

At the beginning of that final university year Bill Packard invited me to join a newly formed group to live in the top floor of an old house in Merivale, Christchurch. We were four men and two women, in 1947 the first mixed flat at a New Zealand university. All were final-year students, two of whom had been with military services. All were keen to work and had outdoor interests. Five had strong classical music tastes, assisted by a collection of recordings of Mozart, Beethoven, Brahms and others. Enid lived less than a mile away and she became a frequent visitor, especially when her friendship with Geraldine Ulrich developed. Don Taylor, one of the residents, was captain of the Tramping Club that year.

One of my best memories of my university years was the broadening of my musical appreciation. Once a week there would be a free lunchtime recital, usually by local performers but on rare occasions boosted greatly by the world-standard Lili Kraus, the Boyd Neal Orchestra and others. Few overseas quality musicians had reached New Zealand during the war and they were welcomed with overwhelming enthusiasm when travel again became possible.

Earle Riddiford had returned from overseas service one year earlier and he had been climbing with Bill Beaven, as described earlier. Bill lived not far away from our flat. Earle and I were both elected to the local New Zealand Alpine Club committee, and after every meeting Earle pressed me to allow him to join our flat. This was resisted by the others for a while, but eventually he moved in, halfway through the year, squeezing into the two rooms that Bill Packard and I shared.

Earle's arrival changed things, mostly for the better. He brought a collection of Benny Goodman big-band records, but also his taste in classical music. He also had a car, a most unusual student feature in those days, and did not mind lending it to me. Most noticeable was the increase in mountaineering conversations. Earle was planning years ahead, not just in local mountains but in the Himalayas as well. He was employed by one of the larger law firms and had been progressing through his degree. He never seemed to mention his work nor do any visible study, whereas the rest of us were serious about passing exams. I sank further into debt; the four other men had salaries or ex-war bursaries.

One weekend Earle and I drove to Dunedin to see Professor Noel Odell, who held the geology chair at Otago University College for five years. Bill Tilman called him Noah, for his advanced age. He had been on several major expeditions and was the last man to see Mallory and Irvine disappearing into the clouds on Everest in 1924. He had also been to the summit of Nanda Devi. We found him supportive but surprisingly casual. He explained that there was nothing magic about the current big names in British mountaineering. In fact they were past it and no young ones were coming on, because the European Alps had been cut off to them for half a generation, through the war and subsequent cash restrictions. He advised us to use New Zealand equipment and plan for at least two expeditions. No one does well first time, he said, owing to their doubts about acclimatising to altitude, strange food and languages and adapting to the scale of the bigger peaks. This was surprising advice but proved to be substantially accurate.

At the time there were about 30 mountain books in Christchurch libraries, and Earle and I had studied them all. Now there are so many I can't keep up, even with those covering Nepal only. Earle showed many signs of not proceeding with a law career; in fact he frequently talked of obtaining a cattle property in South Westland. To me he seemed so unsuited to this that I ignored the faint possibility. I was wrong – he did go farming, only completing his degree much later. He went on three Himalayan expeditions in all.

Bill Beaven and Jim McFarlane often came to the flat and we sometimes talked about overseas ventures. Our friendships leapt ahead. All the talk in the Merivale flat – of bigger mountains in New Zealand and beyond – had to evolve into something. The 'beyond' part was outside my limited ambitions at the time. The New Zealand portion involved, in particular, new routes on Mt Sefton. Looking at this great peak from the Hermitage one sees a substantial ice shelf extending nine-tenths of the way across it, high and frequently in the clouds. From time to time avalanches break away from its frontage, so access from below is risky. There appeared to be a way to it from the left end, but it would take five or so days to reach it from the safer west side. The right end of the shelf is quite near the beginning of the hard part of the north-east ridge of Sefton, but separated from it by a frightfully steep couloir where one would expect frequent rock and ice lumps to fall at great speed. At that time the north-east ridge had been climbed just six times. Two years later I was on the seventh climb.

Earle wanted Jim, Bill and me to get on that shelf and to accomplish a brilliant new route on Sefton. He also had ideas about another new one, less exposed, but meaning a return to the Landsborough and approaching the peak through the complex Douglas River and névé. We agreed to look at Earle's first option, but on the basis of taking enough supplies to the road end so that we could undertake our favoured longer Landsborough choice.

The final engineering examination in those days consisted of a 15-day design and drawing solution for a big imaginary structure. I was in the flat alone one day, working on my design and surrounded by calculation sheets (15 years before calculators were available). Enid arrived off the Fendalton tram.

'Ballantynes is burning down,' she said. 'Look outside.'

At the window we saw a dirty haze over the sky and occasional scraps of charred paper floating down to the lawn. Ballantynes, the largest and most prestigious shop in Christchurch, and perhaps in New Zealand, was about 5 kilometres away.

'Mother and I were in the shoe department of the shop and we could see smoke coming out of the lift-shaft,' Enid told me.

Higher Education

'A male attendant said it was all under control but we did not like the smoke. We hustled out and found our way through more smoke to the goods entrance in Lichfield Street. Dreadful, isn't it?'

Just how dreadful was revealed in next morning's paper. Enid and Vonnie had had a miraculous escape and had no idea of the tragic drama occurring in the back stairs and the Colombo Street frontage. The death toll mounted to 47. Ten days later exams had finished as work began on demolishing the charred skeleton of Ballantynes. I undertook temporary employment for the contractor, Luneys. The roof and timber floors had collapsed and brick walls and buckled steel still stood hideously against the sky, the remnants of a three-storey building.

In those days there were no mobile cranes in the city, and someone was required to climb the charred stairs or temporary ladders to fix wire ropes so walls could be pulled down safely from the ground. I climbed, with a light rope in my hand, high up these walls, then hauled up steel cables and attached the necessary fixing clips. After I returned safely to ground the other employees began pulling the cables. I was amazed how far unreinforced brick walls could move before collapsing. Beaths, another shop across Colombo Street, had a top-floor restaurant and everyone rushed to look out the windows when the walls began to sway. Clambering around the awful wet debris was horrible work. Fire hoses had soaked everything and the smell of decay was always present. Particularly sad was the rear stairway, which was meant to be a fire escape. It was made of cast iron and in the extreme heat four steps had cracked and dropped. Eight bodies had been found under the stair gap. For access to some upper walls I put a scaffold plank over the gap and continued the ghastly mission.

※

Now I had some money and a three-week gap before I was to begin work for the Ministry of Works at Lake Pukaki. This was late December 1947. Jim, Bill, Earle and I left Earle's car at the end of the Mt Cook road and ascended the imposing snow face so prominent from the Hermitage. We climbed the Footstool, Sefton's northern neighbour, and next day went up to Tuckett's Col, the starting point for Earle's notion of access to the elusive ice shelf on Sefton. The intervening gully looked very daunting, with ice bullets shooting down it. These missiles developed a lot of speed as they whistled past, making a more than upsetting sound. Earle fortunately quickly gave away his plan.

We descended to the car and loaded up supplies again for another crossing of Fyfe Pass and a base in the Landsborough. Then we crossed to the next valley system and sheltered under Harper's Rock, an erratic glacial remnant perched on a gravel flat. The size of a two-storey house, it has a welcome overhang on the north side. Ours was about the tenth known visit to that special place.

Some 15 ascents of Mt Sefton had been made on the straight-forward west ridge, by climbing from the Copland Valley to the north. Those who were late on the far more difficult north-east ridge sometimes traversed to this west ridge for the long descent to the Copland huts. The south approach was untouched. We carried a tent and three days' supplies to a high site beneath Mt Thompson, climbing it for a better view of our main objective.

After a reasonable night in our lofty eyrie we looked out on a hopeful dawn. We traversed north below the Main Divide, peeped up at Mt Brunner and decided the rocks separating it from the south ridge appeared formidable. We therefore bypassed these and cramponed up a mixed snow and ice face. As always, Jim and I were together. Bill and Earle were on a separate rope, a good arrangement in a party where all have similar abilities. Generally we kept within visual and vocal range of the other pair. This meant that all had some share in route-selection decisions and avoided the slow, complex manoeuvring when too many are on a single rope. It also meant that if one pair had a safety problem there were two others available in support. We never dreamed of travelling unroped, as is so often done these days.

Suddenly we were on the untouched south ridge of Sefton, with the worst of the rocks behind us. The height was breathtaking. Just below us was the big ice shelf; far below were the Hermitage, flat river terraces and the road, years before an airfield was

Higher Education

considered down there. Our progress was steady and cautious, over an ice bump that still has no name and then up to the icy twin summits. A bite to eat, congratulations, and then we headed down the west ridge towards where it levels off at the more uniform Sierra Range.

Jim was in front, descending steep ice that he was managing quite comfortably, but in these conditions my 10-crampon spikes were not penetrating as well as his were. I had made them in a Ministry of Works workshop, from mild steel plate cut out and bent over to form the spikes. Then I had welded on hard tips and ground them to (I hoped) sharp points. I inspected Jim's bought set and decided mine had to go. Six months later I threw them from a dinghy into the depths of Lake Pukaki, not wanting anyone to inherit them and have a risky problem. I bought myself some orthodox Austrian crampons.

From this exhilarating traverse we returned to Harper's Rock, crossed to the head of the Landsborough and shot a deer for meat. Venison had been on the menu for most of the 18 days. In a short stretch of good weather we made new routes on several peaks, among them Spence, Hopkins and Burns. These are all spectacular mountains from the west (Landsborough) side and had been climbed just once, from the east.

We walked all the way down the Landsborough Valley, appreciating its brilliant topography and its isolation. One diversion was a climb to the bushline for an attempt on a new route on Mt Ward, but bad weather drove us back down. Jim and I returned 14 months later and did complete a new route on Mt Ward. At Haast Pass we located Earle's car, in good order. Bill Packard, who had never driven a car, had successfully driven it from Mount Cook. It was a low-clearance Riley with pre-selector gears, and we were surprised at its unblemished state after this trip.

I was left at Lake Pukaki to begin my first permanent employment. It was early January 1948.

THREE

The La Perouse Rescue

Lake Pukaki is one of the three large supply sources for the Waitaki River, which at that time had just one hydro-electric generation station on it, some 80 kilometres downstream from the lake. There had been almost no hydro development during the war and there was an urgent need to leap into production. A storage dam was to be constructed at Pukaki so that the station downstream could have a larger volume of water sent to it during the winter, when the glaciers at the headwaters do not discharge much melt water.

Bob Semple, Minister of Works at the time, was a great fan of the bulldozer. In the House of Representatives, promoting the notion of an earth dam at Pukaki, he said he would send several dozers to the site to push earth into the river to raise the lake. He was unaware of the need to have control gates at the bottom of the storage level, and that earth dams need quite specific non-porous materials with critical compaction techniques. A spillway is also essential in case heavy rain falls when the lake is already full.

When I arrived, the control gates had been built and excavations were in progress for the construction of the foundations of the main earth dam. I was told I would be the chief surveyor and, until the spillway began, I was to be in charge of the new roadworks. As the lake was raised, some 12 kilometres of existing road would be flooded. I was housed in a standard hut, 3 metres by 2.5 metres, like all single men on the job. It had a simple bed, a tiny stove for burning wood, a table, one chair and no insulation. However, the outlook up the lake was brilliant. The 15 single administrative staff had a cook and we lived reasonably well, especially now that wartime rationing had ended. There were about 20 married men on the site and they had three-room uninsulated dull houses and, like us, few facilities. Altogether there were about 200 men there during the three years of construction. The engineer in charge was Eddie Kalaugher, who was virtually mayor of the minute village.

A few days after my arrival a slightly better house was built for the newly arrived policeman, Ted Trappitt, who later rose quite high in the police world. Usually one bus would arrive each day from Christchurch, and half an hour before bus time Ted would appear at the main office, in civilian clothes. He studied sheets of police photographs of wanted men. As the bus door opened he frequently moved forward to grab some luckless criminal who had sought the isolation for a while of a remote construction site.

In early February 1948, a month after my arrival at Pukaki, I was suddenly involved in the La Perouse rescue.

⫯

The peaks close to Aoraki Mt Cook are named after Pacific navigators. The Aoraki part of the name was formally added in 2002. Some sea captains commemorated, such as Tasman, Drake, Torres and Magellan, preceded Cook. Hicks was one of Cook's officers and his mountain appears just beside Mt Cook. Among the later navigators were Vancouver, Dampier and La Perouse. On the ridge to La Perouse are three peaks named after British admirals Sturdee, Beattie and Jellicoe, who were not Pacific navigators. Mt Low, the last bump on the ridge below the La Perouse summit, was named after Scottish Mountaineering Club member R. S. Low, whose guided party made its first ascent in 1908.

At the beginning of 1948 Mt Cook had been climbed 74 times and La Perouse merely 12. On 6 February that year the south ridge of Mt Cook was climbed for the first time, by Ruth Adams, Edmund Hillary and guides Mick Sullivan and Harry Ayres. Through Ed's inability to obtain leave from his beekeeping at Christmas, when most amateurs are active in the mountains, he did almost all his early major climbs with guides later in the season.

On 9 February the same party set off at 4 a.m. to climb La Perouse. The normal route in those days involved walking to the head of the Hooker Glacier, then traversing the three admirals and Low and onto the final ice ridge. It is generally a long, hard snow and ice climb, with several pitches of fragile rocks at the lesser summits.

These four made good progress on a fine morning until they encountered a small ice wall on the descent of Low, towards the last col before La Perouse. Hillary and Ayres got down the wall but, having found it far from easy, they called to the second pair to divert around the end of it. Ruth and Mick cramponed to a steep slope and were working their way down it when Ruth slipped. She slid down the hard surface, passed the place where Mick was firmly placed and, to the horror of the three spectators, the rope joining them snapped in what was really not a fast fall. Ruth had slid about 20 metres, dropped over a 1.5-metre ledge and was stopped on a projecting rock, the only obstacle to prevent her dropping some 1,000 metres to the west side.

Mick had been given that rope by a client from Europe in 1938. He regarded it so highly that he had locked it away in a wardrobe at the outbreak of war, bringing it out 10 years later for the special climbs he did with Ruth Adams. Although the rope looked to be in good condition, it had probably rotted internally in the damp atmosphere of the West Coast.

The three climbers rushed to Ruth, secured her to the slope and made their assessment of the situation. She appeared to have a broken wrist, possibly a damaged back, and definitely bruising and concussion. The likely back damage meant that a stretcher would be necessary. Without assistance they could not carry her over the long, tortuous route they had ascended. In 1948 there were no helicopters in New Zealand and no climbers carried radios. Getting the news out and assembling the necessary rescue party was to be a prodigious effort. The site was a long day's walk to a telephone, and Christchurch, the nearest large centre, was a further 275 kilometres away.

Ed Hillary stayed with Ruth and spent much of the rest of the day cutting an ice cave and lining the floor with rock slabs, to give some security for the night. His patient regained consciousness but, although cheerful, was unable to walk. The two guides rushed down their ascent route to the Gardiner Hut, where Mick Sullivan picked up food, a cooker and a sleeping bag for Ruth and climbed back up to the accident scene, alone, doing the last hour in the dark. Then three sat in the cave, ate a bare meal and huddled together for the night, two without sleeping bags. In fact Mick spent the next five nights without a bag. Meanwhile Harry Ayres had run down to the Hermitage and reported to the chief guide, Mick Bowie. Immediately a call was put through to Christchurch, so that late on the night of the accident a group of strong climbers received the bad news.

Mick Bowie, who controlled the rescue operation, was approaching the end of a distinguished guiding career. He had once led an expedition to southern China and had spent several years with the New Zealand Army in Egypt and Italy. Also near the hotel were three trainee guides whom Mick brought in from other duties, and they returned in the dark. Equipment was packed for three morning air-drops to the waiting trio. Soon after dawn the guides' party set off for the climb to Gardiner Hut and then on to the accident site, which they reached as darkness was falling, on the second night after the accident. During that day a single-engine aircraft had dropped gear, with precision accuracy, to the three at the accident position. Thus the patient, Ed and Mick Sullivan received a stretcher, medical supplies, one small tent, a very long rope, one sleeping bag and some food and fuel. There was very little they could do for the day, apart from hoping Ruth's condition would improve.

On this same day the Christchurch rescue party had driven to Pukaki in the dark hours of the morning. Bill Beaven, knowing my hut, woke me vigorously at 4 a.m. 'The Mt Cook south ridge party has had a serious accident on La Perouse. Can you come?'

'I've got a busy day, but I should be able to adjust things,' I said. 'You appear quite cheerful for a search party member.'

'Well, yes. It should be interesting. If we act quickly, everyone should get off safely – and it's a good team.'

'Start without me. I'll catch you if I can.'

While Bill headed to the Hermitage in one of the Christchurch cars, I rushed to the chief engineer's house, woke him and explained the situation. He said he would drive me, but first he had to eat. I ran to the rooms of two of my workmates and handed out duties for the next few days. My climbing gear took just a minute to locate.

In this early-morning activity Ted Trappitt, the local policeman, who was not a mountaineer, was woken from his slumbers in his new house. As the police had just been given the responsibility for search and rescue operations, he announced that he was coming too. By then a good friend of mine, Ted was hard to refuse, although I feared that his large, heavy presence on a difficult long ice climb would introduce more problems.

Eddie Kalaugher drove Ted and me to the end of the road at considerable speed. For the last few kilometres La Perouse became visible – a great ice peak towering above multiple shining cliffs. Between the cliffs are steep gullies, likely to be avalanche channels. In fact avalanche cones at their bases could be seen from 20 kilometres to the south. Ted fell silent.

At the Hermitage we obtained more information. Harry Wigley, the pilot, had read a message stamped in the snow: 'OK all well'. He also reported that the three on the site were about a hundred yards on the west side of the Main Divide. Ted looked at me. 'That hundred yards is a relief. It means it is outside my area of police operations.'

I set off alone, some two hours behind the Christchurch party. I carried no food, as the advice at the hotel was that there was enough in the air-drop packages. Fortunately for me the long car journey had taken its toll on the others, so I was able to overtake them before any technical climbing began. I passed some who had turned back, having decided they were unfit for this activity, coming straight from their office desks. The remnants of the Christchurch party were scattered in pairs, with Harry Ayres at their head. He had replaced broken crampons from his run down the glacier the

The La Perouse Rescue

previous day, stolen some hours of sleep and was now on the way up again. The whole tourist operation at the Hermitage was left without guides for a week.

We were surprised to see a long line of steps cut up the face of Mt Jellicoe, not by Sturdee, the normal route. Mick Bowie had chosen a new direct approach to save time, and all of us followed his widely placed footholds in the fading light of the second day after the accident. In the darkness I was relieved to be roped to Bill Beaven, not to a heavy, unskilled policeman. We pressed slowly upwards, assisted by the light of one feeble torch. It was hard work locating the correct positions for boots and ice axes. Every few minutes we were alarmed by the whistles of rocks passing over us at cannon speed.

We were never near a shelter, and debris continued to fall. Strong words were hurled upwards during each barrage. I heard later that Mick, when leading his three trainee guides up there, had been silent most of the way but once called out: 'No bloody mistakes here.'

In those days climbers did not use safety helmets. It reminded me that three years previously I had been struck on the head by a rock, in a very exposed and remote situation. For a few minutes I was unconscious. My companions had made a brilliant recovery effort in accompanying me to a secure place, and then we retreated to the safety of a long walk along a valley floor. Those two friends were Isabel McKay and Ken Tocker, who had been with me previously and also walked with me on many later occasions. The location of that mishap is now marked on maps as 'Hardie's Gut', not at my request.

At midnight on the crest of the ridge our group of eight unrolled sleeping bags and rested until nearly daylight. Two were still on the face below us. With the weather remaining fine so far, the absence of tents and snow caves did not matter. Breakfast was a slender snack in swirling mist. We moved along the ridge, following steps cut by Mick Bowie, and at 10 a.m. we were at the accident site. For the first time I met Ed Hillary.

Thus, 48 hours after Ruth's slide, the team was fully assembled: 16 climbers and one patient. Among the climbers was Gerry Wall, who later became a member of Parliament. He was a medical student, and his patient was soon to be Dr Ruth Adams. His examination confirmed the original diagnosis by the two guides. Gerry suspected a seriously damaged back, so Ruth was put securely in the stretcher, sedated and prepared for the long journey down. We rummaged through the air-drop materials and found that Ruth would have all she was likely to need, but it was more than evident that the 16 climbers would have a hungry journey to the nearest road.

Mick Bowie had given much thought to the two known routes off the mountain. The one we could see by then, over Low, Jellicoe and Beattie, was long and steep, involving risks from further accidents with so many men moving around on rotten rock. The fragility of New Zealand's shattered greywackes is generally well known. With a cold wind coming in from the sea, it seemed that the 'admirals' route could dictate two more nights at above 2,500 metres in doubtful weather.

The alternative was to descend to the West Coast side, where the route off the mountain was technically easier, and by the second night the party would be at Gulch Creek, where a gigantic glacial erratic rock could provide shelter for many of the party. There would be alpine scrub for fuel and we would be secure, but still three days of trackless forested gorge from civilisation. In the interests of getting everyone off the mountain safely, and as fast as possible, Mick chose this second option, down to the sheltering rock and then out via the Cook River.

La Perouse at that time had been climbed only three times from the west side, but in our party was Doug Dick, who had been on one of these trips. In 1938 he had been there in a trio that included David Lewis, later known for his solo yachting and writing. For their expedition-type climb no tracks had been cut through the bush, and for 10 years no one had returned to the Cook River. Carrying a stretcher in this country would be a formidable task, but there were fewer risks of a fatality on this route.

To reach the ridge we had to carry everything upwards to about 30 metres below the summit of La Perouse. Three short vertical ice walls had to be scaled. At each of these there was a confused mess of ropes and large packs, but by early afternoon we were able to begin the slow descent to the west. Two peak-baggers wanted to go up to the summit, but Mick firmly refused.

It soon became apparent that the six – or sometimes four – who were handling the stretcher could not also carry their large packs. Nor could they be roped together to manage all the coils of slack rope on the icy ridge. On a steep slope their heads hit the pack of the man ahead, and crampon spikes tore into clothing and slack ropes. It was decided that the stretcher carriers would proceed unroped, but would hold on to its side loops at all costs. Mick, with one rope and long shaft belays, allowed the carriers to move forward in stages of some 100 metres. The non-carriers did much travelling back and forth, bringing along the gear belonging to the stretcher group.

During a cloud clearing it was comforting to hear Doug Dick explaining to Mick that the ridge ahead would be reasonable, but we would have to divert from it, towards a steep face on the right. We were to expect much loose rock below the face and then great embankments of unstable moraine. At least he knew where we were going.

For the long, steep descents Mick uncoiled the 120 metres of rope that had been dropped from the air with the other supplies. He cut out a large platform, pushed his massive ice axe down to its full length and, with this as an anchor, the carriers descended. Mick was a very big man who said little and moved with a steady strong gait. Although I had met him on many occasions I had not seen him on a mountain. Watching him establishing his anchors gave all of us the necessary confidence to face these situations not attached to normal climbing ropes. With the rope out to its full length, the operation stopped while Mick descended and cut another platform. Crevasses had to be outflanked and falling debris channels avoided. The terrain was beyond the abilities of some of the party and they descended without packs, meaning even more double travelling for those who could handle the situation.

As the light was fading we emerged onto an exposed rocky terrace at about 2,500 metres, where we stopped for the night. As each of us scratched a groove for laying out a sleeping bag, Mick came around and issued us with one slice of cold corned beef and two slices of bread. Then there followed a portion of canned fruit. There were cold pools of water close by, so the raging thirsts of the day were quenched. Several light showers fell, but there was no severe wind. I dozed off a few times and eventually I stirred in the half light with Mick's deep voice beside me. 'Wake up, Hardie. The day's half gone. The sun will burn a hole in your arse.'

I opened my eyes. The clouds were dispersing and the exposed nature of our eyrie soon became apparent. The almost totally unclimbed Balfour Range was just across the La Perouse Glacier from us. The sun later touched Tasman, Malaspina and Vancouver, just to the east. To the west, far below, the barely lit West Coast bush above the Cook River cliffs promised much gloomy struggling before the journey ended.

Ruth had been in a small tent, while the 16 rescuers were all out in the open. At one stage in the night Neil Hamilton had rolled over and committed a terrible crime – he had broken Mick Bowie's pipe. Mick, a heavy smoker, surveyed the damage as he was putting on his boots. 'I had hoped this rescue would have got through without a disaster.' Neil, the only other pipe-smoker present, donated his own Swiss treasure, which Mike puffed at each major stop.

Breakfast consisted of another slice of cold meat and two of bread, but no hot drink. Next we had to descend a long, loose rock gully, which was managed by climbers going down in pairs, using the long rope as a handrail, then scrambling clear at the bottom. Eventually the stretcher was lowered, being guided by just two men to avoid injuring the patient and the fabric.

Gerry, the doctor, did most of the attending to Ruth. She was tightly strapped with just part of her face visible. For most of the time she was sedated so there was rarely any conversation with her. Discussions about the hazards of each future section were held away from her possible range of hearing.

Before leaving the Hermitage, Mick had sent a message to people at Fox Glacier, requesting that a team cut a track through the bush for us, if we were not seen descending the slopes on the east side. He now seemed confident that the track work would have started. He stated that a strong man could struggle through in a day without a track, but there is a big difference between a man travelling alone in hard country and six men carrying a stretcher containing an injured person.

In the afternoon we carried and slid down 700 metres of rocks and snowgrass, aiming at the giant sheltering rock that had been visible most of the day. At 4 p.m. 16 tired men struggled through the first patches of alpine scrub and lowered their packs at the Gulch Creek rock. Here at last there was shelter, and with wood we soon had hot water for the first time. Great billies of tea were produced, damp gear was put out to dry and Ruth was temporarily released from the heat and cramp of the stretcher.

We were settling in for the night when we saw four men coming up the moraine that gave access to the Cook River.

'Are you carrying a body or a live patient?' was their first question.

'She's alive and not too bad, but she has to be carried all the way. Gerry says she has a damaged back.'

'Anxious relatives and hordes of reporters are down at the highway, craving news.'

The first arrivals from the west included Bruce Gillies and Earle Riddiford. They told us that several bush workers were cutting a track nearer the road and that Ruth's brothers were also walking to join us. Just a few hours away were Steve Graham, Ralph Warburton and Peter McCormack, glacier guides who would further strengthen the party.

The new arrivals emptied their token food into the joint pool. They had not been able to bring much because they carried their climbing gear, a tent and their clothing. The editor of the *New Zealand Alpine Journal* was in the party from Christchurch and he wrote in his subsequent erratic account of the rescue that the new arrivals brought up 'tons of food'. Nan Bowie unfortunately copied that piece, without comment, in her book on her husband, *Mick Bowie: The Hermitage years*.

They told us they had had no idea we would be short of supplies. The outside world apparently thought adequate food had been air-dropped with the rope and stretcher. Early next morning two of them turned around to walk to the road with the news of Ruth's state and to report that we needed more food. Bill and I, knowing Earle Riddiford was working for the Sullivans at Fox Glacier, were certain he would be released for this major event, especially as it was Mick Sullivan's rope that had started all the action. Mick worked like a tiger all the way. He fitted in with the other guides and was always helpful to the few amateurs who were out of their depth at times.

Earle's first comment was that the new track would open up some good climbing for our regular four next summer. Bill and I had already shared similar sentiments. In a quiet bedding place the three of us talked about the guides, the equipment, the people who were new to us and the work ahead. I do remember that for the first time we had seen rubber-soled climbing boots. Neil Hamilton had brought these back from Italy after the war. We decided to get some when more arrived. This was the first time Earle met Ed Hillary. Our impressions? He was fit, worked hard and clearly had a very strong friendship with his regular climbing partner, Harry Ayres. The new young trainee guides, Harry Ashurst and Jim Forsyth, also had ability.

The weather was fine and the warmth of dried bags meant we all slept well at Gulch Creek. Mick had us all stirring before daylight, with the reminder that much of the way ahead would involve fording glacier-fed streams, which increase in volume each afternoon with the melting of snow. The sooner we moved the easier progress would be. Carrying resumed, this time on the main La Perouse moraine, consisting of sharp, loose rocks forming a thin covering over hard ice.

In late morning, when the worst of the moraine was behind us, a single-engine aircraft was heard, then seen, coming up the valley. A tiny home-made parachute descended near us. Someone said, 'That doesn't look like much of a food drop.' Tied to the parachute was a handwritten note: 'Wave a parka if Ruth is safe.' We waved. The plane departed. We picked up our burdens and struggled on, still with six on the stretcher and the others relaying the carriers' packs.

Soon the plane returned, did several circuits and a package shot out from an open door. The parachute opened and dropped quickly. Two cartons were broken open and inside each was a giant fruitcake. What a joyous sight! Ruth's father owned New Zealand's largest cake bakery, Ernest Adams Ltd. The cake was carefully divided and consumed immediately.

Soon the valley closed to a steep-sided gorge and we were forced into an area of house-size, smooth, river-worn boulders, originally dumped there by the La Perouse Glacier. With the roaring river lapping their sides it was usually necessary to climb over them. At this stage we could see where the first helpers had been the previous day on their upward passage. There would seldom be 50 consecutive metres of normal stretcher-carrying route. The party had to negotiate great tree roots, hundreds of boulders, awkward bluffs and moss-covered rocks. Frequently the stretcher was pushed forwards, from hand to hand, where there was not space for men to walk together beside it.

Later that day more helpers came up the valley. They included Ruth's three brothers and some skilful bushmen who were helpful with the track cutting. Some food also arrived. The good weather held, but it still took three days from Gulch Creek to reach the road.

At one camp, in the depths of the humid rainforest, we were sitting around a fire before crawling into our sleeping bags when one mountaineer spied an axe and began to chop firewood. Immediately a tall bushman with immense arms bulging from a black singlet leapt up from among us and grabbed the axe. He took a heap of logs and laid into them with great skill, showering us with hefty chips and rapidly producing a stack of firewood. I watched in awe and one of my new associates whispered, 'He's the toughest man on the Coast – won last year's Australia and New Zealand downhand chop. No one must ever touch his axe.'

On the seventh day after the accident Ruth was finally transferred to the comfort of a car, then flown to Christchurch Hospital. She made a full recovery. She eventually completed her medical degree, set up a practice in Melbourne, married a doctor and had three children.

The rescuers and bushmen were given a great welcome at the nearest town, Fox Glacier. Like the others I had a thorough wash and a large feed.

Later I explained that I intended to walk back to the Hermitage and obtain a ride for the 60 kilometres to my work at Pukaki. This involved following the track to Welcome Flat and then crossing Copland Pass, which is some 2,100 metres high, with a short section of snow and some minor crevasses near the summit. Mick Bowie was amazed. 'The Hermitage guides have been offered a ride to Hokitika. They can get a ticket for the railcar to Christchurch and a night out there. You can come with us. If you do walk, can you please avoid the hotel? If the manager finds how you arrived he might not meet our travelling costs, expecting us to walk with you.'

Ah, but I had a plan. Enid was a student waitress at the Franz Josef Hotel, shortly to leave to go back to university. I rang her. Within minutes she and Bett Iles resigned their jobs and they joined me at Fox early next morning. I bought food and the three of us set out for Copland Pass. The weather stayed fine and we had a happy journey. Mick Sullivan and a client overtook us at Douglas Rock, so we were a strong group for the actual pass crossing.

At the Hermitage I deserted Enid and Bett and found a ride back to work, while they went to Christchurch by bus. No one at the hotel realised I had been with the guides on the rescue. Another day later I waved to the guides as they passed in their bus, when I was back supervising road construction.

FOUR

Work by the Mountains

Some two weeks later there was a call from Mick Bowie seeking assistance again. Three young women and a guide had been caught in a storm near the top of Copland Pass, in a very exposed situation on the eastern side. In just one night the three women had died, and the guide ran out to the Hermitage with the dreadful news. All five Hermitage guides went up to perform the unwelcome task of bringing out the bodies, and six of us from Pukaki went to help. We were half a day behind the guides, expecting to climb to near the pass and assist those already up there. To my surprise, at the foot of the climb we found five gloomy guides with three gruesome battered woolsacks, which had just been rolled down the slopes. It was a very silent group that made the three-hour journey to the road, carrying their ghastly burdens.

Nan Bowie's book stated that Mick's guides had to roll the bodies all the way down as the expected 'workers from Lake Pukaki dam construction camp were inexperienced'. In my group of six were two who had been guides on Copland Pass and two expert Norwegian skiers. We were accompanied by Constable Ted Trappitt. With the guides we could have reduced the anguish and actually carried the bodies.

A relative of one of the deceased came to see me and wrote a few times. He was contemplating legal action against the original guide as he was most unhappy about the bodies' recovery and the battering they had received. It was very sad, but I managed to convince him that prosecution would merely extend the agony.

Two weeks later Ed Hillary arrived at Pukaki, requesting a job for a few months until there was a good fall of snow. Then he would leave for some skiing. Sometimes I had him with my survey group, and at others he was working at the main dam excavation area. Together we made some pleasant outings on local mountains. Ed and I both talked of Himalayan ambitions, but they seemed a long way away in 1948, and beyond our price range. We did have two days on skis on the Ball Glacier, assisted by a towrope hauled by a Ford 10 motor. The skis had no edges and the bindings were near lethal if one had a bad fall.

One of the drivers of the Mount Cook Bus Company was a very good rugby player. For some time he had been pressing for a game against the guides, who should have been very fit. The guides could not raise a full team, but they co-opted various waiters from the hotel, the gardener and then Hillary and me. Obtaining transport was no trouble for a match against the bus company. We were delivered to the grounds at Tekapo and played a game of four short sessions. Because no one had regular jerseys there was much confusion. On the sideline were almost all the female members of the Hermitage staff, cheering loudly. There was no referee so there were many arguments about the score and the frequent infringements. A good day ended with a narrow win by the bus company and lots of beer. We were dropped off at Pukaki, then the two buses went on to the Hermitage. Ed's height and fitness made him a very useful addition to the guide's team. We wondered how the hotel guests were treated that night by the tired and inebriated staff. Ed Hillary left Pukaki after about three months on the job.

On another occasion Eddie Kalaugher drove me to Tekapo and, with that scheme's equivalent chief engineer, we looked at the tunnelling shield working in the moraine under the present Tekapo town. Power would be generated and water storage controlled through the tunnel. There were countless difficulties in drilling through the imponderables of an ancient glacial moraine. However, it was completed successfully the following year.

On the way back we stopped by Irishman Creek. My boss pointed to a dip in the ridge to the west. 'If that pass is lower than the Tekapo tunnel outlet, a water-race could run to Pukaki.'

'It looks hopeful,' I replied.

'You go ahead and employ two senior students to do a survey in the coming August holidays. I'll tell head office about it after I have their results.' The final-year students arrived. I briefed them and kept in touch with progress. From this, a few years later, came the Tekapo B power station, which takes all the Tekapo water and drops it some 140 metres to Pukaki, generating much more power than the Tekapo tunnel parent scheme.

Eddie tried me on other possibilities. 'Which West Coast rivers could come this way through a big tunnel?'

'Nearly all drop too steeply in big gorges to be able get here by gravity. Yet there's a lot of water not far away.'

'Next century, with many power stations on the Waitaki, it could even be worthwhile pumping. This is happening in a few schemes in Europe,' he said.

I told him about the Landsborough, which is the only river not running down steeply but is parallel to the Main Divide for nearly 60 kilometres. That valley was surveyed by Mueller in the late 1860s, using a compass. No levels were known in 1948 and the contour map for that part of South Westland did not appear until 1993.

There are many Westland rivers with big volumes of water. The Canterbury side is deficient in water and the situation worsens yearly. Some day there will have to be tunnels bored to replenish Canterbury storage.

Back to 1948. I often amused myself on Sundays biking up the Mt Cook road and climbing mountains on the west side, the Ben Ohau Range. On the summit of Dun Fiunary (2,500 metres) I set out some small sealed packages for receiving cosmic rays, at the request of my brother-in-law Jack Coombs, a physics lecturer at Otago University. These had to stay there for five or six weeks. I eventually climbed that mountain about 10 times – sometimes with Pukaki men, sometimes alone. One companion was Martyn Spencer, who later became a consulting engineer colleague. On one ascent I took a theodolite and I could see the Landsborough peaks over two foreground ranges and some of their spurs were visible, running down to the valley floor, which could not be seen.

On another Sunday I did the same from a summit at the head of Bush Stream. From these and careful studies of my mountaineering photographs in the Landsborough I emerged with heights that indicated a tunnel could take West Coast water from the Fettes junction to a tributary of Lake Ohau, and thence into the Waitaki system. Ed Kalaugher was impressed, but head office took no action. Their notion in those days was that there was abundant water in the Waitaki for the many more stations that might be built there in the distant future.

Eddie's father had attended the 1936 Olympic Games in Berlin. To delight his newly graduated son he brought back a latest-model German optical viewing theodolite. On arrival it was found to have a 400-degree circle, instead of the 360 degrees required in New Zealand. It was shipped back and replaced with the correct model. I did all the Pukaki work with this and it was a delight to use – far better than anything at the School of Engineering in those days.

One of the happier features of life at Pukaki was that radio reception was very good. At that time the four YC stations had separate classical programmes, all listed in the *New Zealand Listener*. I was able to select a wide range of performances and indulge more deeply my love of the major works.

Jim McFarlane worked in Timaru and I was able to entice him into joining me on some weekends, but he had a low opinion of the Ben Ohau Range. The best we did was crossing Elcho Col and making a new route on the Landsborough side of Mt Ward, the highest Main Divide peak in the area. We also managed a winter ascent of Elie de Beaumont on skis, which were taken off about 200 metres below the summit. We traversed to near the west peak of Elie, then returned to the skis. Down on the Tasman Glacier Jim fell and dropped a ski down a deep crevasse. It was just his third time on skis. Down at the Hermitage we reported the loss to the hirer, Mick Bowie. 'Don't worry,' he said. 'We've ordered skis with edges and I'll be dumping all of these.' Since the La Perouse rescue Mick and I had become quite close friends.

In December 1948 Jim, Earle, Bill and I set out for the Cook River, aiming at a number of new challenges in the highest of the

Southern Alps. We crossed Copland Pass to the West Coast again and carried food up the new Cook River track to make a depot for our future movements. Then, from the main hotel, we walked up the Fox Glacier, something rarely done these days with the introduction of ski-equipped aircraft and helicopters. A spacious snow cave was dug and we occupied it for four nights.

From the cave an entry was made into the totally untouched Balfour névé, which begins on the south-western slopes of Mt Tasman. The upper part of the glacier drops vertically nearly 700 metres over rock bluffs, and we had made an entry just above the cliffs. A crevasse-dodging ascent brought us to the Main Divide and a completely new route to the top of Silberhorn. From there it was not difficult to proceed to the top of Tasman, New Zealand's second-highest mountain.

We made some minor climbs and then carried our remaining supplies into the Balfour Valley, below the great cliffs. We climbed up the other side to cross the Balfour Range and descend into the Cook Valley near the Gulch Creek rock, where three of us had been 10 months previously on the Ruth Adams rescue. A climb of La Perouse was completed, most of the way on the route used by the stretcher party. In a short day the food depot downstream was collected. Next we tried Mt Dampier, on what would have been a spectacular new approach. However, a violent storm with near zero visibility turned us back about 150 metres from the top. On the return to the rock we found that 10 or so kea had played havoc with our supplies. Some food and films were lost, a waterproof groundsheet had many holes in it and many stitches had been picked from the ridge of the tent.

Soon the weather deteriorated again and we walked out to the road on the stretcher route. For all four of us it was a most satisfying adventure. We had not reached many summits, yet we had travelled on almost totally untouched ground, seen no other people and lived on our own resources. We saw it as great expedition-type training, avoiding operating from huts on established routes.

Out at the Fox, Geraldine Ulrich and Enid appeared in a party of five who had walked over Haast Pass, years before the road was built on that route. Without much pressure they agreed to accompany Jim and me on yet another crossing of Copland Pass, to return to our respective work locations. Once again this lovely area, with its spectacular scenery and hot springs at Welcome Flat, was a delight to everyone.

For some years I had been interested in climbing Earle's Route on Mt Cook. The name is from an English visitor in the early 1900s, not from my friend Earle Riddiford. Companions of McFarlane or Beaven quality were required for this one, but they were seldom available, because it would mean four or five days away from work. I made a tentative booking with the main climbing guide, Harry Ayres: it would be a new climb for him too. This would be the only time I engaged a guide.

In a patch of brilliant weather Harry rang my office, leaving a message to come up to the Hermitage with my gear. I found him in the bar with Bruce Gillies from Oamaru. It seemed that Harry had undertaken to guide Bruce up the north-east ridge of Mt Sefton, and I was invited. I would be with Snow Mace, another of the guides, and I would have to pay for him. Snow was in the area for a short time and had not done a major special climb, although he had been on the La Perouse rescue. This was to be his last chance for something big – he was to return to New Plymouth the following month. Neither guide had been as far as the east Sefton bivouac, above the top snowgrass level, whereas I had been there and up to Tucketts Col, only 400 metres from the top of the mountain. With some reluctance I agreed and had to give away Earle's Route. There had been just six previous ascents of this Sefton ridge.

Next morning we went up to the bivouac, and in the afternoon Harry and I ascended the complex crevassed route to below the col, under the steep part of the climb. Before dawn the following day we four were on the way, climbing in beautiful conditions, glimpsing the sun rise over the Two Thumb Range. I led Snow on one rope and we had a long wait at the col for the other pair. Bruce was very slow, but Harry said we should still continue the climb. He then led off, meaning that Snow and I had about two hours on the col. It was evident to me by this time that at least one of the ropes would have to traverse the peak, as there would be great problems with four on this loose rock in the dark, coming down the hard way. We had all previously been on the west side of Sefton, which is far easier, so the possibility of a traverse to the other side was not of great concern.

The next section is steep and on fragile rock, with sensational drops down each side of the ridge. Harry continued on, amid calls from Bruce in response to the rocks coming down from his leader, who was really doing a great job. We followed at a distance. Then Bruce was hit on the hand and the pair had to stop, which brought Harry's suggestion that we should pass him. The steep, hard buttress was further ahead, beyond two small steps. I led to the foot of the buttress.

H. E. L. Porter had made the fourth ascent of this ridge in 1926. He acknowledged the difficulties of the loose rock section but he praised the firmness of the final prow, just under the summit. We were making the seventh ascent. When we reached this very firm rock, Snow disliked its steepness, so he wanted us to cut steps around to an ice slope on the right. I knew Peter Graham and David Jackson had led this way. This was the same Jackson who had been my sixth-form master in 1942 and died in the Cass Valley. Our climbing rate slowed even further. From below, Harry called to Snow that if he wanted to experience a big climb he should lead some of it, so Snow took over this role. When Harry reached the foot of the steep but good rock he went that way, not following us.

We arrived on the summit just before 5 p.m., a few minutes behind the other rope. Mirrors flashed from the Hermitage lawn. By now it was obvious that both ropes could not descend our upward route before darkness overtook us. However, we were all happy about the reasonable route to the west, descending to the floor of the Copland Valley.

We set off at a brisk pace out on the vast Douglas névé, witnessing a brilliant sunset. Below Welcome Pass the route follows scree slopes and then snowgrass in the headwaters of Scott's Creek. By the time we reached the bushline it was totally dark. We stopped there and spent the night lying on our packs after eating the remnants of the day's lunch. We talked about the climb. Harry said that Bruce's damaged hand had slowed them down on the last rock section, but otherwise he was happy about the ascent. He criticised Snow for taking the ice bypass and not climbing that rock option.

Mike Mahoney's book about Harry Ayres, while generally an excellent appraisal of an outstanding guide, is surprisingly inaccurate on the Sefton climb. Mahoney states that Ayres took Bruce Gillies off his rope at the foot of the summit buttress, put him with me and then climbed on alone. Ayres would never have done that as a guide, nor would I have accepted Gillies in the circumstances. Mike also wrote that Ayres descended looking for us. News to me. Gillies wrote a brief, accurate account of the climb in the *NZ Alpine Journal* in 1949, in which he made no mention of unroping from Ayres. In fact he praised the final rock buttress, indicating that he did go up that way, roped to his guide. He also stated that we reached the top at about the same time. Harry never kept diaries of his climbs. Given the long time lapse between the ascent and his discussions with Mahoney, his memory may have been faulty.

At dawn, after a drink of water for breakfast, we set off down Scott's Creek. It is a long way down to the valley floor, and Bruce found it hard work – his damaged hand was giving him problems. We then went upstream, aiming, I thought, for Copland Pass. At Douglas Rock Hut we lit a fire and made tea in an old pot we found with dregs in it. This was the only 'food' we could find. To my amazement the others said we would stop for another night. It was about 3 p.m. and we had no food or sleeping bags. I left the rest and did a solo crossing over the Main Divide, reaching Hooker Hut as darkness fell. Again there was no food. I ran down the track to the Hermitage and at a late hour rang Pukaki for someone to come up for me that night.

After an enormous breakfast I was at work next day.

Over the years I went on about four more body-carries or searches led by Harry Ayres. Our relations were always good. In 1987 I was a patient in Christchurch Hospital and he came to see me – he and other supportive visitors lightened my burden. Harry was cheerful and a good friend at that time, exchanging banter with a nurse he had known from his time at Franz Josef. Three weeks later he was dead, sadly by suicide.

⁂

The big spillway contract at Pukaki was put out to tender and Williamson Construction from Christchurch won the job. They built their own camp across the river from the Ministry of Works camp. As I had to set out the initial construction pegs and supervised some of the work, I was frequently in their office.

At a stage when Williamsons were about a month behind their quoted time for progress, the local union boss told us that Bob Semple, Minister of Works, would be on the site in three weeks' time. They planned to do some great stirring for better bonuses, reduced hours and other improvements. My boss was informed by head office of the visit just five days before the event.

The big union chief from Christchurch arrived a day early and on the appointed morning six union delegates took up positions outside our office to greet the man who was sure to be on their side, with a strong Labour government firmly in power. They waited all day and the minister failed to appear. No one told us why. On the second day a smaller delegation waited.

Early on the third morning a woman from one of the sheep stations at the north-east corner of the lake rang Eddie Kalaugher to say that Semple would be on the job briefly at about 11 a.m.

Ed asked, 'Where has he been? We expected him two days ago.'

'He and Mr Williamson have been here. They shot a lot of geese and ducks.'

So Billy Williamson, the private contractor, had beaten the union to it.

Later in the morning I was in the Williamson office when the ministerial car drove past with Semple apparently asleep. I was told that at the main office he got out, shook about 20 hands, stayed about five minutes and then said he was due in Queenstown for a meeting in the afternoon.

My time at Pukaki ended soon after this, as the work was nearing completion. I had learned much about large works and become deeply involved in the whole process of the compaction and testing of materials for building an earth dam. Cyril Loveridge was the engineer handling this work and it was not for another four years, when in England, that I realised how advanced he was in this technology.

FIVE

Passage to London

In December 1949 Jim McFarlane and I were interested in doing big things at the head of the Hooker Glacier on the west side of Mt Cook. After much bad weather we arrived and excavated a substantial snow cave, right at the base of Earle's Route, near where the Empress Hut was later built.

Snow fell for two more days and it was obvious that the rocks on our preferred climb would be covered with ice, so when the weather cleared for a day we decided to try Mt Cook via a mostly snow route. After an early start we sidled across to the slopes just north of the approaches to the low peak and managed to work our way to that summit by mid-morning, much of the climb having been on snow-covered rocks. We were told later that Mick Bowie saw us there through the Hermitage telescope. A mild southerly was blowing and the snow was soft, but we decided to approach the middle peak, which has a crevasse just below it. This is where the Inglis/Doole pair, many years later, spent 13 days, caught by atrocious weather. Both were frostbitten so badly they had to have amputations and both have subsequently climbed Mt Cook. Now Inglis has climbed Cho Oyu and Everest on artificial limbs.

Ahead the soft snow had been blown clear and the surface was sastrugi ice, which in parts required step-cutting. We mounted the high summit after 2 p.m., delighted with the view but depressed by the condition of the other peaks we had fancied for the next week. Our return was by the way of our ascent, though the lower parts were rather unstable from the afternoon sun.

This was the first time anyone had gone along that top ridge twice in one day. It was on the first day of the half-century before the millennium and ours was the 77th climb of the high peak of Mt Cook. It was reached just one more time that year, with Bill Beaven in the successful party.

I was transferred to the Ministry of Works Wellington Hydro Design Office, in a big room with many contemporaries from Canterbury, by then two years ahead of me in structural design procedures. Being rather junior in the vast empire I had difficulty obtaining ears to my views on the Waitaki hydro development. In 1950 the emphasis was on more North Island (Waikato) schemes. Gilbert Natusch was a ready listener and he assured me that further South Island hydro stations, with tunnels to the West Coast would come in a few years. Five years after I left the Ministry of Works, South Island project planning leapt ahead, particularly when the technical problems of a future Cook Strait cable looked solvable. More Waitaki generators were put in place, but no tunnels yet.

Most of my work for that year was in calculations and drawings for the second penstock pipeline, which dives some 600 metres down the precipices at Cobb, inland from Takaka. Sadly, I was never sent there to obtain site information.

For a year I belonged to the Hutt Valley Tramping Club, fortunately joining an outstanding group who went on to reach many worthy posts in mountain and park administration. In the Tararuas I worked on a hut-building project and did dozens of substantial tramps, but I quickly tired of an excess of dark wet bush. I went up Ruapehu several times, being transported from Wellington, asleep, in the back of a big truck with a flapping canvas cover.

Earle Riddiford by now had dropped his job with cattle in South Westland and was back in Christchurch completing his law degree. He was definitely planning an expedition for mid-1951, probably to Garhwal in India, just west of Nepal. He asked me to attend a meeting in Christchurch with him and Bill Beaven to have discussions with F. V. Doidge, New Zealand's Minister of External Affairs in the new Sid Holland government. We wished to begin negotiations about freight, permission, Sherpa hire, inoculations and so on. Indian independence was just two years old and very few New Zealanders had been there since. Doidge was not well informed, but at least the meeting opened the way for me to push matters with one of his senior department men in Wellington. This contact was just two minutes from my office, so I was able to assist in several ways.

The expedition at this stage looked like comprising Riddiford, Beaven and me. Soon Ed Cotter joined us, then Ed Hillary and George Lowe. Harry Ayres was discussed but he could not get enough leave. During that summer the party, without me, had a climbing trip together on the north side of Elie de Beaumont.

I was by now convinced that I did not want to stay low on the ladder of hydro design and the time was ripe for overseas experience. I had paid off my university loan but there would be difficulties in making the necessary financial contribution to the Riddiford expedition. I decided to go to England, preferably by working my passage. Earle sent me a shopping list of a few minor specialist items for his expedition.

Working one's passage had become difficult. Most ships, carrying passengers and frozen meat, signed on their crews at the UK end. In the postwar years there were many desertions at the Pacific ports. Legislation was passed whereby deserters caught in New Zealand were to be taken back by the shipping company that brought them out in the first place. Thus ships' officers would not know until the hour before sailing if there were deserters from their own ship, or if the New Zealand police would appear with crew from a previous vessel.

I applied for leave without pay and vanished to the Wellington wharves in late November 1950. I had told Enid I was trying to get work on a ship. She was by now living in Kent, in England, where she shared digs with her friend Geraldine Ulrich. Both were teaching. I went to four ships in the hour before departure and lined up with a scruffy assortment of men. We were all asked if we had shipping crew documents or British passports, and those with their papers, regardless of talents, were accepted. I was declined.

The newspapers indicated that the next three ships to leave were all sailing from Auckland, so I went north by train with all my worldly goods in a kitbag and a modest suitcase. I found a temporary job at a biscuit factory just five minutes from the main overseas wharf.

From Enid I heard that she had written to the chief officer of the *Rangitiki*, Jack Guyler. This was the vessel on which she had sailed a year previously, and it was now in port. This information reached me on the day prior to its departure date.

I went to see Guyler, who told me to return with my kit at 11 a.m. next day. The biscuit factory gave me my meagre pay and soon I was walking into the ship through the crew's entrance. Fourteen men lounged about, with the purser and the chief officer standing in front of them, studying a long list. The former announced, 'We are taking on nine men. Who has a British passport?'

Six came forward and briefly showed their little books. Without any checking of their crewing talents, they were accepted.

The chief officer then asked, 'Who has black trousers?'

Three of us raised our hands. He pointed to me. 'You're a steward. Go down one deck and report to the chief steward, tourist class.'

I went down and located a vague willowy creature who wrote my name on his list. By this time it was 11.40. He told me a cabin number and where to obtain a white jacket for the journey. 'You're to be in the dining saloon at 11.55 for the first sitting of lunch at 12.00.'

'Who's to teach me what to do?'

'Just watch the others.'

Carrying suitcase and kitbag, I located the cabin and found seven men in white jackets competing to get at the two portholes, only just above water level. The wharves far above were packed with people and paper streamers were being thrown between passengers and farewellers. I did a quick search for a locker and a bunk. I was horrified to hear some of the ribald remarks one of my 'shipmates' for the journey was calling out to unknown people up on the wharf.

Back in the cabin I unpacked my dress trousers and black shoes. The others, it appeared, were all stewards in the same dining room. I followed and watched.

At about 11.58 I found table two as instructed and set it for six,

Passage to London

copying the steward at table three. The loudspeaker announced the first sitting of lunch and presently hordes lunged through the doors, with 20 or so attempting to sit at my table. Passengers had not yet been sorted into first or second sittings, nor had passengers' table numbers been decided. The chief steward tried to eject people and reduce the confusion. Eventually six sat down at my table and I gave them printed menus and took their orders. I followed other stewards through double doors and confronted the cooking and carving team – all overweight, loud and waving great knives and ladles. The ship was moving.

Somehow the meal was served and passengers were asked their preferences for first or second sittings and table numbers. When things settled down that night for dinner I observed that none of those who had survived my first efforts had applied to be at table two. I was faced with two different groups. The first sitting included a young Greek couple, with daughters aged about five and seven, who were going home, disappointed with New Zealand. After two days they stopped trying to communicate with the other couple, who were from England, also returning disgruntled. Those at the second sitting were better communicators.

The unions seemed to have the shipping company by the throat: each steward looked after just one table for six passengers, having one hour to each sitting. We were grossly underworked. For the two dining rooms I reckoned 20 stewards could have been left behind and their accommodation made available for more paying passengers.

On the first afternoon, in the cabin, the others began instructing me about afternoon tea. 'At three o'clock there will be an announcement that afternoon tea is on and we have to serve it. The officers never appear. On the first day everyone comes and they don't have to go to their normal tables. We don't either.'

'Why not?' I asked.

'The more confusion the better, because not so many come next time.'

'Confusion?'

'Yes. The only tips we get in Southampton will be from those at our regular tables. Keep away from them at afternoon tea. For the rest, put cold water in the teapot, break a few biscuits and delay the serving.'

I was amazed. 'Don't passengers complain to the chiefs?'

'They do very little about it. Passengers eat too much anyway, and have no exercise. By Panama most of them know it and they drop out of afternoon teas for good. Then we have more time off.'

Their forecasts were right. Within three days the stewards made a roster that saw most of us miss afternoon teas.

In the cabin that night I was told that on the last voyage a steward had passed on a mild passenger complaint to a chef. Two men had come around from behind the stoves, lifted the steward and held him on a hotplate for five seconds. His screams were audible in the dining saloon. He was badly burned and lay on his belly for a week. I asked if there was any punishment given to the offenders, but it seemed little could be done, with the crew being aboard for just one voyage and the unions being extremely strong in those days.

On the second day I entered the galley with orders for my table. Near the carving bench was a porthole large enough for a man to pass through it. The chef picked up about half a sheep and threw it out to sea. I said something like, 'What a waste when we are going to England where there is still meat rationing.'

'Shut up, Kiwi boy,' I was told. 'That lot in there want big slices from legs. They can't handle chops. You'll see on Christmas Day, when turkeys are cooked, everyone expects a slice of breast and a leg. Ribs and wings go out to the sharks. Now leave me alone.'

Back in Auckland I had worried about being seasick so I had purchased pills from a chemist. Five days out I found them and realised there had been no need; nor was there three weeks later, coming up the English Channel in a rolling winter storm.

Stewards and galley men ate after the second sitting of passengers. Of course the chefs put the quality food away for us, even if something was allegedly 'off' when the last passengers placed their orders. We all ate in the dining saloon, but with stewards and galley staff at separate tables. Because some of the stewards occasionally passed on complaints from diners there was frequently an undercurrent of friction between the two groups. On numerous occasions I saw beautiful slices of pork put away in a warming drawer, apparently unavailable as second helpings for my table.

In the cramped cabin were all sorts of foodstuffs, even including one of the old 70-pound bags of sugar, among crates of chocolate and rolls of cheese. It was explained to me that the crew also had access to a part of the cargo space and nearly every man had a frozen lamb carcass stored below for taking ashore at the London docks.

To the sugar owner I said, 'Your mum will be delighted to get that bag.'

'Hell, no,' he replied. 'I might give her two or three pounds. Most of us have mates in the black market who'll have lorries near the docks. We get a good price.'

I soon gathered that most crew hated this London-to-New Zealand return voyage. Wharf handling of the frozen mutton in Wellington and Auckland was deadly slow. The round trip could take a hundred days, with just two opportunities for tips, and Kiwis were poor at giving them. Calls at Panama and Curaçao were brief and crew time on land was minimal. Trans-Atlantic ships were considered the best, with fast turnarounds, better ships, generous tips and lots of opportunities for importing goodies.

Besides serving the two sittings of three meals every day, I had to clean and polish the saloon portholes, which became surprisingly dirty, even on the inside. It was quite impossible, of course, to touch the outsides when at sea.

Most afternoons I managed to get some fresh air on the tiny forward deck. (The passengers had more generous deck spaces.) It had no chairs or game space, merely some level stretches of steel plate, supporting winches, anchors and lifeboats. This refuge was under the eyes of the officers on the bridge. Very few of the crew ever emerged to this relaxing haven, but I read several books up there. The noise and poor lighting made reading in the cabin nearly impossible.

A well-remembered occasion was when we were told we would heave to next day, off Pitcairn Island. Just before dawn I went up to my favourite place, alone on the foredeck. Away ahead the steep green sides of Pitcairn rose out of a calm sea. I watched as the sun came up rapidly and the sea began to sparkle. Flying fish were leaping off the bow wave, followed by several types of seabird hoping to intercept this prey. Some of the larger birds kept station near the chefs' large porthole.

After the breakfast sittings the ship's actions changed and the throbbing from the engines ceased. Through a porthole I saw two rowboats approaching, although we seemed to be miles offshore. Pitcairn has no harbour. There were many people on board and one man was wearing a black suit. I found out later that he was to be one of our passengers, John Christian, going as far as Panama.

In those days Pitcairn had about 10 ship visits a year. With a population of only about 60 then and fewer now, and no thriving industry, the islanders have few visitors and not much outside income. With the decline of ocean liners and no airport, ship visits have reduced even further. After breakfast I made a brief visit to the deck and heard that there had been a brisk trade in hand-made souvenir items. The temporary visitors were barefoot, in an assortment of bright clothing, and mostly looking more Polynesian than European.

In my meagre baggage I had several books, mainly texts for possible civil engineering work in London. The most apparently useful one was the fat edition of seven-figure logarithms, the basis of all sorts of detailed engineering calculations. What a lot of agony was contained in those pages! Now, a few seconds on a $20 calculator will present all sorts of detailed and accurate answers to complex questions.

Among my other books was the recently published *The Kon-Tiki Expedition* by Thor Heyerdahl. On many afternoons I took this to my favourite place in the bow, read several pages and looked at that immense ocean, full of admiration for those who had intentionally crossed it in a raft made from balsawood. While admiring and envying his journey, I could not agree that the author had proved a South American origin for Polynesians. I had already been convinced by the writings of Sir Peter Buck on this matter.

Most of the stewards were hard Liverpool Irishmen, but one in my cabin was different. Geoff was slow and flabby. He was teased by the others, sent on false missions but not physically bullied.

Passage to London

Once I found him nosing in my little bookshelf, where he found a small Collins French/English dictionary. This was gold to him.

'I'm usually on the Southampton-to-Cherbourg ferry. I have a girlfriend there and she hasn't a word of English. She is beautiful. Can you teach me French?'

I attempted to explain my skimpy, unpractised knowledge of French, but Geoff would not be put off. He came up with several brief and explicit sentences that he asked me to translate. They contained many words that would not be in a school dictionary and that I had never learned. I firmly refused and he mentioned the subject just once more, when France was not far from the starboard bow, two weeks later.

⋅⫼⋅

As we approached Panama, announcements to passengers on the speaker system explained that there were two towns where people could get off the ship. There would be stops long enough for shopping, floorshows and sightseeing. The crew heard separately that some of them would be off for two hours at Panama, and some others at Colon, the other end of the canal. I had occasional glimpses through my cleaned portholes of many other vessels and exciting engineering structures. In the evening at Colon I went down the gangway, purposely keeping away from the stewards, being certain they would be up to all sorts of mischief. I wandered along two well-lit streets in my first experience of non-New Zealand: strange buildings, strong smells, heat, armed police and an exciting buzz.

Back on the *Rangitiki* I saw the steward from the table next to mine being carried unconscious onto the ship by local police. He did not appear at his table for four days. He had not been beaten up but was quite blotto from excess liquor. The chief tourist-class steward spoke to me for the second time on the voyage, asking me to serve the passengers on the absent steward's table in addition to my own. When he did reappear there was no word of thanks from him, just a belligerent enquiry as to whether passengers had tipped me for my efforts.

One evening an officer's steward came into our cabin with a

brief order: 'Hardie, report to the chief officer now.' The others chattered in near alarm, suspecting I was in some sort of deep trouble. Of course I had told no one on board of my private talk to the chief officer before embarking in Auckland.

I put on my white jacket and went into the hallowed officers' area. Jack Guyler sat me down in his office, opened a generous liquor cabinet and for half an hour we sipped and chatted, initially about the voyage 11 months ago when he had met Enid. Then he enquired about my welfare and the general 'roughs' in my cabin. Twice on each passage the chief officer and chief steward inspect every crew cabin, officially for health reasons but mainly to uncover missing stores from the ship.

Jack said that on his previous voyage he had heard, four days out, that a woman of 'flexible morals' had been induced aboard in Auckland and was in the crew's quarters. She was being shared around and making lots of money. The first full inspection failed to locate her – she was no doubt being moved ahead of the inspection pair. Next time they had an unannounced tour, with a third officer standing outside looking along the passageways. She was found curled up in a steel locker. She was secured in a medical room and put off at Panama, where she awaited the arrival of the next company ship bound for New Zealand. Back in my cabin I invented a story about the chief officer needing to check the documents of those signed on as crew in New Zealand.

There was one more stop. This was at the Dutch-administered territory of Curaçao, where the company ships refuelled and the passengers went ashore for half a day. I was on land for two hours and looked at markets and other ships. I recall a large range of liquor on display, and exotic foods and smells – it was much more like Europe than Panama had been. Liquor outlets existed in all sorts of shops. In those days in New Zealand there were rigid restrictions on the sale of liquor.

The mid-Atlantic went smoothly until breaths of winter began to show in the vicinity of the Azores. Niggles from passengers indicated a lot of boredom with the 32-day journey and so few land sightings. But the stewards began coming to life, the main topic of conversation being how to get substantial tips from their table victims. There would be occasional smiles and even attempts at obtaining second helpings from the unco-operative galley hulks. Each man worked out schemes for intercepting his target at the gangway if no payment had been made at the last meal. They discussed amounts and practised what they would say if tips were not big enough.

All this horrified me. At the end of the last meal I managed to avoid my table as soon as coffee had been served. I kept clear of the confusion at the departure gangway, much of it purposely generated by stewards trying to convince people they needed paid assistants.

After the passengers had vanished, the many 'No Entry' doors were opened for crew and it was possible to reach some of the other decks. I went out for my first glimpse of England. Visibility was less than a kilometre. Rows and rows of terraced houses with multiple chimneys discharged dark smoke, and dirty snow lay on roofs and wharves. This was Southampton: cold damp and ghastly. It was New Year's Day, 1951. Exactly a year ago I had reached the summit of Mt Cook in clear air.

The crew remained on board for going up the Channel, around into the Thames Estuary and tying up at the King George Docks. The fog was so thick we did not see the white cliffs of Dover, nor anything else of interest. I explored part of the *Rangitiki*. At the same level as my cabin I found the cheapest passenger accommodation. Six-berth cabins were the same size as the stewards had for eight men. Passengers also had much more luggage space, not to mention swimming pools and a good assortment of games facilities.

Crew members departed with hardly any spoken farewell to their mates. Most seemed preoccupied with transporting their New Zealand produce to covered lorries at the far end of the wharf.

I found the chief officer and thanked him. The purser paid me £24 for the voyage. I put away my dress trousers, returned the white steward's jacket and walked out into the cold, thick air of a London winter. I followed exit signs along a winding passage and suddenly, around a corner, there was Enid, snug in a winter coat and giving a welcoming smile.

Working in London

Geraldine and Enid's home in Sittingbourne was close to where they taught for the Kent Education Authority. I took a room in a house in Ealing and began the search for employment. Enid and I became engaged and decided to marry in late March 1951.

For many days I haunted the consulting engineers who mainly based themselves between Victoria and Westminster. Invariably it appeared that my degree meant nothing to the interviewers. Their concern was, what could I do. What jobs had I had since graduating? There were offers in the hydro-electric world, but because there were no hydro schemes contemplated in England, I would soon be sent overseas to an undeveloped country. However, Enid dreaded spending much of her life in a remote temporary construction site, such as Lake Pukaki, where I had spent two years. It was time to start again on a new career path.

Meanwhile I had heard that Bill Beaven, through pressures from his family business, would not accompany Earle Riddiford to the Himalayas. Jim McFarlane had also declined earlier. This was the last straw, on top of my impending marriage and lack of finance to pay my share of expedition costs. I bought and shipped some high-altitude stoves and other items they required and wrote an explanation to Earle in New Zealand. Enid did agree that when we became more prosperous I would go on at least two major expeditions. In those days it was generally recognised, as Professor Odell had said, that few people performed well on their first visit. There are so many new shocks, such as adjustment to altitude, the months of no outside contact, new food, bugs and long nights of sleeping on the cold earth. If I did well I just might be invited on one of the large free Himalayan attempts, but this would be impossible for a freshman. Earle went ahead on the basis of having a party of four. The others were Ed Cotter, Ed Hillary and George Lowe.

I got a job with a very large structural engineering firm, which had an office just 200 metres from Victoria Station. On the third floor I was given a drawing board in a room with 60 others. A German engineer sat at an elevated desk at the front of the room and, if any of us became involved in a conversation with a neighbour, he would peep over his glasses and soon be beside us, requesting silence and getting on with the work. I was given sheets of architects' preliminary drawings of big buildings. After screeds of engineering calculations I would then add the necessary steel on my own drawings, to make these structural concepts stand up. This involved having to tackle great volumes of the current British loading and structural codes and local bylaws. Many nights I took home these documents to study. My salary was less than I had received in New Zealand.

There were many new towns being built in diverse parts of Britain. The Labour government, just after the war, was more intent on building new houses, schools and shopping centres than in rebuilding the weed-covered gaps so visible after German bombing. Contracts were distributed to dozens of architects, and then went to engineers to provide the accompanying structural, electrical, heating and other necessary details. This should have been very satisfactory but the chiefs in my office had strange ideas. None of us ever saw the architects, nor were we encouraged to visit construction sites. Frequently there can be differing ways of putting together a complicated structure, and discussions with the architect can unravel which points are vital and which can be deviated from to provide a more economical solution. In later life I was a partner in a small Christchurch firm offering services to architects to realise their masterpieces. I tried to be certain that my juniors and the draughtsmen had regular contact with their equivalent operators in the principal's office.

From Ealing I moved to a flat between New Cross and Lewisham, mostly because it was cheap and on a bus route to Victoria. It was dreadful and I was determined to abandon it very soon. Enid gave lengthy notice to her school, but until she found where in London she would work, we held on to my hovel.

We married on 31 March 1951 at a small Saxon church in Lyminster, in sight of Arundel Castle in Sussex. The service was conducted by the Reverend Herbert Newell, a New Zealander who had been employed by the World Council of Churches in Geneva and had retired to be vicar of this small parish. His daughter Margaret was bridesmaid and David Hughes, my friend from past climbing adventures, was best man. In two days added to a long weekend we drove in a borrowed car to Cornwall, then back to London and our squalid flat.

We bought a tandem bicycle and spent several weekends touring the rolling hills of Surrey. Road surfaces were good and traffic densities were quite light. Later in the year I was given two weeks' leave during a school vacation. We trained to Edinburgh and hitchhiked around part of Scotland. We had just one contact there, a very distant relative of my mother. This fine lady was married to a man who had been a cavalry officer in the First World War and now owned a riding school. They lived well and ignored the rationing we had encountered in London. The food was so generous that Enid and I found it too much for our stomachs, having been on slender supplies for so many months. Our hosts took us to a colourful ceremony in the ruins of Arbroath Abbey, where the highlight was the appearance of 10 costumed mounts from the riding school re-enacting a slice of Scottish history. At the time the Stone of Scone was missing from Westminster and was believed to be at Arbroath, from where the English had originally lifted it. After this lightning tour I returned to London while Enid remained for the first Edinburgh Festival.

※

Bill Packard had been on H. W. Tilman's Annapurna IV expedition and had developed poliomyelitis. He was with just one Sherpa, who accomplished outstanding deeds in getting him to civilisation and then to a ship in Bombay. Because Bill was a Rhodes Scholar, the hospital at Oxford assisted him with the latest remedies. They also suggested that a long sea voyage, together with regular exercise, would help his recovery. He and Enid's friend Geraldine Ulrich became engaged and decided to marry in New Zealand, travelling both ways by ship. Before they left, Enid and I suggested we four could eventually share a big house in a better area. Three of us had spent 1947 under the same roof, with Enid less than a mile away, so it should work. We also saw it as a way to give Bill some support. He was still very thin about the shoulders and could not lift his arms above the horizontal.

We found a suitable place at Bickley in Kent, near Bromley, and were set up there when the Packards returned from New Zealand. Enid obtained a satisfactory teaching position at a school just 5 kilometres away. It was a cold, two-storey stone house of Georgian vintage on an acre of land. A glasshouse and small orchard had been damaged by a German bomb dropped on the adjacent property in 1943. I undertook the outside repairs for the first few months, while the other three made the house operate efficiently. There were six bedrooms, two stairways, a stone cellar and a garage.

The Hardies provided and cooked for one week, while the Packards washed up behind us. Next week the duties were exchanged. Many food items in England were still rationed until 1953, so considerable care had to be taken with the catering. Still, we lived very well and soon began entertaining an increasing number of friends. It was not long before most of the bedrooms had short-term occupants.

Enid's father had died in New Zealand one month after we married. Colonel Hurst had had a distinguished career as a soldier and a businessman. When we had a settled house Enid's mother, Vonnie, came to join us for a nominal 'few months'. We all got on so well that she stayed on, from July 1951 until two weeks after the coronation in June 1953.

Lloyd Evans, another New Zealand Rhodes Scholar, arrived three months before the beginning of the next Oxford term. He joined me in outside duties, our main accomplishment being the construction of a quite good grass tennis court, which was a great asset in weekends and on long summer evenings. Lloyd bought a 1932 London taxi, of the black, upright, small-window style. The driver sat in the open front, with a glass screen separating him from the passengers. Back then, once taxis were 10 years old they could not be used for their original purpose, so old models sold cheaply. Oxford undergraduates were not allowed to garage cars within 50 kilometres of their crowded city, so Lloyd kept it at our house for use on visits to Europe, but I could use it for local ventures. This was an ideal arrangement. As visitors' driving licences expired after one year in the UK, both Enid and I renewed ours in tests in the taxi, with the inspector sitting beside the driver in the luggage compartment, on a kitchen chair strapped to the handrails. However, the engine consumed large quantities of oil and its speed was modest.

With this vehicle we made many visits to the Cotswolds for the scenery and history. Soon, with the help of Lloyd, we became engrossed in brass rubbing. Armed with black cobbler's heel bore and rolls of paper, we spent many hours on church floors copying the beautiful array of early engravings. A few years later this became such a fad – in fact an industry – that many vicars locked their churches except at certain times, and requested money from those who were operating commercially. The wear on the brasses can be considerable and the numbers of people became a hindrance to the normal operation of the premises.

During Bill Packard's time at Oxford he had joined the Alpine Club and he soon became close to many of the young climbers who had big ambitions beyond the British Isles. Through Bill, I met many of these men, began attending meetings and eventually joined the club myself. The most significant of these new friends was Charles Evans, who two years later was John Hunt's deputy leader on Mt Everest. Evans turned back 95 metres below the summit, three days before Hillary and Tenzing Norgay made it. He had been on the Annapurna expedition with Bill, and stayed at our house on visits to London. I later became Charles's deputy leader in 1955 for Kangchenjunga.

Working in London

My engineering work was depressing and I could not see myself advancing far in the enormous firm that employed me. I successfully applied for a position with a smaller group, T. & C. Hawksley Consulting Engineers, and doubled my salary. It soon emerged that there were two partners, both history graduates from Cambridge with no background in engineering. One had inherited the business when he was 23, and had invited his university friend to join him. There were four draughtsmen and I found I was the only engineer. Back in the 1850s the senior partner's grandfather had designed a great number of water-supply schemes in various parts of England and he had often been paid with preferential shares in many of the operating companies. Now the firm was employed on extensions and replacements for some of these old installations. There were many good features about my situation, but it was soon clear that it would not provide a satisfactory long-term career for me.

The junior partner had been an officer in the naval reserve at the outbreak of the Second World War. He told me he had been a lieutenant commander on the battleship HMS *Hood* for some months. In May 1941 he was on the bridge heading south, well out in the North Sea. There was an escorting flotilla of destroyers and a cruiser with an admiral on board. They received word that the new German battleship *Bismarck* was in Norway and everyone was on alert. Amid some fog and a smoke-screen the admiral gave the order for the flotilla to turn around to starboard 160 degrees to go back towards base. My boss wrongly signalled 'port' to the *Hood*'s engine room. It takes a long time and a radius of several kilometres for a battleship to turn right around at speed, and it was over an hour before they joined the escorts. Back at base he was given a shore job. The following week the *Bismarck* sank the *Hood* in the strait between Iceland and Greenland. Three men survived from a crew of 1,400. The *Bismarck* was sunk the following week, also with a large loss of lives. With hindsight, the junior partner considered his mistake a brilliant stroke of fortune.

I was aware one day that the senior partner at T. & C. Hawksley was spending many hours searching for something in the basement. Eventually he produced a roll of dusty drawings and explained that he had been commissioned to design a new water-storage dam for the city of Bristol. One had been designed by his grandfather in the 1870s, in an adjacent valley, for the same water company, and he had located the old drawings. I looked at the sheets. They revealed the plans for a grand earth dam, quite large for those years and beautifully drawn but archaic in its engineering methods. Then came the surprise. The partner instructed me to tell the draughtsmen to re-draw it on the site for the new dam. The gate-control walls and spillway structures were made of stone, not reinforced concrete. The gates and the pipe exits were of riveted iron, which in 1952 should have been welded steel. I protested and informed him of the Pukaki earth dam of similar dimensions, which I had witnessed under construction. He was adamant and the drawings were issued in 1870 style.

After construction began, a royal pronouncement stated that the youthful Prince Charles was to administer the properties of the Duchy of Cornwall, and the new dam was near that territory. An instruction came to the firm along the lines that the prince was likely, in later life, to entertain his friends with fishing and shooting on his estates. The new dam must therefore have a fish ladder, so this was added to the drawings. How wrong they were about the activities of Prince Charles!

Like my previous employers, the Hawksleys did not ask their staff to visit site works. I was expecting there would be a laboratory by the foreman's office, with regular tests being done on compaction of the materials, moisture content and tests for porosity, among many other matters. After much lobbying Mr Hawksley agreed that I could visit the dam once – when it was up to about half height.

On a Friday afternoon I joined him in his yellow Rolls-Royce. It was a special design requested by his father and had a fold-down canvas hood. The evening was fine and we drove at great speed with the wind shrieking through our hair, all the way to Bristol. After a night in a flash Victorian hotel we went out to the project site, which was in a lovely quiet valley. I met the contractor and looked at his very limited antiquated equipment. There was no laboratory and no inspection system for the construction.

Earth dams must have a central impervious core of well-compacted materials that are stable and will not develop great shrinkage cracks when they become dry. Sloping shoulders go out some distance to prevent the core slumping sideways when its edges become saturated. Further out is a substantial layer of big boulders to subdue wave action during a storm.

I asked Mr Hawksley: 'How can you be sure the core materials are adequately mixed and are properly compacted?'

He leaned over, picked up some clay in one hand and squeezed it. 'If it oozes out evenly between my fingers then I know it is a well-mixed puddle clay.'

I much preferred the testing and controls we had used in New Zealand. Throughout the day I saw the contractor's foreman looking at each loaded lorry as it arrived on site, reach over and squeeze a lump of clay. I really wondered about that dam. Eighteen months later, in Nepal, I saw an article in an English magazine stating that prior to letting water into the reservoir the land to be flooded was stripped of trees and buildings. Much good topsoil was also taken for use elsewhere. During that process a considerable area of Roman ruins was found. To preserve them an earth bund, or dam, was to be built around them. So far as I know the dam has been successful and Bristol water is satisfactory. It is now a very popular fishing district.

Halfway through that afternoon Mr H politely dismissed me. I arranged a ride to Bristol in the contractor's truck and found a cheaper room for the night. After watching a performance at the Bristol Old Vic I slept well. Next morning I hitched rides to Wells, a city I had not previously visited. I looked in wonder at the beautiful cathedral, and walked around slowly, marvelling at the roof and column construction. I sat and listened to the choir for a few minutes. Nearby were three American women. A man came along to them, leaned over and stage-whispered, 'Get a move on, you dames. We have to do London this afternoon and be in Paris tomorrow.'

Hawksleys celebrated the centenary of their firm while I was in their employment. All the staff and spouses, about 20 in total, attended a delightful function in one of the private rooms at the Savoy Hotel. Each room is named after one of the Gilbert and Sullivan light operas and ours was 'The Mikado'. The most memorable part of the night, now 54 years ago, was that each course was eaten off Hawksleys' gold plate. The grandfather must have done very well with his consultancies and shares in the water boards.

The firm's office was in Great Scotland Yard, a slender street off Whitehall, and just 200 metres from Trafalgar Square. This was an excellent spot for viewing parades, protests and the general buzz of a big city. Theatres and galleries were quite near. Enid, with her masters degree in English, had broadened my tastes in the world of theatre. I did likewise for her in opera, orchestral music and recitals. Frequently in a lunch-hour I would go to a booking office when a show had just opened and purchase upper-circle cheap seats in the best positions for some six weeks ahead. We attended about three live performances each month. Many of our Old Vic attendances were with dozens of pupils from the school where Enid was teaching.

The National Gallery, on the far side of Trafalgar Square, was one of my favourite haunts, particularly when they had lunchtime mini-lectures on some of their exhibitions. The train to Bickley left from Victoria Station. In good weather I generally walked from Whitehall to the station across the parks by a variety of routes. The Hawksleys' office was open from 9 a.m. to 6 p.m. but the partners seldom appeared before 10 a.m. and they had long lunches at their clubs.

Vonnie was in her sixties and had never previously been out of New Zealand. We were delighted that she was adaptable enough to take the train to London and amuse herself while we were at work. She was tested out for camping during a weekend in the Cotswolds, travelling in the old taxi and sleeping in tiny mountain tents. At about this time Enid and I bought one of the first Morris

Minors to be produced. With some trepidation we set off for three weeks in Europe with Geraldine and Vonnie. At that time British residents were allowed to take out of the country just £20 a year. We drove through France, the Dolomite road, saw Venice briefly, drove to Florence and south to a small town, Lardarello, where New Zealand Army engineers had helped rebuild a geothermal power station, after the Germans had demolished it. Much of the knowledge these engineers gained went into the construction of the first New Zealand harnessing of underground hot water for electric power at Wairakei.

At Siena I received word that Priestley Thompson was about to go to Zermatt in Switzerland for four days and wanted me to join him for some climbs. Priestley was a well-known New Zealand mountaineer who had previously climbed in Switzerland. He later held the top job in the New Zealand Forest Service. I drove to the appointed hotel and the others went on to Paris. Although Priestley and I had three days of poor weather we ascended three peaks, without gaining a clear view of our surroundings. Still, it was a joy to feel real mountains under my boots, try the luxurious European hut life and visit an area that had so much mountain history.

I took a night train to Paris and we crossed to Dover, down to our last pennies.

Earle Riddiford came to our house and stayed some three months in late 1951. His Garhwal expedition of that year had gone quite well. Two of them and a Sherpa had climbed Mukut Parbat, 7,200 metres high and previously unclimbed. All had been over 6,500 metres on other mountains. When they reached civilisation there was a cabled invitation for any two of them to join the Mt Everest reconnaissance expedition, which was already in Nepal, under the leadership of Eric Shipton. Such an invitation was an enormous coup for young climbers. It had been initiated by Roly Ellis, who was on the New Zealand Alpine Club committee. The cable to Shipton went via Harry Stevenson, the club's president. There was a long debate among the four Garhwal climbers over which two were to go to Everest. Differing accounts of this stalemate have been published in various books and journals, and aspects of it are still simmering. The four on the Garhwal expedition had never become 'buddies'. As I was not there I leave it to others to write their postmortems, but I wonder about the outcome if Bill Beaven and I had been with them, as was originally intended.

In the end it was Riddiford and Hillary who joined the Shipton party, and both performed so well that they and George Lowe were invited to join Shipton's plans for next year. The reconnaissance expedition had established that there was a likely looking route to the summit of Everest through recently opened Nepal. By then access through the old Tibetan route had been closed to Westerners, although Chinese and Russians were given permission in the next few years.

Late in 1951 a British application was made to the government of Nepal to allow climbers to attempt Everest in 1952. To the great surprise of the applicants they found that the Swiss already had permission that year, and just one nation was allowed there in any one season. How different from the present situation, when there can be 10 or more countries all attempting the same route. The British organisers still wished to have a training exercise at high altitude so they negotiated permission to attempt Cho Oyu, on the Nepalese–Tibetan frontier about 16 km west of Everest and one of the lesser of the 14 peaks over 8,000 metres.

Considerable advances had been made during the war in oxygen and high-altitude physiology, mainly through the need to support air crews on long missions. These findings were largely untried in the mountain situation. Tom Bourdillon was in the Cho Oyu party as the oxygen expert, and Griffith Pugh as the physiologist. As mentioned earlier, few British climbers gained alpine experience between 1939 and 1952, owing to the war and the restrictions on foreign currency. For a few more years this continued. This was one of the reasons for the presence of New Zealanders in various British expeditions during the early 1950s. In our own mountains a younger group had been able to advance our skills, especially on the big problems of snow and ice.

Earle Riddiford visited the Royal Geographical Society office in Kensington and was horrified to find that virtually nothing had been done by way of preparation for Cho Oyu. So Earle himself unofficially took on the duties of ordering and shipping the considerable amounts of food and equipment that had to be forwarded to Nepal. Eric Shipton, the expedition leader, was hard to pin down and reluctant to make decisions on a number of planning issues. Earle found that the oxygen supplies and the physiological requirements were in hand, however, as they were being organised directly by Bourdillon and Pugh. Peter Lloyd of the 1938 Everest expedition also did much work on the oxygen preparation.

For about two months Earle and I went to Victoria Station together in the mornings. Then he went west to the RGS and I walked east to Westminster. Each day he kept me informed on the frustrations he was encountering. It did not look like a good start for the project. Shipton had been brilliant in the 1930s on small exploratory expeditions, where equipment was simple and much of the food was purchased locally. He wrote several books about his journeys and he had hordes of enthusiastic admirers. However, he did not enjoy the large expeditions, where he was tied to one high mountain for six or so weeks. Thus organising such an event from a city office was distasteful to him. Although Earle was not yet familiar with the London scene, he did well in getting the party onto its ship.

The Alpine Club held monthly meetings in its exclusive Mayfair rooms. Earle was invited to address the club on his New Zealand mountaineering experiences. He had a set of slides, but not many of our earlier Landsborough climbs, as these were before any of us owned appropriate cameras. The committee took him to a good restaurant for dinner before the meeting and he arrived just before eight o'clock, in good form. Bill Packard, David Hughes and I from our Bickley house were in the audience. In those days and for 15 more years the club was exclusively male, and to me the members always seemed to be elderly and conservative. Earle was a good speaker, and afterwards several people engaged him in conversation. Of great interest to me was the presence of some special climbers who had visited New Zealand and become legends there much earlier in the century. These included Canon Newton, H. E. L. Porter and Scott Russell. It was a notable occasion.

One day Oscar Coberger arrived on our doorstep. Oscar had a mountain equipment shop at Arthur's Pass and we all knew him as a competent mountain man with a blunt manner, although when it suited him he could be quite charming. He had been interned during the war for his open sympathies with the Nazis. Some months previously we had been so saturated by overseas guests at our Bickley house that we asked New Zealand House not to give out our address to anyone, as we would make our own invitations. Oscar was the only one who broke through this barrier. At the time we had as residents Earle, Enid's mother, Bill Packard's sister and David Hughes. Oscar squeezed in for a week and he proved a co-operative and entertaining guest.

In this book I do not intend going into the Cho Oyu expedition in great detail, but there are a few points that affected me later, especially as I had close associations subsequently with Evans, Ward, Pugh, Hillary and Lowe. Through joint work on the 1955 oxygen development and testing I also had regular contacts with Bourdillon and Pugh. Cho Oyu, not being Everest, received very little public interest in Britain. As *The Times* was a major sponsor of the expedition, that paper printed Shipton's few despatches, but no book was written about it. No one got anywhere near the summit – Pugh and Bourdillon made only minor advances in their sciences because the failure of the climbers to get really high. Earle Riddiford withdrew before the expedition finally disbanded, due mainly to ill-health.

Meanwhile, on Everest, the Swiss made attempts before and after the monsoon. Lambert and Tenzing Norgay turned back about 300 metres from the summit. However, the Swiss party did establish which was the easiest approach to the mountain, meaning the British in 1953 would need to do very little new route-finding. The Swiss had proved access was possible for all but the last skyline ridge. Having Tenzing in the British party would be a considerable asset.

I worked on at Hawksley's, designing and drawing more water schemes, but having an ear to the ground on mountain matters. Bill Packard was a good source and Charles Evans made more visits to the house. We all watched *The Times* for Everest announcements. The first was that Shipton had been invited to lead the 1953 expedition and, to the amazement of British climbers, Shipton named Harry Ayres, the New Zealand guide, as a member of his party. Ed Hillary had made many climbs with Harry and very few with amateurs, and had pressed for his inclusion. The British climbers' grapevine was totally against having a guide in the party. If the guide got high the public view could be that the climbers were 'guided to the top'. I had my own doubts. Although Harry was a great mountaineer he was a chain smoker and I wondered if he would have the necessary lung capacity for very long high-altitude exposure.

There were rumours abroad among climbers – and then in the papers – that there was disquiet about the prospect of Shipton as an Everest leader, when it was evident that the British would not in the future have the monopoly on permits from the Nepalese government. A leader was required who would have determination and focus. Things were happening behind the scenes. At the time I did not have details, but several authors have given snippets of information. In 2003 Mike Ward, who initiated the 1951 reconnaissance expedition, summed it up in *Everest: A thousand years of exploration*. Shipton was removed, but rather shabbily, and was replaced by Colonel John Hunt. Basil Goodfellow, an RGS representative on the Joint Himalayan Committee, played a big part in the change, with Hunt being in some ill-defined way an accomplice. From what I heard at the time, and then later as a secretary at the RGS, and from listening to Charles Evans in high camps on Kangchenjunga, I consider that Ward's was an accurate summary of the events surrounding Hunt's replacement of Shipton. Shipton's biographer, Peter Steele, also recorded the facts of the matter. Some who actually went with Hunt to Everest felt sore about the dropping of Shipton, but also acknowledged that Hunt's leadership style was more likely to put men on the summit.

On the outskirts of much of this at the time, I decided to apply for a place in the 1953 Everest party, knowing I had little chance because of my lack of Himalayan experience. Interviews had been under way for some weeks. This would have been late in October 1952.

I received an immediate reply. John Hunt interviewed me in an office at the RGS. He made a point of shutting the door and cutting off the telephone for an hour. He was quietly spoken, direct and sincere. He said he had high recommendations for me, mentioning Charles Evans and Scott Russell. He disliked taking anyone he had not met, but he had to take Hillary and Lowe, who were still at home, as so many who had been on Cho Oyu said those with New Zealand ice experience were invaluable to the party. He explained that Evans would be his deputy leader and that Charles had pressed for me, so he was in a dilemma, especially as I had no Himalayan experience. Although I had climbed in the Alps and in Wales, as far as the Joint Committee was concerned I was still a New Zealander. I would be next if they agreed to increase non-British numbers.

I said, 'You are taking Hillary and Lowe. Does this put me in front of Ayres and Riddiford?'

'Of course. Riddiford's health was suspect on Cho Oyu and he has just sent me a telegraphed application, which I will decline. The committee and the Climbers' Club would be uncomfortable with Ayres, a guide, in the expedition.'

'What has the Climbers' Club got to do with this?' I asked. I need to explain here that the Alpine Club was rather cautious about accepting new young members in those days, whereas the Climbers' Club then consisted mostly of Oxford and Cambridge mountaineers from whom the next generation of climbers was likely to emerge.

'Norman, many of the young men likely to go have been in the army, where I knew them, or are in the Climbers' Club. The older men on the Joint Committee have to listen to them and try to assess if they will be happy with a guide in their group. No matter what he's like as a person, the climbers would feel their own achievements would be given less credit if they were accompanied by a guide. As leader I would have much difficulty in pairing him with another on his rope. Ayres didn't apply to come on the expedition – Hillary suggested to Shipton he should be invited. No others have pressed for him. I've asked Hillary to notify Ayres of my decision to refuse him.'

Working in London

This and other points were firmly stated. Hunt went on, 'I was once accepted for an expedition in the 1930s and then declined on medical grounds. I've already arranged an appointment for you in Harley Street tomorrow morning, with Lord Horder, the expedition's medical adviser. He will report back to me.'

Horder gave me a brief examination and asked me about my chest burns. Had I been in the war? He said he would notify Colonel Hunt of his approval.

At home I discussed the situation with Bill Packard, stating that I felt I had no chance of being included but that it was an interesting exercise to make the attempt. He said, 'No chance for you at all. Last night Colonel Hunt read out the names at the Climbers' Club dinner. The Joint Committee has to approve the party next week and they are confidential until the committee releases them to *The Times*.'

'Well, are Hillary and Lowe in?'

'Yes.'

'Ayres, Riddiford, me?'

'No to all. A professional would be unacceptable to Climbers' Club members and there is grizzling about the inclusion of Hillary and Lowe. People like Rawlinson, Nichol and Emlyn Jones feel they have been squeezed out.'

Some days later *The Times* announced the names and Packard's information was right. I already knew Evans, Ward, Pugh and Bourdillon, and to me they all deserved their places.

About a month later Colonel Hunt rang me, apologised that I was not in the party and asked if I would do a job for him at the RGS office. I invited him and his wife to come to our house to dine. At the table he explained that several of the expedition were going to Switzerland to try out equipment and were not available for their RGS secretarial work. No expedition members lived near London and the serving military officers had obligations at their bases, especially considering they would soon be absent for five months in Nepal. Could I assist in the RGS office in their absence? Time: about six weeks, no pay. Orders for most things had been placed, but deliveries were beginning. There was a need for inspections, thanks issued, shipping arranged, press and many minor items to keep moving. The Hunts were charming. I promised an answer next day. We were instructed to omit the 'Colonel' title and call him John.

The Bickley quartet went into a huddle and discussed the situation. Then Bill and I approached our employers and, surprisingly, both managed to arrange deals. I was to leave Hawksley's at about 3 p.m. on four days a week, bus to the RGS, which was not far, and work there until about 6 p.m. and Bill was to work other times late on certain days, between lectures he gave at the Geography Department of University College, London.

We found the RGS office was being handled quite well by two very capable women, but in a chauvinist land most equipment donors wanted to present their items to a man and receive appropriate comments from a mountaineer. It seemed that outward letters had to be signed by a man. One of the women was Ann Debenham, niece of the chief scientist for one year of Scott's 1911–13 Antarctic expedition. Frank Debenham later became a distinguished professor at Cambridge. A few years later Ann married Roger Chorley, who was also a prominent climber. The other woman in the office was an Australian, Elizabeth Johnson, who married the heir to Seppelts, the large South Australian vineyard operators.

The job drifted on for many months and even after the expedition had departed I still found that some calls each day were being sent to my engineering office. Hawksley's were very tolerant of these interruptions. I did enjoy being situated in the centre of expedition planning and obtaining an insight into the other operations of the Royal Geographical Society, which was busy with publications, membership matters and its extensive library. The director had a background of exploration in Arabia. None of the regular staff had any involvement with the Everest project. Bill and I and the two women had our own large room and a telephone line, all with a happy co-operative mood in the central Kensington location.

I came away with a deep admiration for John Hunt and Charles Wylie. Although I seldom saw them, I had the job of following the groundwork they had done with their clear ordering of materials, their timing, delivery requirements and acceptance conditions. Wylie was an officer in a Gurkha battalion and had been on a small Himalayan expedition. With that background and consequent language ability he was the ideal man to be transport officer in the field for the 350 porters, then all the mail runners and the Sherpas on the mountain. John Hunt still had army commitments in Germany and was frequently with them or in Switzerland testing gear and talking to the climbers who had missed the Everest summit a few months previously.

Back at our Bickley house, Enid's mother had decided to stay with us in London until after the coronation and return to New Zealand in mid-June 1953. She and Enid accordingly booked spectator seats for the parade on the big day. For a time I ignored this activity, so many months ahead of the actual ceremony.

Enid and I decided to undertake a three-week tour of Spain in our convertible Morris Minor, but this time I wanted a male companion. I suggested Lloyd Evans, the owner of the garaged ancient taxi. Enid invited her bridesmaid, Margaret Newell. Both accepted and planning jumped ahead. Although Lloyd and Margaret were our close friends, somehow they had never met. We were still restricted by the £20 currency limit, so, as in Italy previously, we would be unrolling tents in farmers' paddocks and living cheaply. There were no approved camping grounds in Spain in those days.

One of the many pleasing features of my engineering job was that touring planning could be done from my central location. I attended a very helpful course of lunchtime lectures at the National Gallery. On eight consecutive Thursdays there were talks on the Spanish paintings owned by the gallery. My eyes were opened to the wonders of Velazquez, Zurburan, El Greco, Goya and others. It was easy to find where more and better were on display in Spain. We went there for Easter, a big festival time, and the two following weeks.

Food in Spain was brilliant, cheap and not rationed. Franco's police left us alone. The galleries, architecture and mountains were even better than we expected. In Seville we attended an Italian company's performance of *The Barber of Seville*. It began at 9 p.m. and at the first interval there was a full hour for dinner. By 1 a.m. Enid was asleep, so during the second interval I carried her down two flights of stairs and locked her in the car. I rejoined the others to hear the last act. It was the first time I had seen an Italian company in the flesh, and it was great. While still in Spain our two passengers told us they had become engaged.Lloyd became chief scientist for the CSIRO in Canberra and later received an honorary doctorate from Lincoln University, on the outskirts of Christchurch.

Back in England there were reports every week or so from James Morris on the Everest expedition. Queen Mary died in April. Temporary stands had been erected along The Mall for the forthcoming coronation procession, and the cortege with household cavalry was to pass along part of that route. On a fine spring afternoon we watched the parade of royals in black for the late queen, and the colourful cavalry. I began to regret I had made no booking for the coronation.

On the second of June, the day before the coronation, I took a small pack to work. In it were a waterproof parka, my camera, some food and a cushion. After work at six o'clock I walked the short distance to Trafalgar Square and sat just behind the first spectators who were at the kerb edge. The square filled up during the early evening and a light drizzle began to fall. At about midnight a loudspeaker announced that Mt Everest had been climbed on 28 May. Those reaching the summit were Edmund Hillary and a Sherpa called Tenzing Norgay. That news warmed my spirits. I wondered if any others in the square knew Hillary. Also, I had already read quite a lot about Tenzing, but I had not then met him.

Next morning, about an hour before the procession was due, police cleared a passageway some metres to my right. Hordes of uniformed first aid people, police, sailors, firemen and Beefeaters walked through and took up positions in front of all of us who had stayed the night. There was some minor bickering, but everyone was surprisingly good-natured about it. My photographs show lots of helmeted heads, the household cavalry from their waists upwards and the tops of coaches.

SEVEN

Barun Himalayan Expedition

During the 1953 Mt Everest expedition I had occasional exchanges of letters with Charles Evans and Ed Hillary. After their 14-day walk from base camp to Kathmandu, Ed wrote that he and George Lowe would be travelling to England and asked if they could stay with Enid and me. Evans, eager to avoid the fuss of the great return to admiring Britain, left Kathmandu soon after and went back to the Khumbu to resume mapping the south-west of Everest. Then for a time he became the locum for a Kathmandu doctor who went on a long vacation. The main team and Tenzing's family flew to London, arriving nearly a month after the coronation.

Our lease on the large house at Bickley had expired. Enid's mother was at sea, on the way to New Zealand. We took a flat near St Christopher's School for Girls, at Beckenham, Kent, where Enid had begun teaching English and Latin.

We squeezed the two big Kiwi men into our new residence for three weeks. They were very short of money and initially had no other offers of accommodation, except from Ed's sister, who was married to a doctor in Norwich. Although he visited her briefly, it was too far from the centre of things in London, where a series of lectures about the expedition was being arranged at the very new Festival Hall. There were three speakers each night and, importantly for our pair, they were well paid. George had done much of the movie camera work on the expedition and he spent some time with the studios in the production of the official film.

He briefly entertained hopes of advancing in a filming career but he soon encountered obstacles in terms of apprenticeships and examinations.

A few days after our guests' arrival at the flat, the joint headmistresses of Enid's school invited Ed to speak to the pupils at their morning assembly. He kindly obliged, without photographs or props. He showed some nervousness, which would diminish after several much larger occasions. The joint headmistresses had the unlikely names of Lambie and Dowdie. Immediately after Ed's talk we had to go to a meeting, and Miss Dowdie lent us her car, a pre-war Austin, and four of us crammed into it. Out on a main highway the car lurched and stopped, refusing to come back to life. It took several minutes to locate the problem: Ed's knee had bumped the petrol cut-off tap.

After a month or so a number of post-expedition functions were held and Enid and I attended several. There were a set of dinners, hosted by the Alpine Club, the New Zealand Alpine Club, the Royal Geographical Society and *The Times*. Bill Packard and I organised the NZAC occasion and found a surprising number of climbers with strong New Zealand associations.

In amazingly quick time the film *The Conquest of Everest* had its gala opening, and later John Hunt's book had its launching. The media seem to like to talk in terms of the 'conquest' of mountains, whereas climbers much prefer less aggressive words like 'ascent'. Hunt managed to win his naming battle, calling it *The Ascent of Everest*. There were some very distinguished people at many of these events, but usually not at our table.

Expedition members and a few others were invited to the Outward Bound School at Eskdale in Cumberland, where Eric Shipton was the chief warden at that time. I arranged for my friend Bill Beaven to join us. The weather was dreadful. On the first morning John Hunt said he would walk out to one of the crags to try some rock climbing, and several followed him. Eric enthused that the river was so unusually high that kayaking could be possible.

In thick, driving rain and dirty, fast water I found myself with eight others down at the launching ramp. The kayaks were mostly two-man canvas craft, fragile and eminently tippable. Somehow I ended up with the heaviest partner, Tom Bourdillon, the beginning of a happy, fruitful association. We became afloat quickly, and while we were awaiting the others, George Lowe's craft capsized in deep dirty water. He came up with a roar of laughter and lost his false teeth. We drifted into bad visibility and promptly lost all the others. We paddled past all sorts of obstacles for about three hours, having little idea of the terrain. The other boats had vanished. Suddenly, through the fog, we saw a small weir just ahead. We shot over it without capsizing and were then in calm water, far from visible land, so we turned back to the weir and followed it to its southern end, where we found land. After carrying the kayak for half an hour we met our worried host, in a vehicle large enough to take us and our fragile craft. Some days later, when the stream dropped, a fisherman found George's teeth and posted them back to him.

Shipton invited me to return to Eskdale at a later date, so Enid and I drove there for a weekend the following month. Eric was a good communicator to a small audience and we had many discussions about past mountain matters and future possibilities. The weekend included gentle walks and I gave some elementary climbing instruction to a group of pupils. Although I had good conversations with Eric in the field, there was an air of unease when we were back at the base. We were invited to return, but not long after our visit Eric lost his position with Outward Bound for a series of indiscretions.

In London at about that time I was introduced to Bill Tilman, who had just given a talk to the Alpine Club. He said, 'Ah, a New Zealander. Do you know Bryant or Packard?' The answer, yes, was easy: I had been on the Jackson search with the former and lived four years with the latter. Tilman had been in the Himalayas with both of them. With no further ado he invited me to be in his crew to sail his boat, *Mischief*, to the Straits of Magellan and up the coast of Chile. I was flattered, but declined the offer.

Later, Bill Tilman's first sailing book appeared, aptly titled *Mischief in Patagonia*. A crew of sorts had been assembled, but at Gibraltar some refused to proceed, forcing him to find replacements and head back to England. After a few days at sea this new crew mutinied and he had no option but to put into Oporto.

Another scratch crew had to be located for sailing back home. I have always been glad I declined Bill's request. However, he put to sea with a better crew later and completed the journey. From that voyage and several more he wrote a series of inspirational books on sailing in Arctic and Antarctic waters.

For some months there had been suggestions of a Himalayan expedition sponsored by the New Zealand Alpine Club. Suddenly it became official and applications were invited. Ed Hillary was appointed leader and George Lowe was accepted immediately. Jim McFarlane, Bill Beaven and I applied and were soon approved. We had to make a substantial cash contribution and supply our own equipment as well as being out of paid employment for virtually six months, much of this time being taken up with the sea voyages. Two men from Britain were invited on a free basis, as a gesture of thanks for the places given to New Zealanders on past British expeditions. These were Dr Mike Ball and my good friend Charles Evans, who was the deputy leader. Three others – Geoff Harrow, Colin Todd and Brian Wilkins – completed the strong party of 10.

Ed and George returned to New Zealand for a long lecture tour and for discussions with the organisers of the New Zealand Alpine Club's expedition. Early next year, 1954, they began a lecture tour of the US, with Charles Evans, who had completed his medical assignment in Kathmandu. They prospered in America and made their stay a lengthy one.

Enid decided to keep teaching in England during my absence. Hawksley's considered that as they were a small establishment they needed to replace me, as I would be away for half a year. This was understandable, especially as I had said I would eventually return to New Zealand and would not seek a permanent place in their firm. Enid moved to a smaller flat.

Bill Beaven, Mike Ball and I sailed from Liverpool to Bombay in a comfortable ship that carried just 80 passengers. It was good to be at sea again – and in much more comfortable conditions than as a tourist-class steward. Also on board were three men joining John Kempe, who was intending to attempt peaks immediately south of Kangchenjunga, on the Sikkim–Nepal border. We found after several days that they were particularly interested in

Kangchenjunga, and were regarded as a reconnaissance group for that mountain.

We had Nepalese permission to climb and explore in the Barun area where the main peak is Mt Makalu, some 20 kilometres southeast of Mt Everest. It is the fifth-highest peak in the world and was then unclimbed. There were also other smaller mountains of quality in the district that could be attempted if permission for Makalu was not forthcoming.

In Bombay we met the four who had come from New Zealand by ship. Together we made the long train journey across the Indian plains, then took a ferry over the Ganges and a smaller train to the rail terminus of Jogbani. We were all new to India. The train experience had been fascinating – colourful scenery, new food and smells, dust, crowds and the singsong noise of the railway platform vendors.

These days there is a tendency to equate the word Sherpa with mountain guides. But Sherpas are in fact an ethnic grouping, the name originally meaning 'man from the east' (east Tibet). In the 1950s few Sherpas had any mountaineering skills; in the main they were traders and yak herders, with no knowledge of English. But because they live at altitudes between 3,000 and 4,500 metres, in a harsh Nepalese climate, they are naturally well acclimatised for mountain work. This, and their generally cheerful disposition and willingness to work hard, made them invaluable to large mountaineering expeditions in the area. Today many Sherpas attend formal mountaineering courses and are very competent climbers.

At Jogbani, Hillary, Evans and Lowe appeared. Our Sherpa team was there too. Some of them had been to South Col on Everest and immediately prominent was their leader, Dawa Tenzing (no relation to Tenzing Norgay). It was a relief to be with people who had some local knowledge of India, particularly Charles Evans with his language ability. Our main supplies had also arrived. The 15 Sherpas would be with us all the way, but local hillmen were employed to carry the main loads into the base camp, intended to be at the foot of Makalu.

The approach walk took 15 days. We all adjusted to one another and to the Sherpas quite happily, but there was one disturbing problem. We frequently met returning porters who told us a Californian party was two weeks ahead of us, and was now camped at the foot of Makalu. We knew the Nepalese government allowed just one party to attempt a mountain in any single season, but as we had not passed through Kathmandu the finer points of our permission had not been discussed. We carried no radios and the small villages we encountered had none, nor any telephone services, so contact with the capital was not feasible.

The route followed ridges with brilliant early-morning viewpoints. Usually in the afternoons clouds gathered, and thunderstorms were common. Then for two days we were deep in the Arun Valley, one of the few major rivers that rise in Tibet and cut right through the Himalayan divide.

After crossing the Arun at Sedua the party divided to explore three separate unmapped valley systems. As Evans, McFarlane and I could all operate a photo-theodolite, the RGS had supplied us with three of these instruments. An acclimatisation period is essential before attempting a high mountain, so this arrangement suited all of us. We could look about in new country and accumulate the benefits of higher altitude. The Hillary group, including Jim McFarlane, would go with the main baggage to the Barun Valley and establish the base near the cliffs of Makalu, recording the terrain as they went. I was in the party that went up the Iswa River, while Charles Evans explored the Choyang Valley, the adjacent one to the south. It was hoped these valleys would have crossable passes at their headwaters and that after 15 or so days we would all gather at the Makalu base to confer.

Nepal had been closed to Europeans, particularly surveyors, for hundreds of years. Some of the major peaks, visible from hill stations a hundred or more kilometres away in India, had been fixed and their approximate heights calculated. Some of the infilling valleys had been sketched by Indian staff of the British surveyors. These highly trained assistants, counting their footsteps and using compass observations, did remarkably well in solving countless problems – not just in Nepal but far into Tibet – some 120 and more years ago.

The main peaks in our area had reasonably good fixes for

location, but precise altitude calculations were problematic. Heights relative to sea level were based a way off, near Calcutta. Over these big distances factors such as the curvature of the earth must enter the sums. Light rays at high altitude have a slight curvature downwards (known as refraction) and the extent of this was not detailed until surveyors took instruments to very great heights and did reverse observations back to a known baseline.

The basic map we used had four fixed mountains on it, located from India. They were Everest, Lhotse, Makalu and Chamlang. In 1933 a plane made two flights over Everest and Makalu and, from photographs taken, some sketching had been added, giving a broad indication of glaciers and rivers. These were just horizontal views from the cockpit, not aerial mapping as it is known today. The 1921 and 1935 British Everest expeditions on the Tibetan side had a surveyor in their parties, so there was a reasonable chance that summits on the Himalayan divide, visible from the Tibetan ridges, would be shown in their correct locations. For our purposes it was necessary to link our work to all four of the peaks located from India, and establish conformity with the northern 1921 and 1935 triangulations.

I was one of four climbers in George Lowe's group. With us were six Sherpas. We worked our way up the Iswa Gorge, with thick rhododendron forest and few signs of a track, other than occasional indications that men and animals used this route during the monsoon when grazing was possible. There were peaks up to 5,300 metres on the ridges to the north and south. As altitude was gained the forest slowly changed to large pines and silver birches, which gradually gave way to dwarf rhododendrons, azaleas and junipers. Winter avalanche debris still clung to the cliff bases so few flowers were visible. Deep in the valley there was little use for the theodolite, although I did some sketching for map detailing. It is a beautiful valley with the great features I had long been hoping to see.

Towards the head of the valley a large glacier appeared, starting at the impressive face of Chamlang, a giant upthrust wedge 6 kilometres long, at about 7,300 metres for its entire length. It looked most formidable. A high pass on our right seemed to be accessible, by which we should be able to join the main party in the Barun in a few days. We explored the main glacier and sighted a pass on our left, which would allow the Evans group also to use our exit. At the head of the valley another pass was visible. I was to climb it from the other side 18 months later.

In 1961 the highest summit of Chamlang was climbed for the first time, by a Japanese team. There are still many more challenges on it and the mountain is not far from the main modern trekking routes.

We made a successful crossing to the Barun base camp, feeling we had advanced in our acclimatisation and I had begun a corner of the mapping work. One kilometre up the valley we made contact with the Americans. They were from the Sierra Club and had designs on the very steep Makalu ridge, which began behind their camp. It has prominent rock buttresses, which appeared to be most difficult obstacles to surmount when carrying up high camps. However, they were a cheerful group and we saw various of their members as the weeks passed. In 1960 I was on another expedition with Larry Swan, their biologist. In the expedition also was Bill Long, who later went on four Antarctic expeditions and often stayed with us in our Christchurch house.

It seemed that Ed Hillary had already talked to their leader about access to the mountain, and we were to attempt a route further up the valley, well clear of their area. There were now no problems concerning the absence of clear permission for the New Zealand expedition. As it turned out, the Americans did not get very high on Makalu and their particular ridge was not climbed until many years later.

Our base camp was empty when we arrived, apart from one Sherpa and our doctor, Mike Ball. The Hillary group was expected back next day. We took the opportunity to catch up with washing and mending gear. I considered I was reasonably fit, but I had lost a lot of weight and had mild dehydration problems. Back in London, Ed and George had sung the praises of Griff Pugh, the high-altitude physiologist who had been on the Cho Oyu 1952 and Everest 1953 expeditions. Griff had recommended large quantities of water to be consumed daily, and had firm ideas about diet for a high-performing body. My two informants had repeated some of these things to me, but punctuated them with tales of Griff's fast cars, his crashes and lady friends. They themselves, unaccustomed to having a non-climber in their party, had not taken Griff's advice very seriously. Now on this, my first expedition, I had failed to do so also.

On our approach walk the location of clean water had been a problem. In New Zealand I had drunk from almost any stream when thirsty. There were possibly greatly diluted pollutants from deer, chamois or possums, but one's body probably adapts to such things. In Nepal on the approach walk the debris at each habitation put one off casual drinking, especially the droppings of cattle, pigs and hens near water sources. Sanitation facilities for humans were nearly non-existent. In those days we rarely carried water bottles, so we usually had drinks of boiled water only morning and night in the camps. It was easy to become dehydrated.

Early next morning Ed Hillary and a Sherpa suddenly arrived in camp. Ed was carrying no pack and looked exhausted. The news was alarming. Jim McFarlane had spent a night deep in a crevasse and had serious frostbite in his hands and feet. He would have to be carried down to base camp, and probably on to Kathmandu. Ed had cracked or broken ribs in trying to extract him from the crevasse. Jim was now in a higher camp, quite unable to walk.

George Lowe and Mike Ball left immediately to attend to Jim at the upper camp, a long distance up the Barun Glacier. All hands would be required in a big carrying job. While gathering our equipment and supplies we heard the details of what had happened.

Ed, Jim, Brian Wilkins and five Sherpas had been to a col on the Tibetan frontier, in cloudy conditions with a cold wind blowing. Jim had stayed there doing some map sketching while the others, apart from Brian, walked down to their camp at the Barun Glacier. Later, on open névé snow that appeared fairly uniform, Brian had suddenly dropped through a snow crust and fallen about 20 metres to a shelf, where he stopped. He was roped to Jim, who had no warning and failed to hold him. Brian was hardly injured, as his drop had been restrained — but not stopped — by Jim's sliding action on the surface. But then Jim, when he came to the opening, had a free fall, and had suffered concussion and bad bruising.

Brian left Jim, lying on his pack, with crampons still on his feet. Fortunately Brian had his ice axe and was able to work his way along and up the crevasse, eventually emerging on the bleak surface. He rushed down as fast as he could and gave the bad news to Hillary. Ed, with five Sherpas, two sleeping bags and two ropes, climbed back up to the accident site and managed to find it in the fading light. They lowered a rope to Jim, but he was unable to attach it.

Then Ed tied two ropes around his waist and was lowered through the first hole, where he saw that the crevasse was like a big bottleneck, with a small hole at the top and overhanging both sides. He was lowered down, attached at his waist only, by the Sherpas in a series of jerks. He had no foot loop or harness, so the full weight of this big man was applied through the chest attachment. All the time the loaded rope was cutting into the edge of the top snow lip. On the top the Sherpas found themselves getting too close to the hole. They held him suspended for some time, so Ed was able to talk to Jim. Then, after a lot of shouting, they pulled Ed back up and at the top lip, with the rope passing through the now deep groove in the compacted snow, the destructive forces on his chest cracked three ribs. Communication had been extremely difficult through the snow hole and it was bitterly cold on the surface. If he had used a loop in the rope for a foot support, or the more common smaller slings, the weight on his chest would have been reduced and he would have been able to manoeuvre himself at the exit hole at the top.

In total dark and a freezing wind a rope was again dropped to Jim, who this time did manage to tie himself to it. He was pulled up to the lip but was unable to assist himself through the hole and the others did not rescue him at the edge. So Jim was lowered back down. Two sleeping bags were dropped to him and he called that he would get into them. Those at the top of the crevasse went back to their camp, a long way down. Ed was in considerable pain from his rib damage and it had been a long day, when the climbers were just beginning their altitude acclimatisation.

Barun Himalayan Expedition

Next morning the same six, with Brian Wilkins, went back to the crevasse. Brian descended by his previous upward route and found Jim suffering from concussion, not in the sleeping bags, without gloves and still wearing crampons. Brian was pulled up to the top and came out safely. Jim was again lifted to just below the surface but again he could not be lifted over the lip, so he was lowered until the escape hole could be enlarged with ice axes. Cascading lumps of ice dropped 20 metres but fortunately did no damage. Eventually Jim was pulled out to the surface. Then began the haul down to the first camp, where Jim was put in a sleeping bag and given food and liquids. Ed then descended to base, where he found our Iswa group and more Sherpas.

Soon the Evans party also arrived from their more southern valley, giving us adequate manpower for the next stage. The carry down to base took three days and involved everybody. Jim had limitations from several days of concussion, and his crampons being left on in the crevasse had restricted the blood circulation in his feet. It was decided he should try to recuperate for six days in the relative comfort of base camp.

After a short rest some of us began a half-hearted examination of Makalu, on the glacier approach about 3 kilometres away from the Americans' line. A Camp 2 was established and, while Charles Evans and Geoff Harrow made advances on the main mountain, placing the first supplies at the intended Camps 3 and 4, George and I climbed an ice summit of 6,700 metres. On our return we found that Ed was in camp and far from well, in considerable pain from his rib injury. However, next morning we all climbed up towards Camp 4, with Ed's health getting worse. He and I started down next day, encountering immediate troubles. Others joined to assist but Ed collapsed completely. The combination of altitude sickness and rib damage was too much for him. There was no option but to abandon the mountain, and all assembled to carry him back to the less rare air of base – a journey of four hard days.

Decisions? The two doctors decreed that both McFarlane and Hillary required several days' rest before contemplating the 15-day walk to Kathmandu. This was years before helicopters arrived in Nepal to facilitate high-altitude rescues. As Jim would need carrying all the way, a message was sent out to Sedua to engage a trio of strong men to take turns at carrying him in a basket on their backs. Evans also requested that some strong liquor be purchased. On a cold mountain, alcohol can give a temporary boost but it also opens pores and results in heat loss. But Evans advised that with Jim in the safety of base, in warm surroundings, a few rations of liquor could enhance circulation in his extremities.

It was evident that one of the doctors needed to accompany the evacuating party to Kathmandu, and one man returning to New Zealand should escort Jim all the way home. Thus Jim, Ed, Brian and Mike were to leave us after five more days. I put in a plea to at least get some surveying done, with the accessible Barun peaks now well within range. The remainder would pack up base and depart over the plateau and Hongu to reach Khumbu before the monsoon was due, usually in the first week of June. They hoped to climb some summits on the way. I would try a Barun–Imja crossing and also meet them in the Khumbu. No one had crossed the col I contemplated, and I knew Eric Shipton had looked at the other side and declined to attempt it. If my route failed I would follow the others via the Hongu.

When I was nearly ready to depart a strong suggestion was made to me that Brian and Mike should join my survey team, as they would shortly leave without climbing anything of significance. They would have to return in five days to begin their escort journey. I said my farewells to Jim – we had not been able to climb together on the whole expedition. In New Zealand he had been my main climbing companion and for the expedition to end this way for him was tragic. He was carried to Kathmandu, flown to Christchurch and spent a year in hospital undergoing a series of not wholly successful skin grafts. He was released with his feet 5 centimetres shorter and no outer tendons in his fingers. Still, Jim went on to have an outstanding engineering career and became a very successful sailor. In his later years Bill Beaven and I sometimes crewed for him on his 9-metre yacht.

Barun Himalayan Expedition

On the way up the Barun, Sherpa Pasang Dawa and I made a diversion to look at the accident site. Well back from the hole I drove Pasang's axe firmly into the ice and tied my rope to it. Armed with the appropriate ascending slings I crept to the edge of the hole and looked down. It was a nasty place, with such bad memories. I went back a few metres and there were indications of the existence of the crevasse, including quite a chasm near the place where Brian had climbed out, further along. Should Brian have seen it in the first place? However, light conditions can make a difference and when Brian dropped through the hidden hole there were clouds about and the climbers were on their way down from their first sortie at that altitude.

Writing this in 2005 I looked up what I wrote for the *New Zealand Alpine Journal* in 1954. The account of the expedition covered four pages and showed it to be a rewarding and very successful trip. Between Lhotse and Makalu there are eight peaks in the 6,500–7,000-metre range, and between them high cols, all over 5,800 metres. Just one point had a name, Pethangtse, a peak that looks most spectacular from the Tibetan side. Many parties in recent years have commented on how formidable it looks from the north. Mike, Brian Urkien and I climbed Pethangtse together, a very satisfying first ascent. Then, in various other combinations, we went up six more. Among other things I established a frontier surveying station where I tied observations back to the 1921 work.

Mike was full of praise for Urkien, the Sherpa who had been attached to him for the whole expedition. I was very happy with Pasang Dawa. It was Pasang who had carried out Bill Packard four years previously when Bill had collapsed with polio. Pasang alone got him out to Kathmandu and then by train to Bombay. As Pasang lived in Darjeeling, and Urkien in Khumbu, we decided to exchange Sherpas, as it would be far cheaper for these men to get back to their homes. In addition I knew that Pasang would be a most useful nurse for Jim's carry to Kathmandu. Urkien was with me for three subsequent expeditions and I lived in his house for three months. A truly great friend.

The Wilkins and Ball group left, much happier now after a

short burst of climbing. With their departure I parted with the last European food and joined the three Sherpas and their cuisine. I had seen that Evans, at base, often declined our hard dehydrated carrots and potatoes, preferring tea or hot water with tsampa – roasted barley ground to a coarse flour. I had no trouble with the change and considered I was more healthy from it. Perhaps by then I was thoroughly acclimatised. On all subsequent expeditions I sought out tsampa and had no major health concerns.

⫶

Now, with just three Sherpas, survey gear and a week's supply of food, I was alone at the head of the Barun Glacier and had to consider how to reach the next valley to the west. Urkien and I managed the ascent of a difficult peak on the Imja divide to the west. The descent to the Imja was utterly impossible. We moved camp to a higher location, quite near the col, which overlooked the route that Eric Shipton had declined in 1952. From there, in thick cloud, the two of us climbed what I believed to be Cho Polu. This should have given us a view to the Imja for our crossing, but we saw nothing. Two years later, when plotting survey results from other stations, I realised that the point we reached was not the actual summit. Survey photos from the south showed a slightly higher bump. I think we did not climb Cho Polu after all.

We then had a serious look down the crossing route. It would have to be straight down one of the many steep, fluted gullies. Without packs two of us went down about a quarter of the way and came up again. There was no overhanging avalanche risk above the route, but it was the type of place where broken icicles could sweep down at enormous speed and do great damage if they made contact. From the appearance of the vast cone of debris at the bottom it was evident that the whole slope must send down extensive volumes of snow from time to time. I worried all night, but in the morning decided we would attempt it. The alternative would take a week and we would be on short rations.

With all our gear on board and joined by one long rope, we four set off, descending on a straight course all the way. Twice in unsavoury places I left in an ice piton. Near the bottom there was a crevasse to negotiate, and then a long scramble over the old avalanche debris. We were successfully out on the Imja Glacier with another great array of peaks to admire. Looking back up the fluted slopes we decided it seemed just about impossible as a crossing route. I understood Shipton's reason for refusing it. Further down we erected a comfortable camp, in the knowledge that not far away there would be yak tracks and the Sherpas' own home villages. Near the tents was running water, so we would not need to use fuel to melt snow.

We walked past the approaches to Island Peak and left the active glacier near the three huts of Chukhung, the first buildings we had seen for five weeks. People appeared, and after a relaxing drink we bought arak (a strong distilled firewater) and meat. Then suddenly we met Geoff Harrow and some of our original Sherpa team. On the way to the Hongu they had made the first ascent of Baruntse, 7,168 metres. Colin and Geoff had achieved it one day, with George and Bill two days later. As the others had no knowledge of my progress, Charles Evans had awaited news of me at a camp in the Hongu. I despatched my Sherpa team to their various homes, one day to the south, and made a solo crossing of the Ambu Lapcha, a pass of 5,787 metres, east of Ama Dablam. From the pass I could see a wide basin with five small lakes in it, and a ring of spectacular peaks around the skyline, with Chamlang and Baruntse as the brilliant backdrops.

Charles was easily located, by the nearest lake, in a very peaceful setting. The water was close to zero. I plunged into it, but briefly. (In 1984 I dived into an Antarctic lake to qualify for an unusual award. The water temperature there was just below zero.) I washed clothes and listened to the description of the events that had occurred during my absence. I stayed the night and we talked for hours. Charles suggested I delay my passage back to England and join him for three weeks, walking west as near the Tibetan frontier as possible. We would have a few days in Kathmandu and be together for visits to some Indian cities. It was a most attractive invitation.

He was now the expedition leader and would have to spend

time at the main Sherpa village of Khumjung, paying our employees and clearing the mail. Four others who would be walking to Kathmandu could revise our departure bookings. They would also take our two theodolites, as our next journey, during the monsoon, would be in cloud all the way and mapping would be impossible. I agreed to this proposal. We were so remote that outside communication was impossible, but I wrote a letter of explanation to Enid.

We crossed the high pass to the Imja together. Strangely, Charles and I had been on the same expedition for nearly three months but had never been linked by a rope, nor even been involved in the same project. The Imja Khola opened out into large grazing pastures. At Dingboche we saw sprouting barley terraces, protected by rock walls. Cheerful women called out to us as they hoed rows of potatoes. Some were using ice axes. The route took us through Tangboche, whose monastery on its brilliant site was familiar to me from dozens of photographs and the Everest film. From there the track dropped to a deep gorge and the Imja joined the Dudh Kosi, where the warmth and moisture of the monsoon were giving a boost to early flowers and grasses. Another easy climb up a track, big enough for loaded yaks to pass, and suddenly we were in the broad, nearly level valley occupied by the substantial adjoining villages of Khumjung and Khunde. It seemed to me an idyllic plain formed in a high glacial hanging valley.

Colin and Bill were still in the Hongu. They walked a long way down the valley to ascend another worthy summit, Nau Lekh (6,363 metres), and followed our route to the Sherpa villages two days later. In total the expedition had climbed 19 peaks of over 6,000 metres, all first ascents. The mapping had been reasonably successful. However, Jim McFarlane had received injuries that might ultimately prove serious.

The five-day Dumji festival was held early each June, coinciding with the beginning of the monsoon. Potatoes and seeds planted weeks previously began more rapid growth. At the conclusion of the ceremonies all animals were taken up to higher pastures and the home fields, free of grazing, were left for the growing of hay. Ceremonies were held in temples, in courtyards and at the cairns marking the entrances to each village. There was much hospitable entertaining in an atmosphere that was delightfully informal. The very young and the ancient all mixed together in a happy mood. Gifts, mainly of food, were given out, much liquor flowed and the odd dog sniffed around, picking up spillages.

At the gompas (temples) the lamas wore their ceremonial costumes and from time to time some of their extraordinary headgear was worn to act out a special event. Long brass Tibetan-style horns joined the sounds of a large drum and noisy cymbals. Practically everyone wore some colourful Tibetan clothing, and the women sported quality jewellery. In 1954 most of the men still had pigtails and also wore simple colourful necklaces.

I found much to examine in the construction of the houses, the stone walls, the gates and the water channels. Very few nails or bolts were used in the houses. Beam junctions were carefully shaped and wedged or doweled into fixed positions. Roofs were made from pines slabs held down by rough rocks. Stairs to upper floors were usually a hazard for Westerners, always being in the darkest part of the house and short of headroom.

It was a most relaxing time for me. Khumjung was such a delightful village and the Sherpas were so hospitable: I understood why some of the few earlier visitors had praised it so highly, and I decided I had to return at some future date.

EIGHT

Private Expedition

Charles Evans and I engaged six of our regular Sherpas to come with us for the long walk on a new high route to Kathmandu. We changed money to small denominations, as any purchases would be at high-altitude pastures, where no one would have a bag of cash change. We read our mail and wrote replies, as well as excuses for delaying our returns. Much of our high-altitude clothing was also sent away with the descending group. Our departure from Khumjung was in a daze of chang from well-wishers. Chang is a local beer made from millet or, more recently, rice. I enjoyed it.

One hour away, in Namche Bazar, we gathered our rather staggering octet and turned right, leaving the main track that descends to Chaunrikarka and then Kathmandu. We went up to Thami and then crossed another high pass, the Tesi Lapcha, which was new to me but familiar to all the others. Then we were in the Rolwaling Valley, which becomes forested lower down. Near the top of the pass I had a short glimpse of a snow leopard stealing its way among large glacial rocks. Travelling involved descending a glacier, then along a moraine, through patches of pasture and then on to a track in the forest. All the side-streams were now swollen and dirty from monsoons.

At these altitudes one does not encounter the downpours of Calcutta. The monsoon brings a thick, damp fog for most of the day, with sometimes brief clearings at dawn. Drizzling rains are frequent, and as the temperatures are warm there is much melting of snow and ice. Even though it is warm, if one is travelling in snow the feet can become extremely cold, because one sinks further into the snow rather than staying on the frozen surface. Also the dampness of the warmer snow penetrates the leather and gaiters more easily.

We stopped at the village of Beding. Not being on a main trading route, this was a more primitive settlement, and lacked the adjacent grazing grounds and potato paddocks of Khumjung. Two great peaks are just north of the town. One is Menlungtse, which is totally in Tibet, and there is a reasonable pass over the frontier, quite close to the village. In thick cloud we crossed the pass and descended to the next valley, hoping to be far upstream of any possible Chinese patrols. Charles had no serious ambitions to climb the mountain, but he did want to make his own assessment of possible routes for the future, if the time came when Chinese authorities would allow expeditions to come that way.

We were in the same place where Shipton and Ward had seen and photographed yeti tracks in 1951. We had both seen those photos, and those that Shipton took of the surrounding unclimbed summits, but we waited one day and the weather did not clear enough to allow us to explore. Being north of the main range, we had hoped there might have been breaks in the cloud.

Our return to Beding was uneventful, except that before the village we stopped at a large area of young bamboo and picked dozens of shoots. Boiled, they tasted very like asparagus. There was also by now an abundance of wild garlic. For this journey the only Western food we carried was instant coffee, some sugar and a few remaining bars of chocolate. We were eating tsampa with the Sherpas and drinking a lot of chang. The Sherpas would eat the first young fronds of one variety of fern. We tenderised them in a pressure cooker and enjoyed them. Mushrooms were also available above the top forest limits. Several varieties grew wild during the monsoon and these were always welcome. I enquired how they knew which were safe to eat.

'If they grow out of a heap of old yak dung, it means they are right for yaks, so good for us.'

'But if there are yaks nearby, won't they eat them first? I asked.

Apparently in the high pastures, where there are wolves and some snow leopards, the yaks and especially their calves are kept in a corral at night. While the animals are being milked in the morning the children run around the grazing places and pick the mushrooms from the old dung patches before the yaks are allowed out.

From Beding we walked down to the Bhote Kosi, initially in heavy forest, where for the first time I encountered large numbers of leeches. So long as one kept boots on and checked exposed skin from time to time they were no great problem. Next we went uphill again and walked almost to the Kosi headwaters. Two small villages we passed had the intriguing names of Lamabagar and Hum. We were back in Nepal but very close to Tibet. For the rest of the journey westwards we were almost always in country unknown to our Sherpas, and two or three times a day we would encounter shelters temporarily erected by Bhotia people who were occupying high pastures during the warm wet weather. They would be grazing crossbred cattle and sometimes sheep and goats.

Their shelters consisted usually of eight poles placed firmly in the ground and a simple roof frame lashed to them. Sheets of bamboo matting were unrolled over the framing to form a roof. Young bamboo can be cut and split while still green, then it is woven into large sheets, which are made into roof parts or big mats for spreading out grain and vegetables to dry. These temporary structures had no bracing and just rudimentary walls. Still, they shed most of the monsoon drizzles and formed a base for the animal herders to live. The higher-quality roof rolls would have some birch bark behind the bamboo weaving.

On one occasion we were inside one of these shelters when Charles, beside the woman attending the fire, called to me, 'Do you eat liver?'

'Yes. I'd like some if it's available.'

I could smell meat being fried in butter. Soon it arrived on a plate, along with potato slices. It was delicious, particularly as we had not eaten any meat since our yak stew in Khumjung. I commented to Charles that the liver appeared to have no veins.

'It's yak's blood. They cut a hole in the carotid artery and drain off about two litres. This has salt added to it and is heated over a fire. When it goes solid it can be stored or cut into slices like liver.'

'How about the yak? Does he bleed badly?'

'No. They tie him to a wooden frame held down by rocks. After the cut, a patch of moist tsampa poultice is put over it, and the animal's head is pulled round the other way. He is held there for an hour or so, and then released, and he staggers off to join his mates.'

On another occasion we saw a nak (female yak) tied to one of the wooden anchor frames. We approached to observe the local surgeon in action. But, no. It was a mating with an Indian bull, both participants being rather reluctant. The yak is really a creature of the high Tibetan plains and they are not very healthy in the lower Nepalese forests. The European and Indian cattle have problems above about 2,000 metres. There is a vast expanse of country where the crossbreed can live and work successfully. The plough and packing animals are mostly crosses and there are names for the considerable range of fractions of these. The females are fertile so they produce calves and milk. The Indian bulls at these heights are usually kept in a corral for protection and fed hay by hand. If a group of nak get near a foreign bull they give him a hard time.

While researching this book I found the following, written in the back of a 1981 diary, dreamed up when I was alone in the Yak and Yeti restaurant in Kathmandu. I wrote it to my second daughter:

> Dear Ruth,
> It's truth.
> I saw a yak that every Sherpa calls a nak.
> But it's hard to tell
> I truly swear,
> When their private parts are hid by hair.
> But yak or nak, dzum or dzos
> Each grunting hairy creature knows.
> Which way you spell it, no matter how,
> They cannot stand a Hindu cow.
> They've humps and bumps
> Are full of fever.
> Frankly, I can't stand them either.

On My Own Two Feet

Charles talked about a peak near us, Choba Bamare, which stands some 600 metres above the main range, being very visible from much of the high track when walking from Kathmandu to Jiri. In later years I walked that track 10 times and I recall a thumb-shaped peak standing up from a nearly level line of ranges. We decided to approach it. Local yak herders directed us to a track that would lead to the grazing ground near the mountain, but they gave arm-waving descriptions of avalanches. Our very primitive map indicated that the mountain was on the frontier, but no one seemed to know just where Tibet began.

We stayed in the fog-bound area for three days and eventually went right round the great thumb without seeing a simple way to the top. The snow basins were damp and soon our feet were cold and wet. The steep rock ridges had big buttresses with a sprinkling of new snow. On two occasions the cloud cleared to the north Tibetan side for just a few morning hours, but we did not want to press the peak without obtaining a glimpse of its overall content.

Two of our Sherpas and a local man had been at our high camp, while the other rested at a small village. They had bought a sheep at a very low price, killed and skinned it and were preparing the first meal from it. Several metres of intestines had been cleaned, then filled with tsampa, blood and finely chopped wild garlic. When cooked and sliced they were very like the English black pudding.

We left the area and proceeded south on an interesting high route, then west and a big drop down to the Sun Kosi, which is another of the rivers that rise in Tibet. In the 1960s the Chinese built a road following this from Kathmandu to Lhasa.

We encountered a major track that passed through the frontier village of Kodari. Instead of following the river down towards Kathmandu, where the road now goes, we climbed again and took a high route that brought us through more pleasant pastures, until eventually, coming down a long spur, we could see some of the hills in the Kathmandu basin.

Private Expedition

Charles had previously told Dawa Tenzing we would try to come out this way, but he gave no forecast of a date. At the entrance to a small village we met a smiling Dawa, typically holding a big black kettle full of chang. We got out mugs and began drinking. Then he pulled out a bag from his pack. It was mail for the two of us, the first for five weeks.

We sat on the wet grass with our mugs and were immediately absorbed in our news. At about the third item in Charles's heap he suddenly gave a loud whoop shout: 'Norman, look at this!'

It was a cable from John Hunt in London, and as far as I remember it read:

> To Evans or Hillary. HMG [the government of Nepal] has given the [Joint] Committee permission for climbing Kangchenjunga in 1955 and 1956. Will one of you lead a reconnaissance next year? I expect to lead main climb in 1956. Expedition costs will be met by the committee. Kempe report is inconclusive and climbing route is far from solved.

Charles jumped up and said: 'The answer is yes! Will you come with me?'

Yes indeed.

John Kempe was the leader of the British expedition that was attempting summits just south of Kangchenjunga while we were in the Barun. Three of his men had been with us on the boat to Bombay. With the cable was a message from Ed Hillary: 'Not me. Over to you, Charles.' Ed had seen the cable in Kathmandu two weeks previously.

However, a letter from John to Charles said that the army was not very keen on his having leave for two Kangchenjunga expeditions in a row, especially as they regarded that climb as much less significant than Everest. John's views on the merits of Kangchenjunga were very different. In addition, for Everest in 1953, John had used a great amount of young subaltern time during the months of preparations. He was considering early retirement from the army anyway, and a future meeting would clarify the whole matter.

There are 14 peaks in the world of over 8,000 metres in height. By this time six of them had been climbed and applications had been made for attempts on most of the others. It was likely all 14 would have their first ascents in the next three years. K2 and Kangchenjunga were regarded as probably the two hardest. The British had made the first ascent of Everest but none of the others. Among mountaineers, Kangchenjunga was regarded as an enormous challenge and a great prize.

The arrival of that cable was most fortuitous. During the day's walk to the city we discussed all aspects of the proposition. With no roads or airstrips in east Nepal, the starting location would have to be Darjeeling in India. Tentative assembly dates were fixed and Sherpa numbers established. Clearly, Dawa Tenzing would again be the sirdar (head Sherpa) and our present team of six would be the core of the support. Having this much arranged saved the problem of trying to communicate with them in their village of Khumjung, which is more than 20 days' walk from Darjeeling.

Dawa had walked out with the Lowe party, who, with Hillary, had all now left Kathmandu. Jim McFarlane and Brian Wilkins had caught a flight that would, by various connections, take them to New Zealand.

In 1954 there was just one hotel – of sorts – in Kathmandu. We were invited to stay in the British Embassy, where Charles was well known and he was also close to the Gurkha recruiting officer, Colonel Lowndes, who had an establishment there. After the partition of India the British Army gave up its Indian regiments but made separate arrangements with the Nepalese government to retain Gurkha units and build training camps on Nepalese territory.

Charles immediately rang London and agreed to lead the expedition. He also asked the big question that would affect all planning: Would there be enough money available for oxygen to be taken, so the reconnaissance could go quite high? The answer was not wholly clear, but he was told for certain that John Hunt would not go on the 1955 venture.

Our Sherpas departed. I cleaned myself up, wrote letters in several directions and then began a tour of Kathmandu, conducted by Lady Summerhayes, the ambassador's wife, in the embassy's second-best car, a Humber Pulman. There were just six cars in the city. The Embassy Rolls had been carried in by 120 porters.

Its wheels were taken off and two long telephone poles lashed to the chassis. The walk took four days. A tortuous access road from India was completed three years later.

Kathmandu was a wonderful, clean, quiet place, but Charles said it had declined since his first visit in 1950 with Tilman. Local Newari tradesmen had been selling handcrafts then, but now there was an abundance of mass-produced Indian goods in the shops. There were some open drains on the outskirts, but the population was small and the monsoon rains flushed things away. The buildings had real character; the shops were unrushed, with tempting smells and modest prices. There was one electrical generator for the city, so candles and kerosene lamps were lit at dusk. Each time I have returned I see what I consider to be depressing deterioration. Now there are traffic jams, noise and the smell of burning diesel. Uncontrolled building has produced a great jumble of structures and styles.

After Charles had completed numerous business and social chores we walked over two more passes to reach the Indian rail terminus at Raxaul, where we were the guests of Dr and Mrs Strong, who managed a mission hospital. Charles knew them well and he spent several hours performing medical tasks where the Strongs needed his expertise, including a throat operation.

During the last year of the war Charles had been the doctor to a British Army unit in Burma. He completed various instruction courses in Indian army bases and, during brief leaves, made short Himalayan visits. Thus he became fluent in Hindustani and developed a considerable enthusiasm for Himalayan travel. He wrote a book about his army experiences, *A Doctor in the 14th Army*, which was published posthumously in 1998. He slowly dictated the book during his last years as he was slowly losing mobility from the effects of multiple sclerosis.

After Kangchenjunga he returned to his surgical career but found his fingers no longer capable of the fine work involved. Eventually he diagnosed his own sad problem. He gave up mountaineering and took up deep-water sailing. Although wheelchair-bound, he was appointed principal of the University of North Wales, then vice-chancellor of the University of Wales.

He had a turn at being the president of the Alpine Club and he was later knighted. In 1957 Charles married Denise Morin, who translated Jean Franco's *Makalu, 8470 Metres: The highest peak yet conquered by an entire team* from the French. Her mother had translated the bestselling *Annapurna* by Maurice Herzog six years previously. Denise was also enthusiastic about sailing. After Charles was incapacitated she sailed their boat to the Caribbean once, and later down to the Straits of Magellan. Charles died at the end of 1995.

I was privileged to have such a friend, and to be taken to some of his special Indian cities was a delight. I will not give a detailed description of our journey, but mention three incidents. Charles's arrival had been mentioned in many Indian newspapers and, among other things, he was asked to speak to a Rotary club in one city. He was introduced as the man who turned back 95 metres from the summit of Everest. He was then asked all the old questions: Who reached the top first, Hillary or Tenzing? What about the decoration given to Tenzing, when Ed had a KBE? How about Hunt's lesser knighthood? Charles tried to divert them with the news that permission had just been given to attempt the third-highest peak in the world, now the highest unclimbed mountain. But no, the questions went back to Everest.

Afterwards I asked him about the constant emphasis on Everest.

'It was the same on the American tour and similar in England,' he said. 'I'm used to it. In the 1930s if a German said he was going to the Himalayas, he would be asked, Kangchenjunga or Nanga Parbat? If you told an Englishman you were going, he would ask, Everest again? You'll see. With our expedition next year the Germans will know where we are, even if no one else does. Those were the mountains that Germans had attempted in the 1930s. British emphasis had been on Everest.'

In Lucknow he wanted me to see an old museum. He said many of the artworks were taken from galleries by the British when they departed. Some were also removed by Indians if they appeared too pompous. He wanted me to see a selection of really early ones, claiming that paintings back in the days of the East India Company showed the British rulers wearing Indian clothes, sometimes turbans. For about 50 years relations were good, until the British Army arrived and, soon afterwards, the senior officers' wives, with their English class distinctions and snobbery. I pointed out that Indians have class distinctions that are probably as bad. Charles claimed that the senior Indians, 200 years ago, had thought the British were beyond that sort of thing and that they would set a good example to Indians. They were greatly disappointed.

In Delhi we stayed in a hotel owned by Robert Hotz, who was on the Himalayan Club committee. He invited about 10 members for dinner, including Peter Aufschnaiter, who had been leading a German Nanga Parbat expedition when the Second World War began. All members of the party were interned by the British in India. Aufschnaiter and Heinrich Harrer escaped and walked to Lhasa, as recounted in Harrer's book, *Seven Years in Tibet*. Aufschnaiter did not want to return to Europe and was now doing engineering work in India, particularly in irrigation projects. We had a long talk about engineering and surveying in Nepal, where there was much need but no money.

Seven years later, Harrer spent a fortnight with me in New Zealand, and that stay resulted in his joining Philip Temple for their successful New Guinea expedition.

Again Charles rang London. Issues were becoming clearer and responses more favourable. He flew back to resume his work at Liverpool Hospital. I went by train to Bombay for an uneventful shipboard return to England.

The ship reached the Liverpool docks on a fine English summer morning in late August 1954. There to greet me were Enid and Charles. Amid hugs and greetings I was told that Tom Bourdillon and Wilfred Noyce could not go on our 1955 expedition, but would be available for John Hunt in 1956. They felt they could not commit the time to both, and had declined Charles's invitation. Would I still go, and would I undertake the oxygen duties?

NINE

Preparing for Kanchengjunga

Enid seemed to be not too greatly disturbed by my acceptance of the Kangchenjunga invitation. She knew Charles well and felt that he and I would have a lot of input into the project and not be pressed into difficult undertakings by sponsors or committees. While I was at sea the Joint Committee, chaired by Sir John Hunt, had given Charles an almost totally free hand to proceed as he saw best.

The thought of the oxygen being my responsibility was daunting, with my lack of familiarity with the equipment. Tom Bourdillon was available to give me advice and had already placed orders for his modified oxygen sets to be manufactured by Normalair Ltd at their factory in Yeovil, in Somerset. If I accepted the responsibility I would be employed at Yeovil, and be paid. I looked at Enid and she smiled. It was evident that Charles had already explained all this to her, and arranged my modest salary at the factory. On the actual expedition there would be no salaries.

Charles informed me of his tentative list of expedition members, and I was the only one with an engineering background. I agreed to take on the oxygen position, especially when Charles also said he had arranged a committee to meet me most Friday afternoons at Yeovil to review progress. They would be Tom Bourdillon, Griff Pugh and Alf Bridge, the latter an engineer from Normalair. I knew them all as experienced mountaineers. Tom and Griff had been on the Cho Oyu 1952 and Everest 1953 expeditions.

The job would begin in December 1954 and we were to sail

Preparing for Kangchenjunga

for Bombay in early February. I needed a paid job from August to December, in London. I was accepted by an engineering firm that had offices near St James's Park tube station and water-supply contracts operating in many parts of the world. I was allocated the administration of the Qatar team, which had several vehicles, pumps, drills, mobile generators and all sorts of data-recording equipment. This was years before oil was found, deep below the shallow-water searching level. I had to buy and freight specialised goods to Qatar and keep the field group active. As I had little background with the British firms involved in making these goods, I did struggle. Perhaps an experienced stores officer would have been more successful.

One of the London staff had been an air force officer stationed on the African Gold Coast during the war. He had not seen much action, but the station was necessary, as U-boats did pass down that way from time to time. My colleague had a rifle he no longer used and had been looking for someone to whom he could donate it. Knowing I was to return to the Himalayas, he insisted I accept it.

'What if an abominable snowman puts his head into your tent?' he said.

'If it exists it would be dreadful to shoot one of the last of a rare species,' I replied.

He countered with, 'Buddhists don't eat meat. You could shoot the odd wild sheep or a rabbit or something. I shot a python up a tree once, as well as a leopard.'

My colleague brought the rifle to work and I was stricken. It was an Austrian Manlicher, dated 1880, made by Steyr, with a clip magazine for five rounds and an aperture sight. It was modest in weight. There are bharal – wild sheep – in the Nepalese mountains and they are good for eating, so I did take the gun and did indeed fell some bharal. (Sherpas, although Buddhist, are not too fussy about not eating meat, especially if someone else kills the animal or if it has fallen over a cliff.) In New Zealand I have shot a few deer, chamois and pigs with this rifle. Now it resides in my son-in-law's collection.

However, the rifle did cause me later troubles at Indian Army checkposts near the Tibetan border. If I had had a very long metric spanner I could have unscrewed the butt to shorten it and kept it in a kit bag out of sight. From the past I was accustomed to carrying a rifle, but in 1955 it stirred up questions on many occasions.

While in London I was asked to give lectures, for no fee, to some schools, the Institution of Civil Engineers and the Mountaineering Club at the Sandhurst Military Academy. For the latter, train tickets were posted to me and there was all the pomp of an officers' mess. I showed slides on these occasions and talked about Makalu, surveying and Sherpa villages, but never a word about being over the ill-defined Tibetan border a few times. Some years later I was told that the future Ugandan president, Idi Amin, had been an officer cadet in the audience at Sandhurst that night.

Charles's expedition list was firming up, although some still had to confirm leave from their employers. He had invited Colin Todd from last year's Barun party, but his professor would not part with him again. A few months later Colin was killed in Dunedin in a road accident. I asked for Bill Beaven, but Charles said he was too slow to acclimatise. I countered that Bill had climbed Baruntse comfortably and that the New Zealand Barun group the previous year had started very late because the three senior members were lecturing in America. This had left a short acclimatising time, which would not be the case next year. Sad to say, Charles did not contact Bill.

There would be nine in the party, six of whom had been to the Himalayas previously. Of these, only Evans, George Band and Tony Streather had been really high. Joe Brown had a big name for new rock-climbing routes in Wales and he had been to the French Alps briefly. Neil Mather had a fondness for fell walking over very long distances. John Clegg, the doctor, had climbed several times in Switzerland and he had a fund of good songs.

Tom MacKinnon, at 42, was the oldest, a Scotsman with two Himalayan visits. John Jackson had been on many Himalayan tours while in the air force in India and he had been the main mountaineer in the *Daily Mail* 1954 yeti-searching expedition.

Tony Streather needs special mention. He left school early during the Second World War and went to India after hearing

Preparing for Kangchenjunga

that the British Army there would take officer-training cadets at a younger age than in England. He rose in seniority and at partition in 1947 he went to the Pakistan Army. While there he was asked to be the transport officer to a Norwegian expedition attempting Tirich Mir (7,710 metres). The portering system broke down below the top camp so he carried a load there. Finding nothing to do, Tony went on to the summit, using the support of his officer's cane and wearing a golf jacket, to the amazement of the summit party resting on top. He left Pakistan and joined a British Army unit, dropping in rank from colonel to captain. In the Korean War he received a decoration.

When Everest climbers were being considered in late 1952 Streather was taken for trials to Switzerland but was dropped for his lack of knowledge of mountain techniques, yet he had been higher than any other in the whole selected team. Houston's 1953 K2 expedition took him as transport officer and he went to their top camp and had many good words written about him for assisting the survivors of an accident high on the mountain. I was very happy to know of his inclusion in our team. He could go high and our transport would be in capable hands.

•||•

The Normalair company in Yeovil was in the same location as Westland Aircraft, where naval planes were being assembled and tested. Normalair made the breathing apparatus for pilots and for submarine escapes, as well as many other procedures that had secrecy embargoes on them. I shared a workroom with one of the submariners.

Manufacturing of most Kangchenjunga equipment was well in hand. The oxygen cylinders were a new design and proved to be highly successful. The only fiddly part was the flow selector and regulator, which needed to be robust, light and unlikely to freeze in extreme temperatures, as had happened on occasions on Everest in 1953. I assembled various parts, wrote a manual for their operation and devised packing cases and their transport, right up to 7,000 metres, where they would be opened.

One test was eagerly awaited by all concerned. A large room had a specially designed decompression room built inside it, complete with windows so observers outside could see if the occupants were having problems. On a workbench inside the chamber I was to have a closed-circuit oxygen set and the open-circuit ones ready for simple tests. Before starting, temperatures were dropped so the atmosphere would be realistically cold. Then, dressed in mountain clothing, down jacket and gloves, I sat on a stool beside the bench. Two pilot trainees and their instructor came in with me as subjects for this test on the effects of low pressure. On the walls were a telephone and several breathing masks if required. No one was allowed into a decompression chamber alone and safety procedures were elaborate.

The suction apparatus outside was started and soon we were at the equivalent of 7,500 metres. I used a special spanner for changing bottles, unscrewing a tube and blowing through it for blockages. The regulators were tried at all flow rates and the sets put on and off my back. The closed-circuit valves had to be opened and shut without problems and the soda lime canisters had to be able to be changed with ease. This last test always seemed inappropriate to me, as each canister weighed 5 kilograms and I had never heard of anyone on a mountain actually carrying such a heavy spare, when the first one should give a good flow rate for eight hours. The additional 5 kilograms would have been an unwelcome burden on top of all the other necessary climbing gear.

The pilots were talking into recorders and they had to write imaginary instructions onto worksheets, in order to test the effects of oxygen shortage on their brains. After an hour the pressures were returned slowly and we assessed our work. All my equipment had performed satisfactorily. I was not surprised that I had a headache, and was also relieved my tasks had not been too complex – one of the pilots had written utter rubbish on his sheet, and the other had several mistakes.

In normal breathing one takes in nitrogen and oxygen. On breathing out, the nitrogen is expelled along with carbon dioxide, but a lot of oxygen also passes to the outside. With the closed-circuit set, when one is breathing just oxygen, there should be no nitrogen in the system unless a mask or tube leaks, permitting outside air to enter. The outward breath consisting of carbon dioxide and oxygen passes through the soda lime canister, where the carbon dioxide is intercepted while the oxygen goes on to re-enter the body. This in theory should be economical because no oxygen is lost and there is a reduction of weight of oxygen cylinders carried. Something of this sort is now used in spacecraft, where a pump and filtering system, along with temperature controls, keeps reasonable breathing conditions inside the craft. Carbon dioxide is removed and the oxygen is available for re-use.

With an open-circuit set one breathes oxygen from the atmosphere but can get an oxygen boost from a cylinder on one's back. It is less cumbersome but wasteful of oxygen, as three-quarters of the oxygen is breathed out into the atmosphere.

On the mountain the closed-circuit systems have big tubes like elephant trunks hanging from the breathing masks. These go to the soda lime tank and then back to the mask again. To breathe, one has to push air through the system and when the oxygen comes back inside again it is warm, as it has already been through one's lungs.

Tom Bourdillon and senior staff at Normalair were convinced that Tom's design of the closed-circuit system had a great future in Himalayan mountaineering. Griff Pugh said little and I felt he was sceptical, like Evans. Griff was more forthcoming on giving adequate safety instructions to oxygen users, the health of the climbers and the need to drink high volumes of water during the whole expedition.

It was decided that we would use mostly open-circuit sets, but would take along two closed-circuit sets as a contribution to Tom's research.

The Friday afternoon gatherings at Yeovil were very helpful for me. Tom and Alf Bridge, and usually Griff, were intensely interested in all aspects of high-altitude oxygen use and were constructive in their comments. Alf had never been to the Himalayas, but he had been a notable rock climber in the 1930s. As a permanent employee of the firm that owned Normalair, he was able to smooth the passage of our various developments through the official channels. Alf was also the expedition secretary, working from the RGS office, again with Ann Debenham. Meetings of my oxygen group were quite informal, and I was required to ring Charles Evans each week to keep him in touch with our progress.

For one weekend the whole Kangchenjunga party had booked a hotel in the mountains of Wales. I brought an open-circuit oxygen set to demonstrate and allow everyone to try it. There was no need to demonstrate the complexities of the experimental closed-circuit sets, as most would not be using them on the mountain.

Everything was packed and sent to the wharves at Liverpool. There was so much to do, with clearing one's work situation and making tidy domestic arrangements, that there was no opportunity for farewell parties. I left England not knowing if or when I would return. I had been approached by the Ministry of Works to return to New Zealand, all expenses paid, but I would have been bonded to a hydro-electric construction site in the Waikato, and this did not appeal to me or Enid.

I opted instead to have the expedition pay for my return to New Zealand. I arranged for Enid and our friend Joe Macdonald to join me in Nepal in September, after the monsoon. Then, in December, all three of us would go home.

TEN

Kangchenjunga

The expedition has been described in one book and in two journals. *Kangchenjunga: The untrodden peak* by Charles Evans was published in 1956 by Hodder & Stoughton. Here, I summarise the main events and in a few instances record some additional points that were of particular interest to me.

On 12 February 1955 the nine-strong party assembled at Liverpool. The ship carried 80 other passengers and I remember little about them. We spent an hour most mornings in Charles's cabin on serious Hindi lessons. Having Evans and Streather both competent in that language was most valuable. I took it very seriously and put in extra time at the subject. Twice we alternated the lessons with a medical and an oxygen refresher talk, going over the instructions that had been discussed in Wales.

On one Mediterranean afternoon Charles came to me in private and said, 'I have just found that two of our party have never worn crampons and we are going to one of the biggest ice mountains in the world. I want you to take them with good Sherpas and give them four days on some hard ice as an early acclimatising trip.' He told me their names. I was surprised at this information, but it was not particularly unusual in those days. We tended to regard crampons as being just for ice work or very crusty snow. Today they seem to be used in a broad variety of snow conditions.

At Aden, Charles rang ahead to Bombay enquiring about details of our rail journey across to Calcutta. At a meeting he confirmed what had been mentioned in England – that our baggage would occupy a full goods van. This would not be attached to the express train but to slow trains, taking four or five days. Streather wanted to take the express train to Darjeeling to begin the hiring of Sherpas and porters. Charles needed two of us to accompany the goods van. He reminded us that a German team three years previously had lost their baggage for two weeks. Tom and I, having earlier Indian rail experience, volunteered for this task. Charles would proceed by a different route to New Delhi to clear some formalities.

At Bombay we checked our hundreds of packages and had our van sealed. We noted its number and description and waved to the others in their first-class rail diner. Our slow trains went by a different route, often stopping at outlandish places where food was not available. At every stop, day or night, one of us would get out to watch the reforming of the train after a lengthy shunting performance, making certain that our van came with us. At least I had practice for my developing language skills. After five days we reached the rail terminus of Siliguri, where six trucks had been sent down the hill to meet us. Three hours later we reached Darjeeling with all items intact. We were short of sleep and had mild upsets from the range of irregular food sources encountered on the way.

Darjeeling is a popular hill station, high above the hot dusty plains. We stayed for four days on the spacious grounds of the Henderson family, who had a large tea-growing estate. Jill Henderson was the secretary of the local Himalayan Club and we greatly appreciated her hospitality and her recruitment of Sherpas and porters for our journey. Early one morning we drove to a remote lookout to obtain a distant glimpse of our objective, far above the haze and foothills clouds. On the same day we were entertained to lunch at the Planters' Club in their interesting Victorian building.

One of the club members at the lunch function read out the frequently quoted statement by Sir John Hunt: 'There is no doubt that those who first climb Kangchenjunga will achieve the greatest feat in mountaineering, for it is a mountain that combines in its defences not only the severe handicaps of wind, weather and very high altitude, but technical problems and objective dangers even higher than those we encountered on Everest.' It was emphasised that on Everest in 1952 Tenzing had been to about 300 metres from the summit, so the basic route-finding for 1953 was just on the final ridge. For Kangchenjunga no one had been within 2,500 metres of the summit on the Yalung side.

The Sherpa team was virtually the same as had been with Charles and me in the Barun; just two were new. Dawa Tenzing was sirdar again and did an outstanding job all the way. In Darjeeling, Urkien gave me a headband he had bought in the bazaar and a small bag of genuine barley tsampa. He remembered how Charles and I had usually added tsampa to our tea the previous year. I did the same all the way this year and, apart from throat and chest problems at one stage, I was healthy all the time.

On the long walks I sometimes used the headband, but they are inappropriate in complex climbing. They are commonly used throughout Asia for carrying heavy loads. A long leather strap goes under the baggage and its top end is worn high on the bearer's head, just above the forehead. The load has no shoulder straps as we know them. The headband gives total freedom for the arms but one cannot move one's head, which is usually pushed slightly forward. I have subsequently used it a number of times in New Zealand, but I let it drop to my chest when my group meets others – it causes too many comments.

I was disappointed to see that Urkien had cut off his pigtail, but Dawa still wore his.

Forty-five (and again 50) years later I visited Darjeeling and was disappointed. The tea plantations had all been taken over by Indian planters and the Planters' Club had lost its records of everything more than 30 years old. The town was crowded and noisy, and the haze of the plains appeared to have crept higher up the foothills. Darjeeling still has several select high schools plus the Himalayan Mountaineering Institute, and is an important centre for the Hindu and Buddhist religions.

Kangchenjunga is on the frontier between Nepal and Sikkim (more recently a province of India). Permission to operate in Nepal was clear, but for many years mountain climbing in Sikkim had been forbidden. Several Himalayan peaks, especially Kangchenjunga, are regarded as sacred, through the belief that they are the ultimate dwelling places of spirits after a series of uplifting reincarnations. As the actual summit was astride the frontier it would be tidy to have permission to tread it, although the actual climbing would be from the Nepalese side. Charles obtained a day visa to enter Sikkim to interview the maharajah at Gangtok. I drove with him as far as Kalimpong and waited for him there. Charles returned disappointed. We were not to enter Sikkim in any part of the journey and were not to stand on the summit, but the precise distance from it we could reach was not defined.

Back in Darjeeling, on 14 March, our caravans moved off, having about 230 men on the first day and another hundred one day behind us. It was a joy to be walking in Nepal again. For two days we had brilliant views of the mountains ahead and we tried not to be overawed by their immense vertical scale. Much of the time the trail was deep in valleys with no outward vistas. On the eleventh day we arrived at the terminal of the Yalung Glacier at a little over 4,000 metres, where we stopped for a major reorganisation of our transport. The Darjeeling porters were barefoot and they were all paid and discharged at this stage of the journey. We had engaged 16 Sherpas for work high on the mountain and they were issued with quality equipment. A further 14 were given ex-army clothing for work lower on the mountain, also for cooking and mail running. As the terrain became difficult from here on, all loads would have to be relayed in four-day round trips to the climbing base camp.

Charles had an obligation to write a fortnightly article on our progress for *The Times*. He struggled to find any drama to report, so his bulletins were gentle descriptions of the pleasant mountainous country we were seeing. We were early in the season and noisy winter winds kept blowing snow from the high summits in the area we were approaching. Most mornings dawned fine, but on many afternoons the party would be walking under thunderclouds.

George Band, who had done an excellent job in organising the expedition food with Neil Mather, crossed a high pass to the nearest village, Ghunza, where he engaged a few well-clad porters for firewood deliveries and other duties. He arranged for the later purchase of supplies of tsampa and some edible yaks to go in April to base camp. This enterprise also gave them useful acclimatisation experience.

I went to the range on our east side, with John Jackson and Joe Brown, for four days of climbing on major snow and ice peaks, reaching two summits of Koktang, a little over 6,000 metres. It is a complex mountain by the border of Sikkim and none of its summits had previously been climbed. We all benefited from this diversion and enjoyed being part of a smaller group on a mountain.

The others of the party were opening the rather difficult route up the main glacier, which has no undisturbed ablation valley at its sides, as exists on the Everest approach. Thus they had to be out on the active moraine for some days before approaching a possible base camp. This activity up to 5,000 metres was also useful for acclimatisation purposes, although there were technical problems on ice and fragile moraine even down at that level. In one place the access down to the glacier was so loose that they put in a hundred metres of fixed ropes to support the carrying teams.

All this action was happening at the end of March and temperatures were bitingly cold. We could hear violent screaming winds on the exposed slopes far above us. On two occasions tents were torn by the wind gusts and once the dome tent used by Sherpas was lifted off its occupiers and deposited, rather broken, in a hollow 200 metres downwind.

My second activity in the Yalung was to have two days working on surveying problems. Charles wanted to know the heights of various features on the mountain, for planning the location of higher camps. I established two theodolite stations, made many observations and then retreated to a sunny spot to produce, via seven-figure logarithm tables, the many heights required. From my viewpoints nearly all of the features of the south face of Kangchenjunga were visible.

At the head of the wide Yalung Glacier was the third-highest mountain in the world. K2 had been climbed by two Italians in 1954, so Kangchenjunga was now the highest unclimbed mountain.

From my top survey station the climbing problems looked most formidable. Part of the Yalung Glacier was fed on the left from a very steep active icefall that flowed in two long halves. To the right were extensive walls of avalanche debris, and further to the right more cliffs, which were too far away from the main objective to be useful for us. The main feature feeding the debris was an ice shelf at nearly 7,300 metres, spread right across the impressive face. At the left end of the 'great shelf' a secondary steep glacier drops down to feed the lower icefall. If one could reach this shelf there would probably be reasonable climbing through to the rock faces that begin at about 200 metres below the final summit. That top portion, having severe rock ribs separating snow gullies, looked hard, even from my position 11 kilometres away.

The Kempe party, having the same view in 1954, thought there was a possible chink in the armour. A hard rock, massive at the bottom, separated the lower icefall from the avalanche debris under the cliffs. They went most of the way up this buttress but, when it ended at the extremely active icefall on their left, they turned back. We referred to this as Kempe's buttress. His team had also looked at the other side of this icefall and wisely rejected it. Two of them tried the cirque at the head of the valley and considered it to be very dangerous.

There had been three attempts on Kangchenjunga in the 1930s, by large, competent mountaineering expeditions, and all failed by a considerable distance. Two German groups had tried from the Sikkim side in the early days when permission on that approach could be obtained. The third was a predominantly Swiss party, which also contained Frank Smythe. Through a telescope on the hill behind Darjeeling he examined the slopes we were now considering. In *The Kangchenjunga Adventure* he wrote in 1930:

> But a minute's examination was needed to assure us that it was futile to seek a way from the Yalung Glacier. Though only the upper part of the route was visible, the long sloping ice shelf the climber would have to ascend is exposed to avalanches of ice and stones, while the icefall up which the party would have to go to reach the shelf looked unassailable.

Kangchenjunga

They ignored the Yalung and tried the north-west approach, but retreated after a death in an avalanche.

A few casual visitors had reached the lower Yalung, and one other, besides Kempe, got 250 metres above the main glacier. This was in 1905, when Aleister Crowley believed his mystical powers would enable him to tread the summit. While he was in a tent near a group of climbers and porters, an avalanche swept all of them some distance down the slope and their cries were audible from the camp. Crowley did not go the short distance to assist a rescue. Three porters and a Lieutenant Pache were killed, while two climbers did manage to escape. Crowley remained in his tent and later wrote: 'Not that I was over anxious in the circumstances to render help. A mountain accident of this sort is one of the things for which I have no sympathy whatever.' Three days later Crowley left for India. There, to reinforce an order on a mountain, he pulled out a pistol from under his pillow. Three months later he was advised to discreetly depart from India because he was under suspicion for shooting an Indian in a back street in Calcutta. The Alpine Club blackballed his membership application. A feature called Pache's Grave, in memory of the dead lieutenant, appears on early maps.

In the year 2000 Enid and I were part of a musical tour of Bohemia. On the second day a well-intentioned chap sat beside me in the coach. He said, 'I hear you're a mountaineer. I've read *The Third Eye* and a book by the famous mountaineer Aleister Crowley, the great mystic.' I groaned. Three days later we became friendly and I discovered that he played the bagpipes very well.

⁂

I shared a small tent with Urkien during the survey work. George Band and a Sherpa arrived and said Charles wanted us to select a tentative base site near the foot of Kempe's buttress and to leave a tent as a marker for loads due to begin arriving that far up the glacier. We were to go up the buttress and push into the icefall beyond the Kempe turning point.

The night spent at the suggested base site was extraordinary.

Several times the glacier vibrated with lengthy shakes like an earthquake. It was a bright moonlit night. Three times, perhaps a minute after the boom and shake, the moonlight vanished and we were in darkness. Just minutes later it would settle and the moon would reappear. Undoubtedly we were too close to the avalanche cliffs. In the morning we found 5 centimetres of powdered snow on the tents and equipment. When avalanches hit the glacier, great clouds erupted and spread down the valley. We were right in their blast path – no place for a base camp.

In the morning the four of us struggled up the steep rocks of Kempe's buttress carrying a camp, which was far from easy on the exposed cliffs. After a terrace was selected the Sherpas returned to the glacier while we listened to the rumbles in the very close icefall. For an afternoon and the next day we worked at the great ice chunks, like three-storey houses, cutting steps and edging around crevasses in very difficult circumstances. In the afternoon some of the route would be lost with the partial collapse of a serac across our path. It was far too difficult and out of the question for Sherpas carrying the loads they did.

Late on the second day we emerged through the worst ice problems, and up on the left I saw what appeared to be an alternative route that bypassed all the horrors. If the other side of this route was feasible it would be better to approach it from a base camp nearer Pache's Grave, well away from the avalanche cliffs and the horrific icefall. George and I discussed the alternative approach and decided to recommend it to Charles by radio. We requested Sherpas to bring up two rolls of rope ladder for placing on the worst vertical faces we had ascended. We also suggested that Charles should come up to see the state of the icefall.

While loads kept advancing up the lower glacier, Charles and Jacko (John Jackson) joined us and repeated our climbs. They agreed that the situation was most dangerous and that the alternative route, not visible from below, was very hopeful. Charles and George, who had been many times through the icefall approach to Everest, said this one was much steeper and much more active.

We retreated, picked up our camps and went searching for another base. High on the next rock bluff down the valley was a safe situation, away from the crackling and shuddering of a glacier campsite, with water and still in view of the summit. This diversion, to check the Kempe route, had taken a total of six days, but it was time well spent. We would finally abandon the potentially lethal direct approach and I found how well George and I co-operated in the difficult sections. He had been the youngest in the 1953 Everest team. With me he was always an entertaining, hard-working and very competent companion.

Charles sent the two of us off again, very happily. I had thought we would be rested, but he wanted us to reach the same place above the lower icefall, using the new approach. There were some difficult steep sections, but they were far more stable than the previous continually active icefall. We put in place some 150 metres of fixed rope on the worst sections. Then we went up some less mobile slopes until we reached the couloir we had seen from below. We called the col at its head the 'hump'. The couloir became known as the 'gully'. We, the front pair, while looking at alternative ways through crevasse mazes, travelled alone. Once the route was found to be workable, ladders and ropes would be brought to the locations where safeguards needed to be placed. We proceeded to a safe level area suitable for Camp 2.

We returned to base camp, which was expanding rapidly on the new Pache's site and materials were arriving for use higher up the mountain. No real time had been lost by our examination of the Kempe's buttress route, as the main activity of relay groups was still further down the main Yalung Glacier. The timing of the whole project was governed by when adequate supplies would have arrived at the final base camp. For the first time in 12 days we were all together again. Charles stated that I was to be his deputy leader. He had approached me much earlier about this but awaited the assembly of the whole team before announcing it. In my diary I recorded being 'greatly honoured to work for such a leader'.

⫯

I went down the glacier and was away for three days for a rest. On my return I found that Charles Evans and Joe Brown had gone up and put in a tent for Camp 2, about an hour past the hump. This meant a large amount of a likely route was opened up. Soon we were all involved in escorting loaded Sherpas attached to our climbing ropes. In total, nearly one and a half tonnes of materials were to be placed, and mostly consumed, above base camp. Between lower camps, loads could be about 20 kilograms each. For top camps these would reduce to less than 12 kilograms. It therefore took a huge amount of planning and escorting to move everything to the appropriate locations – few outsiders realise that much of the time climbers spent on these large expeditions was in load-escorting duties.

One of the complex issues on big mountains with many camps is arranging the right number of tents in their appropriate locations, to cope with the daily movements of people. Charles made advance forecasts of the movement, and at base camp he noted instructions detailing where men and tents were to be placed, at each future camp of the whole enterprise. The moving of the supplies between base camp and Camp 2 took about two weeks and the technical difficulties on the route were so great that Sherpas were always kept roped to a climber. The same occurred at higher lifts, where two Sherpas would be linked to one climber.

We had four small mobile radios capable of communication between camps if line of sight was possible. Modern radios are about a quarter the size of those we carried in 1955. More of these sets would have been beneficial. There was no way of transmission to the outside world, and that suited me, but it was not universally popular. On modern expeditions small mobile phones and satellite repeaters have brought dramatic changes, not always desirable in my view.

Above Camp 2 there was a uniform slope, which had many crevasses yet was likely to be more free from avalanches and it did provide good direct progress. For two days I undertook the oxygen preparations – in two weeks that equipment would be required. Crates were unpacked, cylinder pressures checked and sets assembled for higher camps. Practically all parts had come this far undamaged, but some cylinders had lost a small amount of pressure. All the party were in good health. Of course there were high-altitude headaches, some snow blindness and sore throats, but having so many experienced men in the team made recognition and treatment of ailments much easier. John Clegg, our doctor, seldom went as far as Camp 2 and generally stayed at base. This role had been defined for him at the outset and he was happy about it. Fortunately he did not have many medical problems in the early stages, but there were always some men who needed a rest at base camp.

The weather was normal for that area and in April the high-altitude winds seemed to be decreasing. Dawn was usually calm and clear, but by noon there would be clouds and poor visibility. Often by 3 p.m. snow would be falling. Being aware of this we had brought about a hundred small coloured cotton flags. During the approach walk bamboo poles had been cut and these, with flags attached, were placed on our snow route to mark any change of direction or the edge of a crevasse. They were of great value when descending in white-out conditions.

By now Charles had an excellent build-up arrangement progressing. He asked me to wait for him at Camp 3 with two of the most experienced Sherpas and prepare the two closed-circuit oxygen sets. This would be the trial he had promised Tom Bourdillon. On summit attempts we would not use the experimental closed-circuit sets. Tom and Charles had used them three days before the summit on the Hillary and Tenzing climb on Everest, but the valves froze and they turned back at about 95 metres below the top.

Charles hoped to put Camp 4 on the great shelf, where we would stay a night. After another complex struggle with crevasses we did finally reach the shelf and erected a small tent. Next day he and I, without Sherpas, went higher on the direct line towards the snow gully we called the 'gangway'. Here we found a small well-placed terrace that looked to be a safe situation for Camp 5. From there, reasonable slopes were visible for some distance above us. Charles then decided that the expedition would make an attempt at reaching the maximum possible height that could be interpreted from the Sikkim summit restriction. There was no problem about the legality of our route, as it was totally in Nepal. It was just the actual summit that was on the boundary.

A Camp 6 would be required to place climbers within range of their goal. From the slopes beside Camp 5, we thought the snow and rocks under the summit were not as formidable as we had earlier presumed, but the skyline pinnacles seemed forbidding. Charles and I agreed that with the high camp placed well up the gangway the summit should be within range in about five hours, keeping to the preferable mixed rock and snow patches below the pinnacles. However, we were anxious about what we could see above us for the siting of the future camp.

Having used the closed-circuit sets from Camp 3, we had two days' climbing with the assistance of oxygen, from about 6,500 metres to well over 7,600 metres. For the first 20 minutes each day we had received considerable boosts from the equipment, but it soon became uncomfortably hot and pushing air through those clumsy closed hoses was hard work. At each minor obstacle the hoses, which went down to below our waists, were an awkward menace. It would be impossible to do any complex rock climbing with them.

After the first tepid half-hour I brought in the rope and Charles came up to sit beside me. I turned off the flow and took off my mask. I told him I was desperately hot in my chest but still cold in my feet. Charles said he felt the same. On Everest he and Tom Bourdillon had stopped every half-hour to cut lumps of ice to place on each other's soda lime canister to cool it.

Tom had requested that there be no insulation around the canisters so they would keep to air temperatures. He thought we would be comfortably warm. We cut lumps of compacted snow for each other and piled them on the sets to cool them. Because of the risk of nitrogen entry we had shaved our faces around the contact areas of our masks. Nitrogen in the system could result in poisoning if the cylinder ran out of oxygen. This danger meant we rarely stopped, and communication with our climbing partner had to be by signs, with masks still in place.

The weight of the canisters was another problem, as was condensation from our breathing, at the lowest point of the U-shaped tube. I found that after a long session I could hear bubbles blowing through water at each exhalation. When we did stop to converse or cool off the other man's set, it was also necessary to drain the outward tube by pointing the mask down to the snow, sometimes tipping out about a quarter of a cup of water.

Closed-circuit sets were far too complicated for our Sherpas, and we never asked them to try them. After our two-day trial we packed them away and worked with the reliable but wasteful open-circuit apparatus. I did bring out one of the other sets for a later move between camps.

Charles and I now had a position for the second-highest camp, number 5. We looked up the gangway and there seemed no convenient terrace for the top camp, and it would be vulnerable to any rubble falling from a wide arc of the upper mountain. Charles did not want men staying for a long time at that site. Our descent to Camp 4, where we were alone, was uneventful, and Charles went into quiet planning mode, occasionally thinking aloud. Before an attempt on the top peak could be launched there needed to be six more days of carrying supplies for higher camps. He had to select the summit men, and then allocate load-carrying escort duties to all of the team. There was time to go right down to base camp, decide the final programme and then move up again.

It became apparent that Charles considered George and I were the best for going to the top, but in case of our failure or bad weather he wanted a second pair. He said Joe Brown and Tony Streather should be added in some combination. I interjected forcefully, 'You must put yourself into one of the pairs. You're the best all-round mountaineer in the party. You've been on about 10 Himalayan visits and never stood on a major peak, except being first on the south summit of Everest. You missed the top Everest by 95 metres through oxygen failure, and little credit has been directed your way for that effort. You have the ability and you deserve it.'

He responded, 'No, my place is to be responsible for putting in the top camp and then descending to occupy the next one, to be in a supporting position if anything goes wrong with your groups. Camp 6 will be in a risky situation.'

At breakfast he blurted out: 'I think Tony should be with you.'

'Delighted,' I said. 'I'd happily go with him, George or you.'

Three hours down from Camp 4, Tony and Neil were directing two Sherpa groups in upward movements with their loads, at altitudes of about 6,250 to 7,000 metres. Explaining that prospects for a summit ridge attempt were bright, Charles said to Tony, 'I want you to team up with Norman, to be one of the assault pairs.'

'I'm happy with that if you two are likewise,' Tony confirmed.

Charles suggested Tony and Neil could go down to base for a general meeting and rest, but they declined the offer. Tony quoted Charlie Houston, who thought that acclimatisation gains could be easily lost by short drops in altitude. Houston was the leader of the 1953 K2 expedition, where the whole party had waited several days in the highest camp through a lengthy storm. He was then regarded as the main American authority on high-altitude physiology. I met him in Chamonix in 1990 and discussed this point with him, and he still thinks that if one is healthy it is best to keep at middle altitudes for quite a long time, up to three weeks or so. Above 7,000 metres deterioration can be rapid for most people. Houston also gave glowing reports of Tony Streather on the K2 expedition.

On the radio Charles asked the others to gather at base camp the following afternoon. Just before that camp Tom MacKinnon saw us coming, climbed up a short distance and requested a talk. 'You two must be thinking about going for the top. Don't consider me in it. At 42 I don't have the fire in my belly of some of the young ones. I'll carry and escort right up to the top camps if required.' It was good of him to say this. He was a hard worker and an excellent expedition companion, but he had never sought the work of establishing new routes. One needs a few Toms on a large expedition. His statement reduced the numbers of those who could be disappointed by Charles's pending announcement.

It was generally assumed by the others that as we had found a feasible place for Camp 5, we would be considering going higher. Seven of us gathered in one big tent, where Charles, with planning lists in front of him, announced his programme, summarised something along these lines:

> I think the upper part of the mountain will be difficult. The
> first pair might possibly not reach the turning point below the

summit. It could end up like Everest, where the first pair turned around short of the top. I intend putting in Camp 6, having a two-man tent. The first assault pair will have a night there and next morning go as far as they can. If they reach the top that will be fine. They are to turn around and descend to pass Camp 6, converse there with the next pair, and then they will escort the second pair's two Sherpas, taking them down to Camp 5 that afternoon. On that same day the second assault will go up to Camp 6, settle in and get the report of the first party as they pass on down. Next morning they will make their attempt. George and Joe will be the first pair, with Norman and Tony next.

There was a surprising silence for about five seconds, then laughter and congratulations. I was happy to be officially included but uncomfortable about Charles not being in one of the pairs. I had already made this point privately to Charles and now said to the whole group, 'If any of the four at any stage feels not up to it, he should give way to Charles.'

Again he was not having this and repeated that he would select the Camp 6 site, descend to 5 and watch us as far as possible, to be in position for any rescue if needed. I found this stoic acceptance by the others of all decisions a little surprising. In New Zealand I had been used to people of generally similar abilities discussing such matters, thus clarifying the issues and helping avoid later complications.

No one came to me about the decisions announced by Charles. Tom urged me to push the mountain hard. We agreed that John Hunt, for the following year, had so praised his 1953 Everest team that they would probably all be invited for 1956 and our group would be largely omitted. One of us should either climb the mountain, or get so high he would have to be on Hunt's invitation list.

I thought hard about the day for the first assault. I was not convinced about having just the one tent at Camp 6, and I needed to work out their oxygen allocation. I asked Charles about their turnaround times on that intended day. He suggested they turn at about 1 p.m. and aim to reach Camp 6 no later than 4 p.m. That would give them just enough time to descend to 5, leaving Tony and me alone in the tent. On this basis I agreed on the single tent. Tony, the transport officer, was not consulted at this stage as he was still operating between Camps 2 and 3. Confirming this, Charles said just two sleeping bags would go up to Camp 6. Because of the exposure, he did not want many men there at any stage.

At the large meeting at base camp I had suggested we should not state in letters home the names of those selected for the summit parties, and I believe everyone kept to this. The reason behind my request was related to the flurry of unequal decorations and erroneous reports that came out of the Everest climb. I said the announcement of success, if any, should not be made until Evans was in Darjeeling, so he could give all announcements and be available for the inevitable 'Who got there first?' The Everest success message had gone out by code on Indian checkpost radio, and the leaders were out of contact for some 12 or more days.

A plane from the Indian Air Force had recently flown over the mountain and an observer had taken some photographs, which were sent to us via our fortnightly mail runner. On these the couloir by the hump was now clearly visible, but it had not been in sight from the valley floor. There were hints of it in a Kempe photograph, but its significance and ease had not then been apparent. However, another Indian shot showed a large detail of the top slopes of the main peak and confirmed Charles's forecasts of difficulties on the skyline rocks. In clear light the following morning George and I spent about two hours with the photograph, binoculars and theodolite telescope, looking at the details of each feature of the final rock section. I was hopeful that there might be enough snow patches between the snow gullies to avoid the delays of taking off crampons for the rock ribs. I did not welcome the possibility of facing big rock climbing wearing full oxygen kit. Keeping on the snow would be preferable for me and, I was certain, for Tony.

The north-west wind that had screamed across at high altitude for weeks had diminished with the spring conditions, as is usual. The calmest weather tends to be between mid-May and the first week of June, as the monsoon penetrates northwards. We gathered our supplies and went upwards. At Camp 3, where the main oxygen stores were now situated, I stayed to start those, including Sherpas, who were going to Camps 5 or 6. Each man had an individual crash

Kangchenjunga

course on the use of the equipment, and most of the spares were also taken up.

On one occasion I brought out a sketch I had made of the summit approaches, from the Indian Air Force photograph, to discuss with Tony. I went on at some length about the merits of one option versus others. Suddenly I realised Tony had been quiet for several minutes. He said, 'I run the transport and you are the mountaineer. I'll support you all the way, but mountain decisions are yours.'

Tom MacKinnon, John Jackson and a big team of Sherpas left fully laden for the long lift from Camp 4 to Camp 5. There was new snow at that height and they made very slow progress. Some did not quite make it and several dumps of gear were deposited at 60 and 100 metres away from their destination. Jacko had fogging troubles with his glasses when using the oxygen mask, so he removed his goggles, which, in his case, were not highly protective models. He soon had bad snow blindness. The party descended to Camp 4 in some disarray. They were meant to go on to Camp 3, but some were unable to face that next downwards stage. Thus 11 men spent the night in accommodation meant for eight. Tom MacKinnon was the last to arrive, as dusk was falling. On his rope was Pemba Dorji, who had collapsed twice just above Camp 4.

For two days a violent storm, coming in unusually from the south, caused almost all movements to stop. Snow built up at all the high campsites. When it eased, a team descended with the still ailing Pemba Dorji, and instructions to get him right down to the denser air and medical attention at base.

After the planning meeting at base camp the previous week, Charles had typed instructions for each group, along with the movements of tents and oxygen supplies. Each of us was given a copy of these sheets. I still have mine. The two-day storm delay upset the dates but the main instructions still applied. First assault, as well as Evans and Mather, went up to Camp 5 and were dismayed to see that a small avalanche had either covered or moved the loads deposited just short of that camp. They searched but did not recover everything. There was now a possible shortage of oxygen and Sherpa food.

At Camp 3, Tony and I heard this bad news on our radio. On the previous night I had had coughing and breathing troubles – so bad that Tony connected a nearly empty cylinder and fed me a low-rate oxygen boost. It made a great difference. Soon I became warm with my chest comfortable, and I slept well. Next day Tom and Jacko arrived from above. Tom, a pharmacist, examined me, radioed the doctor at base and obtained approval to give me auriomycien. This, with the low-flow oxygen for sleeping, did wonders.

At our camp we had all the oxygen required for our attempt and for the Sherpas to get it to the top camps, but now there were no more spare cylinders. By radio we told Charles we were still coming up to be the second assault. When we did move I reverted to closed-circuit to Camp 4 only, partly as it would not use much of the rationed oxygen, but also because its heat might further clear my chest and throat. I travelled well and had no more troubles of that description. The rest at Camp 3 had helped Jacko's eyes and he was able to assist another upward lift.

The original plan resumed its course, but with dates changed. First assault, with Evans and Mather, went up the gangway. George carved out a narrow platform for the erection of the two-man tent of Camp 6. We estimated the height of the camp to be at 8,200 metres. The summit is at 8,586 metres. Their support group went down to Camp 5, leaving George Band and Joe Brown in residence. Meanwhile Tony and I, with two Sherpas, came up to Camp 5, which again was full to the brim. This was probably the hardest of the ascents between camps – not technically difficult but a big lift at that altitude. I foraged in the debris but found few of the lost supplies. We, the second pair, had enough oxygen for one push to the top. The weather seemed to be settled after the storm and we were all physically well again.

Next morning, 25 May, Tony, Urkien, Aila Tenzing and I set out for Camp 6. At one early stage we obtained a glimpse of the top pair much higher in the gangway. The ascent for us was steep and direct, but it was also rather obviously the likely path for any rocks or ice falling from above. We arrived at the tent, which had collapsed as expected, because the others had removed their anchoring ice axes. After putting it up again we melted snow and all had hot drinks. From there we could see a long way up the gangway, with no sign of the first pair coming down. This concerned me greatly. By late afternoon I feared there was a real possibility there had been an accident. I also knew their oxygen would have been exhausted if they had been consuming it at normal flow rates. It seemed unlikely they could arrive in time to descend to Camp 5 as intended. To avoid having four, or possibly six, in that two-man tent I sent the two Sherpas down, unescorted. This was just the second occasion when Sherpas undertook the full journey between any camps, without being attached to one of the climbers.

Jannu, the great peak to our west, was visible from all our high camps. Now we were a little above it and the awareness of great altitude was even more apparent. The tent, sited on the small platform cut by George the previous day, overhung the ledge by about a quarter of its width. On the upper side, small lumps of fallen snow were pressing onto the tent fabric. I cleared some of these.

As the light faded I had my last look up the gangway, then went into the tent and munched at a meagre meal. At this height I found I had no great desire for food and we were too worried to eat much anyway. We climbed into the sleeping bags and discussed where to search in the morning. With no radio at Camp 6 we could not converse with Charles. From the hummock behind Camp 5 he would be able to see us going upwards in the morning. If he saw no sign of the other pair he would be likely to take a companion and a tent and come up to Camp 6, but that would be without oxygen, as we had the last cylinders. A rescue looked full of hazards.

Half an hour after dark we heard a shout outside. Charles, standing out in the cold above Camp 5, also heard it. George and Joe were just above us, having climbed to the defined turning point about three metres below the true summit. We gave our congratulations. I removed their crampons as I leaned out from the tent entrance. Joe was in considerable pain with snow blindness. Because of the limited space they sat outside with hot drinks until we could squeeze our gear and the bulky cooker into a corner. Tony and I were already in the two sleeping bags and, as the newcomers were wearing their down jackets and trousers, we decided to remain that way. More drinks continued from a precariously tight cooking situation. The other two had on their boots and did not untie their climbing rope. The cramped situation meant no one had much sleep. George and I talked for hours. Joe was too involved with the pain in his eyes.

They had gone up the gangway with relative ease but turned off to the right too early and confronted difficult rocks that were very steep. Returning to the gangway, they selected an initially better route, higher and to the right. Joe was leading most of the way. They mounted some awkward rock pitches and after a while reached the crest of the west ridge, where they encountered a violent wind. Sure enough, they found the pinnacles and rock steps visible on the aerial photographs. They turned the first obstacles on their right. Higher up, the west ridge was again impossible and the wind unrelenting, so they went to the right again. Looking up, they saw a rock wall that had a number of substantial cracks in it. Joe led up one of these, placed light rope runners to support his climbing rope and ascended, suddenly finding that he had emerged just below the top of the mountain. George followed and they were there. They had taken off their crampons for most of the rock climbing. There was a convenient flat shelf on the Nepal side, just below the true summit. They stopped there after seven hours' climbing.

After taking photographs they departed shortly after 3 p.m. They left one anchored sling at the top buttress to give me support if I led that way next day. Quite soon Joe's oxygen ran out, so he dumped the equipment; his eyes were also having problems. During the rock work he had taken off his goggles and for some of the time George had removed his gloves. On a snow crest between two rock ribs George's oxygen also finished, so his set was abandoned too. They therefore descended slowly and with great care. In the tent at Camp 6 Joe was often groaning with the pain in his eyes and George's fingertips were more than just tingling. The tent was two metres long and 1.3 metres wide on a platform barely a metre across, which meant that one man was in a precarious bulge if any stitching gave way in the night.

We discussed their climb in some detail. I was just hoping George and Joe would be well enough to go down in the morning without our support, in which case Tony and I would still have our day. I put a question to George: 'What's your opinion now about continuing with the climb into mid-afternoon?'

'Well, the top was just up there above us,' he said. 'You know how it is. We heard you two were still coming next day, but there was a chance you might not locate enough oxygen. Joe was very keen to keep going. The weather might not have been right for you.' I agreed they were fair comments.

At daylight we somehow started the cooker and consumed a few biscuits and more drinks, but the restricted space made every move difficult and, with the reduced air at that height, all movements were slow. Because the other pair had kept their boots on all night I suggested they start their descent to Camp 5. They were happy to do this without our assistance. Then it was our chance to put on our frozen boots and prepare the oxygen sets. Each of us had a large cylinder and a small one, operating in open-circuit mode. The small cylinders were screwed in for immediate breathing, and the larger ones tied with frozen webbing until they were required. I went out to see that George and Joe were moving freely down the gangway.

It was about 8.15 a.m. when I led off from the once more collapsed tent. Traces of the others' steps were occasionally visible. I cut little scratches, with two strokes of the axe blade, enough for the five inner spikes of the crampons to obtain a grip. (Crampons with two front points were not available until 1957.) On the right we recognised the false approach the previous pair had made before going upwards again. With not much more of the gangway remaining, we turned right, going from one steep patch of snow to another, wearing crampons and scraping small steps.

After about an hour of good progress Tony called to me from below that my windproof jacket was flapping. I stopped, turned off the flow valve and swung the oxygen set around from my shoulders. As I did so the free cylinder bounced off and whistled past Tony's head at an enormous speed. The frozen webbing, which had been tied in the crowded tent when the brain was working slowly, had defrosted and was not tight enough in the growing warmth of the morning. The cylinder had worked loose and was lost forever.

I put the set back on and left the flow valve turned off on my small cylinder. I climbed upwards on no oxygen, thinking I was doing reasonably well. Tony had been about 15 metres behind on the rope, but soon he prodded me with his axe and said, 'You've slowed down too much.'

'Sorry about my dreadful mess with tying that cylinder,' I replied. 'Just now I thought I was doing quite well with my pace.'

'You're the mountaineer and have to stay in front. Take my unused big bottle. I'll finish my small one on a lower rate. When I run out I can take over the remains of your small one.'

That made sense. Also, with Tony giving me his 7-kilogram cylinder his load would be lighter for ascending on a lower flow rate. We changed and moved on again. The difference was considerable, although the flow rate was only two litres per minute. With the oxygen I became warmer, I moved better and everything looked much more positive.

I led over more rocky obstacles to the bottom of a prominent snow rib that is normally visible from base camp. After some minutes on this we met the others' steps again, and then the oxygen set left by George. High on the rib I deviated from their route where they had gone up to the windswept skyline ridge. There were enough snow patches for us to proceed to the right on the face without the delay of taking off crampons. We stayed all the way below the west ridge and the pinnacles. Around another small ridge I suddenly saw the rest of the upper mountain. Behind me Makalu and Everest were showing clearly above the top of the west peak of Kangchenjunga, so we must have been about 60 metres below the summit. I brought Tony up, removed my mask and said cheerfully, 'We're going to make it!'

'Which is the top?' he asked. From just below the complex skyline it was not easy to identify the precise high point, but from below and in the photograph I had studied the small details so often that I was able to tell him.

I pointed out the awkward rocks above, which Joe had led at their final stage. George told me it was a 'v. diff' on the British rock-climbing scale. I went through more snow patches to the foot of that problem and, still wearing crampons, scratched my way up part of it. The rope sling was visible on the skyline and I did not like the situation. With crampons off I could make it, but I was concerned about Tony's experience on such a face. Besides, I had wanted to get up without the assistance of that sling. I looked down towards Tony to see if he had a secure place to sit and remove his crampons. Then I saw a further snow shelf, off to my left, invisible from where he was waiting. I went down, told him to keep his crampons on, and led across some minor firm rocks. Soon we were on the snow that led up to the main southeast ridge between the first and second peaks of our mountain. Far below an enormous face was the Zemu Glacier, in Sikkim, where the Germans had tried so hard in the 1930s.

Our short ridge was not difficult and the wind was modest. It took just a few minutes to reach the place where George and Joe's steps were evident on the platform a few metres under the true summit. More congratulations and thanks. How wonderful to be on such a brilliant mountain, and with such a very special friend! We sat, with great smiles on our faces, and ate more than we had been able to face at dawn in the tent. Jannu was now far below us. Makalu, Lhotse and Everest stood out, above a continuous cloud bank, 130 kilometres away. We had reached our platform at 12.15 p.m., taking four hours from Camp 6, an hour better than Charles's estimate.

While Tony changed oxygen cylinders I took several steps to the west, from where I could look to the distant brown hills of Tibet. Part of the Zemu ridge could be seen and it looked difficult. There were clouds over our base camp, so we would not be visible for the others of our team. We stayed on the small terrace for 50 minutes.

I met Reinhold Messner at Chamonix in 1990, at the fortieth anniversary of the first Annapurna ascent. He had climbed all 14 of the 8,000-metre peaks. He said a small blue bottle was still on that platform, and he read our expedition name on it.

We returned by the same route as our ascent, and very soon Tony was out of oxygen. I still had quite a lot and offered my bottle, which he declined firmly. According to him I was the one with the techniques to stop a fall, so I needed to have my wits in operation. At two brief rests I held the mask on his face and we moved off again. On the hard parts I stayed close behind him holding the coiled rope and used a rock piton in one awkward situation to safeguard the descent. Out on the gangway we found that our steps had been covered by wind-blown snow and it was necessary to scrape them off with our long axes.

Since those days there have been dozens of improvements in mountaineering equipment and in food and cookers. I agree with most of them. However, I am not comfortable with the very short ice axes. I acknowledge their place for steep face work, but for downhill step scraping or prodding the edge of a crevasse, one long axe in the party can be useful.

Back to the mountain. We returned to Camp 6 in good time, thirsty and tired. We melted two cookers of snow and soon decided to stay the night. With room to move this time, we should have been comfortable but my diary records a not very restful night. In the morning the lower gangway presented few troubles. Charles and Dawa Tenzing came a few rope lengths up to greet us, with welcome liquids and kind words. Until then they had not known that we too had climbed the mountain – or at least to the terrace below the summit. However, among the congatulations we heard the sad news that Pemba Dorji had died at base camp at the time we were at the top. Charles was anxious for all of us to get off the mountain as soon as possible, particularly to assure Pemba's friends that no one had been on the precise summit and there was no wrath from the Sikkim gods for any of our actions.

From a lower camp through binoculars the previous afternoon Jacko had seen us arriving back down at Camp 6. In the morning John Clegg at base camp had watched us begin our descent from that camp. This news had been distributed by radio, so there had been no concern about our safety. We collected all the important equipment and personal gear and went down. Charles and some Sherpas went ahead and reached base one day before Tony and me. At Camp 4 Charles saw Urkien waiting and invited him to go down, but no; he said he would wait for me. The weather

Kangchenjunga

was warmer and the cloud cover intensified with the approaching monsoon. Our boots sank further into the snow and beside Camp 1 a major snow bridge had collapsed, forcing us to make a long diversion to achieve a safe exit.

Charles, Tony and Jacko looked grey around the eyes; everyone seemed rather withdrawn. Pemba Dorji had just been buried and two men using piton hammers were chipping a Tibetan inscription on a large rock. The two doctors stated that death had been from a blood clot in the brain, accelerated by the climb to Camp 5.

I wondered about Charles's reaction to the decision of the first summit team to continue their climb, but I did not ask him and he made no comment. In fact the subject was never raised by any of the expedition, and the fact that four had summited, rather than just one or two, had made it more an overall expedition success. In later years many have asked me, after I had given a lecture, how it was that in a well-planned expedition, four spent the night in a two-man tent with only two sleeping bags.

When the burial formalities were over the atmosphere brightened, but we were all very tired and most had lost weight. In one day we packed up, cleared our rubbish and departed. At the terminal of the Yalung Glacier, in the balmy atmosphere of only 4,000 metres we stopped for two days. With running water and firewood available, we washed and laundered, had haircuts and prepared for the next stage. Here I was to part company with the others, who were preparing for the 12-day walk to Darjeeling. I wrote several letters, as it would be six or more weeks before I would again be near a mail service. I wrote oxygen reports for Tom Bourdillon and notes for Charles to assist him with the official book he had undertaken to write.

For me the separation was very emotional. We had been a good team. I would go to New Zealand at the end at the year and wondered when I would see them again. Every five years since, they have held a reunion in Wales, and on two occasions Enid and I have attended. Tom MacKinnon died early, so I did not see him again. I spent many hours on these brief occasions with Charles, before his death in 1995.

There was no misreporting of the news of our climb – in fact it was scarcely noticed. My precautions about not revealing summit names had been quite unnecessary.

I packed up and, with three laden Sherpas, took the wet, cloud-covered track to Ghunza.

The intended 1956 expedition was cancelled. Kangchenjunga was not climbed again for 22 years, when an Indian Army team took advantage of the changed political situation in Sikkim. They ascended it from the north-east by the route attempted by the German climbers in the 1930s.

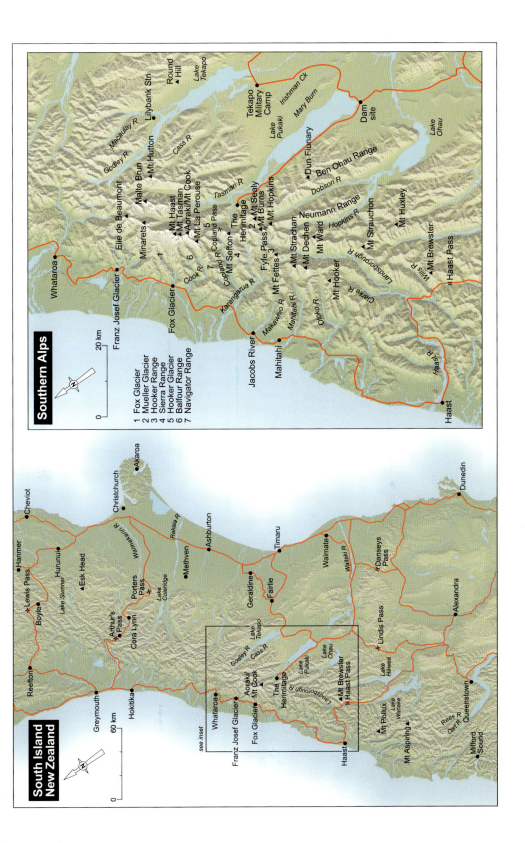

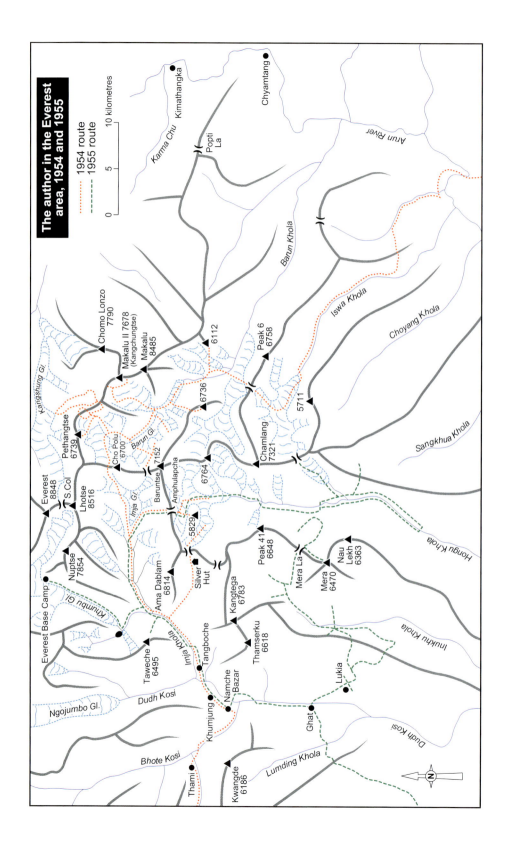

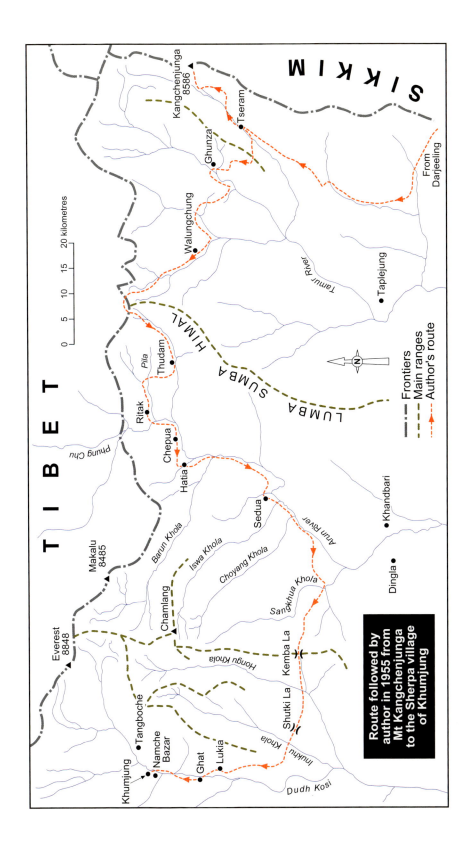

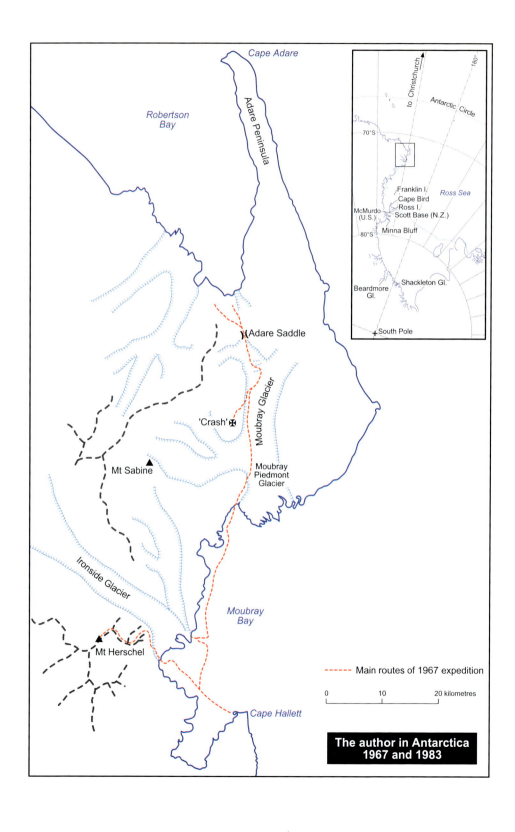

The deer cullers' Boyle Base Hut, built in the early 1930s, still stands in 2006.
Enid Hardie

Jim McFarlane and the author with dried deer skins near Arthur's Pass, 1945.
Enid Hardie

Mt Elliot, photographed during its first ascent, in 1947, by Norman Hardie, Bill Beaven and Jim McFarlane. Mt Dechen is partly obscured.

View from the summit of Mt Burns, 1948. Jim McFarlane on the right.

Above: *Jim McFarlane, the author, Earle Riddiford and Bill Beaven, resting up in the Landsborough Valley, 1948.*
Bill Packard

Right: *Jim McFarlane approaching the final summit of Mt Cook on New Year's Day, 1950.*

Left: *The injured Ruth Adams being supported by rescuers, just below the summit of La Perouse. The author is on the left of the stretcher, and Edmund Hillary on the right.*
Jim Glasgow

Above: *The senior guides in the La Perouse rescue team, Harry Ayres and Mick Bowie.*
Jim Glasgow

Bill Beaven on Fettes Peak, looking towards Dechen and Strachan.

The author reached the summit of Mt Sefton in 1948 and 1949 by the two ridges shown.
Colin Monteath

The author and Jim McFarlane climbed all three peaks of Mt Cook in 1950, returning the same way. This was the first time anyone had gone along the top ridge twice.
Colin Monteath

Left: *The author using a photo-theodolite in Barun Valley in 1954.*
Colin Todd

Below: *Mt Makalu in the Himalayas, taken from the summit of Mt Pethangtse, 1954. The Sherpa Urkien is on the left, with Brian Wilkins.*

Above: *Charles Evans, Tony Streather and the author posed for a* Times *photographer in London in 1955, just before leaving for Kangchenjunga.*

The Times

Right: *Charles Evans, leader of the Kangchenjunga expedition, sketching in the Yalung Valley, 1955.*

Above: *The route pioneered by the Kangchenjunga expedition, showing the Yalung face and the camp numbers. The ridge in the foreground obscures the extensive cliff of the main mountain.*

Right: *The summit of Kangchenjunga, showing the routes taken by the two parties.*
Indian Air Force

Climbers in the bypass corridor between Camp 1 and Camp 2 on Kangchenjunga.

Charles Evans on a rope ladder at the lower icefall.

A party ascending the slopes of Kangchenjunga near Camp 3.

Above: *Charles Evans resting with a closed-circuit oxygen set near Camp 4.*

Left: *Tony Streather and Urkien erecting Camp 6, where four men spent one long night.*

Opposite top: *Streather on the terrace just below the Kangchenjunga summit.*

Opposite: *The view west from the terrace below the summit of Kangchenjunga, showing major peaks in the distance.*

Chamlang Makalu Lohtse Everest

Above: *Building a footbridge over a glacial torrent at a tributary to the Arun River.*

Below: *Crossing a similar bridge built by the party in 1955.*

Urkien

A Bhotia man stitching his foot with darning needle and string.

A local porter scraping off dirt with his kukri, Tamur Valley.

Sherpa women removing seeds from pine cones for the Himalayan Trust nursery.

Left: *Carrying in one of the prefabricated panels of the Silver Hut.*

Right: *Mike Gill and Ed Hillary working on the hut.*

Below: *The last section about to be attached.*

Desmond Doig tries on the supposed yeti scalp.
Mike Gill

The first ascent route on Ama Dablam (6,828 metres) was on the right ridge, then up the central snow face.
Mike Gill

John Harrison, pictured here during a climbing expedition north of Lake Hawea in 1965, replaced the author for the 1961 attempt on Makalu. He died in the Mt Rolleston avalanche accident in 1966.

The author with his Japanese charges at the start of the Mt Fuji climb, in December 1960, on his way home from the Silver Hut expedition.
T. Mori

Posing for Japanese media on the roof of the television station on the summit of Mt Fuji.
Keiko Kawai

Tel Satow, leader of the party of Japanese women climbers who visited New Zealand in 1961.

Keiko Kawai, another of the Japanese women climbers, pictured in the Crow Valley.

Bill Beaven, Heinrich Harrer and the author on Mt Rolleston during Harrer's two-week visit to New Zealand in 1961.

John Harrison

Farewelling Harry Gair's sledging team in 1962.

Instructing Americans in crevasse rescue, 1962, with Wynne Croll above.

The Hillary party's camp on sea ice near Cape Hallett, 1967.

Signposts at the South Pole, 1983.

Above: *The author in a sledge-hauling group in Antarctica in 1967, after the expedition's snowmobile had broken down.*
Mike Gill

Below: *Snowcraft instruction near McMurdo Base.*
Guy Mannering

Penguin rookery at Cape Hallett, with Mt Herschel in the background. Part of the American base is visible at the extreme left.

That party that climbed Herscel in 1967 arriving at Cape Hallett. Sir Edmund Hillary is closest to the US Navy Hercules.

Norman and Enid Hardie in Khumbu, Nepal, in December 1974.
Norman Macbeth

Taking a breather at 5,200 metres in the Gokyo Valley, 1974: Frank Davie, Norman Macbeth, Ruth Hardie, Sarah Hardie, the author, Ken Tocker and David Hughes.
Ang Temba

Father Christmas visits the South Pole in 1983.

Supply ships unloading at the Hut Point ice wharf, 1984.

Inside a Himalayan Trust school in Nepal, 1980.

The author with his 1955 Kangchenjunga oxygen set at his residence in Christchurch in 1999.
Colin Monteath

Visiting the Silver Hut in its new location in Sikkim, 2000: Mike Gill, Jim Milledge, the author and John West.
Bill Packard

Ex-presidents of the New Zealand Alpine Club at the unveiling of the Hillary statue at Aoraki Mt Cook, 2003: Hugh Logan, Norman Hardie, Sir Edmund Hillary, Dave Bamford, Gordon Hasell, Geoff Gabities, Charles Tanner, John Nankervis.
Colin Monteath

Invitation to the Kangchenjunga jubileee celebrations 2005.

ELEVEN

West to the Khumbu

I wanted to walk by a new combination of high routes to the Nepalese province of Khumbu, generally keeping close to the main range and not crossing into Tibet. Memories of the last year's travelling with Charles Evans were still strong, but he could not possibly come this time. We had discussed the route I wished to take. Charles looked at the Sherpas who were to be with me, and the size of their bulging loads. He offered me another man, but I declined.

The expedition had abandoned much food and equipment at base camp and on the mountain. Of course much had been picked up by our employees, sometimes for their own use, or possibly for later sale in the Kathmandu bazaars. Early on I examined the Sherpas' loads, which seemed very heavy and bulky. Each had been issued with boots, ice axe, sleeping bag, windproof clothing, goggles and a large New Zealand pack. In addition I now found that they had accumulated plates, cutlery and mugs, climbing ropes, a large screwdriver, rubber tubing from the oxygen gear, two big tins of biscuits, several kilograms of sugar, many empty tins and two kerosene cookers (but virtually no fuel for them). The only food I had requested, apart from expedition supplies for the first two days, was instant coffee. After that time I would rely on wild foods and minor purchases along the way, as I had done in 1954. We kept some of this surplus equipment, and traded the rest for fresh food along the way.

John Jackson was consulted on track and food details. During the previous year he had walked about eight days of the route I was proposing, but he had diverted into Tibet for three of those days to avoid swollen rivers in the wetter Nepalese highlands. Jacko had encountered no problems and saw no Chinese patrols on the way. However, he had felt very vulnerable. In those days Tibet was closed to Westerners, the Korean situation was nasty and few governments had recognised the communist government of China.

The first day, 6 June 1955, was not difficult as we gradually worked our way through high-altitude pastures where plants were putting on their rapid monsoon growth, preparing for early flowering. Conditions were damp and visibility was limited. In mid-afternoon we put up our two tents and a fly in an attractive sheltered basin. This gave me the opportunity to assess our situation.

We had no theodolite, as I had sent it with the main team to Kathmandu, to be brought to the Khumbu with the returning party after they were paid off. Surveying would be just about impossible until the monsoon clouds vanished in late September, when Enid and Joe Macdonald were to join me.

Two easy passes of a little over 4,500 metres had to be crossed, the highest being the Mirgin La. Between them were green basins with an abundance of dwarf rhododendrons in flower, azaleas, buttercups, junipers and, lower down, small pine trees. The light was not good enough for successful photography. By this time I had permanently attached my headband to my pack and it was easy to reduce the pressure from the two shoulder straps, which did the work most of the time. In the evening, by a clear stream, I inspected my feet. I knew that two of my toes were dark brown to black from a touch of frostbite. John Clegg had seen them before my departure and expressed the opinion that there was good live tissue under the surface blemishes and that I would probably have no problems from them. He was right. After a few days the colour slowly faded. John had wanted to load me with heaps of medication, which I had declined, so I was relieved I had not needed it.

On the second afternoon we descended to about 3,500 metres

at the small village of Ghunza, appearing like a mini-Swiss town from a distance. On closer acquaintance the dirt and smells confirmed that we were in Nepal. Camp was put up in a small yak pasture and I wandered off to inspect the village. It had been built in a gorge where the river was narrow enough to allow the construction of a high-quality permanent log bridge and was on the intersection of important trade routes. As there was no large area for growing crops, it seemed that trading and supplying porters were the main industries. At that time almost all the men were away carrying out the returning baggage of the Kangchenjunga expedition. In one house I saw one of the colour-coded boxes that had originally housed our hand-held radios. It had reached Ghunza before me – I had seen that box three days earlier, as we were sorting loads for the final party separation.

I was asked into many houses but accepted just two invitations, knowing from the past that on entry I would have a wooden bowl of chang handed to me and that negotiations on any item would not begin until I had at least sipped the third drink. One would not have to drain the first two offers, but one was required to take at least a substantial draught each time. I enjoyed the drink but knew from the past that some brews were much more powerful than others and there was no way of telling in advance.

In the second house I was given a beer made from maize, warmed to about body heat and served in a wide bamboo vessel. A thin bamboo tube served as the straw, and this was quite successful until near the bottom, where sediment tended to limit the flow. The house had shelves and cooking pots very similar to those in the Khumbu, but the outer walls were mostly of roughly split wood, not the massive stonework seen in the higher residences further west.

In the camp I reprimanded Urkien mildly for purchasing too many local foodstuffs. We should eat most of the expedition food first, to lighten our loads. Even I was carrying about 25 kilograms and the others had more than 35 kilograms. But the wise Urkien always had an answer: 'An empty tin with a lid will buy three pounds of potatoes and I thought you would like a real egg instead of that powdered stuff.' Well, at least he was casting off some tins rather than spending my money.

Proceeding west from Ghunza a down-valley route descends to a deep gorge and then one climbs up, following the Tamur Valley, taking three days in all to reach the next important village, Walungchang Gola. A shorter route exists by climbing to nearly 5,000 metres and crossing the Nango La. This alternative is usually used by the local people. Two men were going that way so we engaged one of them for two days to share our loads and to keep us on the right route in the anticipated drifting monsoon mist. It would all be new country to my Sherpa trio for the next 10 days. As expected, it was a pleasant journey, apart from the struggles of my companions for the first three hours. Urkien diagnosed the problem as 'too much chang and potatoes. They'll be better when we are eating tsampa again.'

Down in the Tamur Valley we found ourselves on a major track for the first time in many months. This led to the Tipta La, on the Tibetan frontier, one of the few places in east Nepal where the terrain is gentle enough for laden yaks to make the crossing. Suddenly we saw nearly a forest of prayer masts and then were in the very special village of Walungchung. I believe I was the third Westerner to enter this valley.

Sir Joseph Hooker, the eminent British botanist, spent several days there and wrote a detailed description. Hooker had been in the Antarctic with James Clark Ross in 1841, and, sailing north from the Ross Sea, he stopped in New Zealand, where he spent many months examining the distinctive flora. His name is securely on maps at a glacier, a Landsborough range and Mt Hooker, so prominent from the Haast Pass road. Hooker's sea lion also bears his name. In 1848 Hooker spent most of the year in Nepal and Sikkim, exploring many valleys and recording the flora. Later he wrote *Himalayan Journals* in two excellent volumes that are still frequently quoted in botanical publications.

As in Ghunza, most of the houses in Walungchung were made of wood and the roofs were of long shakes. I was not surprised to see pigs and hens, as Hooker had mentioned them a century earlier. This must be nearly their altitude limit, as they do not

West to the Khumbu

thrive in the higher Sherpa villages such as Khumjung. On one side was a colourful Buddhist gompa and a very prominent radio aerial. Jacko had told me there was an Indian Army checkpost in Walungchung, and I decided it would be polite to call first, rather than letting them hear about me and then sending a search team looking for me.

The post was in one of the better houses in the small village. Two officers gave me a chair and ordered servants to stop staring and bring some tea. Then conversation began – where to, where from, nationality and why a rifle? They had not talked to any non-Asian for a year and they had many questions. Rumours from the expedition's Ghunza porters had told them that Kangchenjunga had been climbed, but they did not know the names of those who had reached the summit. As Charles Evans would not yet have reached Darjeeling to make announcements, I did not want news to leak out through the radio at this Indian watching station. I found an excuse to go outside, where I found Urkien and instructed him not to mention the names of those who had climbed Kangchenjunga.

Back in the checkpost the major revealed that he had met Charles in Kathmandu after Everest was climbed. 'And how about Doctor Pug?' he asked.

Who could that be? I wondered.

'Shy, I think, very tall, with red hair, so obvious in an Asian city.'

'Of course, Griff Pugh.' I was able to talk at length about Griff and the work I had done with him on oxygen equipment.

They had also seen Jacko when he passed this way the previous year. 'Did Evans or Jackson reach the summit?' they asked.

I embarked on an explanation of the fact that all announcements had to be made through the leader, that *The Times* in London, as major sponsor, had the first option on news and photographs, through the complex arrangements of the Joint Himalayan Committee. This brought a range of other questions.

'We see you have just three Sherpas with you, on a *Times* expedition. Last year Jackson passed through with 11 Sherpas as part of the *Daily Mail* yeti search. Does that mean the *Daily Mail* is a better paper than *The Times*?'

I explained that the *Times* sponsorship ended for me when I left the main party. At the end of the monsoon I would get some small support for surveying work, from surplus funds from the 1953 Everest expedition. I also explained that the two papers were vastly different. Since 1921 *The Times* has generously assisted British Everest expeditions, seldom interfering with their administration. The *Daily Mail*, by contrast, was merely exploiting the current curiosity about the existence of a most unlikely creature.

The Chinese had moved into Tibet just three years previously and the Indian government was most anxious about this change to the north. Army checkposts had been established in the Indian province of Garwhal and in Sikkim, where Indian influence was strong, but Nepal was an independent country. The government of Nepal did not then have enough army or radio facilities to place watching stations, so India took on this responsibility on a temporary basis. There were limits on their numbers, no firearms were permitted for Indian employees and local trade between Nepalese and Tibetans was to continue. Traders could be questioned but not detained.

I asked if they received newspapers, and they replied that they were not issued with any regular supply. One would occasionally arrive in a private package with the fortnightly mail runner. Books? They had virtually none. Did I have any to spare?

I carried Carlyle's *French Revolution* and both parts of Shakespeare's *King Henry IV*, and I did not want to be separated from either of them. *War and Peace* was with the theodolite bag to be located next month. At present, with busy days and carrying no lights for reading, the Carlyle was taking some time. They had not heard of the Hooker visit in 1848 and thought that Jacko in 1954 had been the first European visitor to the upper Tamur Valley.

⋅⋅⋅

The Sherpas with me, besides Urkien, were Aila Tenzing and Gyalgen. The better-known men of the main expedition had been attached to individual climbers and were not available for my private exploit, so I had asked Urkien to select two from the remainder. Aila had been to the top camp on the mountain but was not an outstanding climber like Urkien. However, I soon found he was talented at finding the chang locations on our route, and his village was the one nearest to our starting location for the later post-monsoon surveys. Gyalgen was small and shy, great at locating edible vegetables and a good small-scale cook. At about this stage I found that his wife was Urkien's sister.

I spent the night in the village headman's house, sharing a room with a junior lama. Between us we had a small amount of Hindi. Urkien was unaware that I had had a modest meal with the Indians, and he sent up a generous plate to my room. On finding I had company he then had delivered a saucer of quality English biscuits from his pack, to the great pleasure of my companion.

In the morning I gave some mail to the checkpost and eventually the letters did reach England. We began walking again, having changed the fourth man to another local who knew the route ahead. We ascended a deep valley with a noisy river beside us, following the good track that crosses to Tibet at just under 5,200 metres. I walked near the front to be certain our 'guide' turned left before the climb to the Tipta La. He stopped at a large cairn where a meagre route did seem to go westwards. He explained that if we went that way it would be higher and in deep snow. He wanted me to choose the Jacko track, which meant three days in Tibet, passing through two villages where there might be a Chinese patrol. I insisted on turning the hard way.

We passed through more high-altitude pastures with yaks in residence for the monsoon. At the top level of forest we spent the night under a giant overhanging rock where the many smoke stains on the walls indicated it had frequently sheltered visitors. In the morning we ascended rocky slopes and then soft snow, which hid any sign of a track. Visibility was bad all day. I recall crossing at least three apparent passes, in very confusing country. I looked at my compass and tried to find if the next river system flowed north to Tibet, or west or east. Finally we came down from a snowy ridge to a pass that loomed out of the fog. It had cairns and prayer flags on it, and the next river flowed south-west. I breathed many relieved sighs. About five years ago I saw a satellite-based map of that area, and I think the last pass was the Umbak La of some 5,100 metres and we had been in an undefined corner of Tibet.

Our tired group pushed through damp snow, occasionally passing a cairn that indicated we were on the right course. Soon after we reached short vegetation that was clear of the snow we stopped for the night. We consumed the last of our expedition food and topped up with the coarse-grained tsampa.

At dawn, for the first time, there was a clear sky for one hour. Makalu and Chamlang were not far away to the west, and in the foreground was a very deep gorge where the Arun River flows from Tibet. This glimpse towards familiar country illustrated the amazing size of these features. All the rivers crossed so far had their headwaters at the frontier watershed. But the Arun drains an extensive series of tributaries in Tibet, including the Kangshung, on the east face of Mt Everest. On the next day we would drop right down to the Arun, cross it and climb quite a way up the other side of the gorge.

Half a day before the Arun is the unusual village of Thudam, deep in a heavily timbered valley. All the residents seemed to be involved with the paper-pulp industry. From a vigorously flowing river small water-races had been built, and hollowed logs directed water steeply down to rotating waterwheels. From each wheel a reciprocating action pounded a block of wood back and forth over a rock deck, until the wood was converted to pulp. All the moving parts were made of wood and the lubrication was simply water. Each main axle had about eight grooves cut in it for the rotating blades, which must have been very difficult to construct from the available tools.

Because water splashed in all directions the pulp was saturated. It would then be swept to another platform and, after partial drying, pressed by hand to cannonball size and allowed to dry further. When a large number had been stacked, a yak caravan would be loaded with saddles and a whole line of animals would depart, bound for one of the monasteries in Tibet, for further processing to writing paper. There are other places in Nepal that use the same process, and paper from these sources is frequently available in the shops of Kathmandu. Thudam is at about the lowest limit for yaks in the district. Transport further down the valley is usually by direct manpower.

The Arun River is too wide for a timber bridge – I estimated it to be over 45 metres in span. The local people had built a suspension bridge out of bamboo, similar to those I had seen the previous year. This one sagged badly and many strands splashed in the raging dirty water, just a metre below the single wood poles at walking level. It seemed so fragile that I told my party to halve their loads and cross one at a time. I strapped rifle, ice axe and umbrella vertically to my pack to allow my hands to be free to grip the main bamboo cables. Then I led over the bridge and waited for the others. In the middle, Gyalgen froze. Urkien went back to him, reaching over to take his pack and then crossing with him, with Gyalgen's eyes clamped shut. The other half-loads had to be collected. As Gyalgen was in no condition to face two more crossings, I went back with his headband.

The whole operation took two hours. One very disturbing feature of the big bamboo suspension bridges is that the wrecked one never gets removed. As you cross the latest version, below it the sight of a broken bridge dangling down a bank to the raging water is most disconcerting. There is no safe way of testing a new bridge. One must hope that when failure occurs it is caused by forces of wind and water, and not by the weight of humans and their loaded backs.

Such bridges are completely impossible for any animal to cross. A steel cable bridge and a metre-wide wooden deck would have shortened many yak-traffic trade routes and made available a few more grazing pastures. In the lower Nepalese foothills there are now a number of steel suspension bridges.

The climb up the other side of the river was hot and steep. We were down at about 2,200 metres and the atmosphere was uncomfortably humid. The Arun cuts so deeply down that journeys near it are all in steep country, as most tributary rivers have also chopped enormous cuts through the mountains to meet their draining river.

At the end of a long day we entered a larger village, Chepua, where Jacko had told me to expect another Indian checkpost. The man in charge was Captain Singh, who was most hospitable and wanted hours of conversation.

I was reminded of an episode related to the 1953 Everest expedition. The mountain was climbed on 28 May, and James Morris, the *Times* correspondent, rushed down the valley to reach the Namche checkpost to report the news on 2 June. Asked about progress, he said the weather had not been ideal and the party would be withdrawing in a few days. James had a message written down and asked that it should be sent out by army radio. The message mentioned several items about the weather, but it was in fact in a prearranged code that confirmed the summit ascent and revealed the climbers' names. Thus the first news reached London just in time for the coronation on 3 June. In the next few days the post carried many uncoded congratulatory messages both ways and then, as the party walked out to Kathmandu, they were again out of radio contact until they reached the city.

The Namche checkpost officer was co-operative and happy about it all, but some weeks later there were complaints and exchanges between Delhi and Kathmandu. Indian checkpost officers were instructed not to transmit coded messages for a third nation, bypassing the government of Nepal. These posts still exist but are now operated by Nepalese Army staff.

Captain Singh and one of his assistants at the Chepua checkpost took a great interest in my rifle and the ammunition I carried for it. They politely – and firmly – asked to borrow it for a day. I was reluctant and said, 'Surely, you are in the army. You can use your own.'

'We were trained to shoot, but HMG [the Nepalese government] will not allow us to be armed.' I already knew this from the Walungchung post.

After some discussion I handed it over, with five of my 15 rounds. I was concerned in case they tried to confiscate it altogether. Then I was asked if I had seen any game animals on the way. I had seen a few footprints, but the only large wild animals had been near the terminal of the Yalung Glacier, back at the beginning of my walk. Visibility was so limited and we had made so much noise, I was not greatly surprised.

West to the Khumbu

I told my Sherpas they could have a day of rest and buy some fresh food for the next stage. I had with me two fish lures and a long string, and spent the morning in a long walk through bamboo forest down to the Arun River, where I cast my crude line into the water. However, it was so dirty with melted glacier debris that no fish would have been able to see my tempting lure. Much further down the Arun, nearer its confluence with the Ganges, I have seen big mahseer – a highly regarded sport fish – being caught.

In the afternoon Captain Singh and I continued our long discussions. They see few visitors, apart from Tibetan traders, who don't speak English and have very little Hindi. Late in the day his assistant came back, rather glum. He had glimpsed an animal, which had vanished in the mist. The rifle was returned to me, but no bullets. I took out the bolt and told Urkien to hide the rifle in his tent, with the entrance tied.

Progress down the valley was hot, wet and slow. There were few conifers in the forest but an abundance of bamboo and rhododendron – and now leeches. In the second morning from Chepua we came to the Kashua Khola tributary, where the bridge had collapsed. This was just a short span, built from small trees and sturdy bamboo poles. Two local men offered to rebuild it for us, at a considerable price, but it looked well within our capabilities, so I refused to pay and our quartet set to work. The two who wanted payment joined us, as they also wanted to make the crossing.

Before long another five men arrived on the opposite bank, so I threw them the end of the climbing rope and had it rigged as a temporary handrail. On our side a cluster of sloping poles were put in a hole on the bank and held down with heavy boulders to make a cantilever nearly halfway to the other side. From its end more poles were pushed to a big round rock, and with some green bamboo lashings the structure was completed. On the way up the hill on the other side the Sherpas learned that the locals often deliberately wrecked the bridge when they knew an expedition was coming and then demanded payment for building a new one. Twenty minutes up the valley there were two big rocks where one could jump across the river. Ten days previously the French

Makalu expedition going home had apparently paid for a bridge, which had gone by the time we arrived.

For just a few hours we were on the same track we had used 15 months previously, on the way to the Barun Valley. From the Barun outlet to the last big river all our walking was at altitudes of 2,000–4,000 metres, where conditions were humid. Rampant growth emerged in all directions, but there was little food for sale. Corn cobs were just forming, rice paddies were flooded and hens were sitting on their eggs. In two more months there would be a food surplus. However, there were still patches of wild garlic, ferns, spinach and, on the passes, mushrooms. Milk, butter and a dubious yoghurt could be purchased, if one visited a number of houses to find who had a surplus.

River crossings were a continuous problem. The main Himalayan range is like a giant spine with hundreds of ribs running off it. Between each rib is a dirty glacier-fed torrent in full flow early in the monsoon season. Our next river was the Iswa, which drains the south face of Chamlang, so familiar from the previous year. One short bamboo bridge, barely clear of the water, spanned to an island and then another crossed to solid ground. The second one was swaying because the walking limb was under about the top 15 centimetres of roaring water. Everything was saturated and slippery.

Urkien and I tied a few straggling ends with yak-hide thongs and we ran out the climbing rope. We relayed all the loads, because Gyalgen, Aila and our one extra hired man were reluctant to cross even without loads. Gyalgen came last, when Urkien did a final crossing to reclaim his thongs and release the rope.

Our small caravan continued westwards until we met the valley of the mighty Dudh Kosi, which drains numerous glaciers in the Everest area. We had crossed several more passes and rivers, and built another bridge. Of great interest were the changing environments encountered every day. In the valley floors rice was the main crop, and buffalo, pigs and goats were seen near the villages. As one climbed towards the next pass the crops would be maize and millet. At the colder summit any sheltered arable land would support potatoes or buckwheat. Huge differences in altitude, over just 6 kilometres of terrain, dictated these differences. Villages on the valley floor largely adhered to one of the many variants of Hinduism, while at high altitude we saw the carved stones and prayer flags of Buddhism.

Down in the Dudh Kosi, near Jubing, we joined the normal access route for Everest parties. In less than a day we were in the minor sleepy village of Lukla. It was not on the main track and it existed because it had some arable terraces and was on the beginning of a high track leading to the unmapped valley to the east, approaching Mt Chamlang. We would be based there much later, for our survey work. This was Aila's home and we left him there, for re-employment in three months.

Lukla is vastly different today. The Hillary Himalayan Trust desperately needed a landing strip for light aircraft, so it bought some Lukla land, which was very steep. For several weeks in 1966 a Sherpa and New Zealand team laboured on removing rock walls, filling hollows and then dragging smoothing logs over the clay and mud. Then the filled areas were roughly compacted. Finally a small aircraft came in to land on the undulating surface, which averages about eight degrees from the horizontal. Its altitude is 3,000 metres. Without much enlarging it is now a very busy airport, taking sometimes 20 or more flights a day. Nestling between big mountains and being on such a slope, it can be a frightening destination for a timid passenger. I recall one time when I took off from Lukla, I could see the broken fuselages of three planes that had collapsed for a variety of reasons. The wrecks remained there, owing to the absence of any transport large enough to lift them. Lukla now has a booking office, waiting rooms and even hotels.

Urkien, Gyalgen and I walked up the Dudh Kosi Valley very quickly. The other two were just hours from home and they were in a hurry, particularly because the Dumji festival still had one day to run. Being very fit and acclimatised to the altitude, we had no difficulties going almost non-stop. At Namche Bazar I was on familiar ground – that was where Charles and I had left the main route to travel west 13 months previously. I called on the Namche checkpost, saw familiar faces, and promised to be back soon for a long talk. In the town on that occasion were Norman Dyrenfurth, whose father, Oscar, had led the 1930 Kangchenjunga expedition, and Erwin Schneider, who was also on that expedition. There was much talk about the mountain. They were hoping to gain permission for an attempt on Lhotse (8,386 metres), now the highest unclimbed peak in the world.

We climbed the big hill above Namche, which still had numerous giant pine trees growing on it. From the pass at the top, through the mist, we saw the lovely town of Khunde, and to the right Khumjung, familiar from last year. It was almost like being home again.

In Urkien's house there was suddenly great hilarity. The other men from the expedition had not yet got back, so numerous wives burst in for news. Chang flowed, of course. There were smiles and congratulations in all directions, but they had to be broken by a sad excursion to Pemba Dorji's house with the tragic news of his death at base camp. This dampened the final day of the Dumji festival, the annual event I had first seen the previous year with Charles.

Pemba Dorji's widow hired several monks and the head lama from the Tangboche monastery to conduct six days of mourning – about 11 hours a day. Prayers and mantra were read almost continuously, to ensure the deceased's smooth passage to his next reincarnation. The chanters were all paid and fed during these days. A drum and two reed instruments were part of the performance, although not played with great skill. Because of the intermittent thumping of the drum, the whole village was aware of the sad ceremony under way.

On the fifth day of mourning the rest of the Kangchenjunga Sherpas arrived home from their walk to Darjeeling, train to Raxaul and 16-day walk home via Kathmandu. Their route had taken 35 days, and mine 27. They, of course, had had to accompany the main party out to the roadhead at Darjeeling, where they left the others, bound for England. Charles Evans had been able to confirm compensation money for Pemba Dorji's widow by telephoning London, and he arranged for Dawa Tenzing and Chanjup to travel with them for three weeks of eye-opening experiences in England.

With the arrival of this group in the village I received the first mail for seven weeks and my surveying box. In private, with the sirdar's wife and his brother Annallu as witnesses, I counted out the compensation money, which would be handed over along with Pemba's wages and his issued clothing and equipment. It was a generous, straightforward arrangement.

Four of us went promptly to Pemba Dorji's house, which by now had 20 red-clad worshippers mostly squatted on the floor, in the weak illumination of about 10 butter lamps. I invited the widow outside to tell her in private the amount of the payment being made to her, so she could put most of it safely aside for herself and her two children. She sent messengers down the hill to Namche and announced even bigger ceremonies for next day.

The holy men performed all the new day and everyone in the village was given one rupee each and a ball of cooked rice. There were something over 300 people in Khumjung and Khunde in those days, as well as visitors from other villages. Apparently the trip to Namche involved buying rice and also having some big notes changed to single rupees. Three households cooked rice most of the night, and then rolled rice balls a little larger than cricket balls. The nearest rice-growing paddies were some six days' walk away, so rice cost more than local grains. I compared notes with Annallu, who confirmed my thoughts that more than half the compensation money had been spent. Throughout the mourning period copious volumes of chang had been drunk, but most of this had been brought in by other villagers, who called to pay their condolences. The atmosphere had not been totally glum.

At the end of Dumji all animals have to be moved to high-altitude pastures, some of which are four days away, and up to 5,200 metres. The whole of the home area was then available for growing and cropping hay. With the animals away, any gaps that had appeared in the rock walls around the arable land could be left unmended until harvesting time. Potatoes and buckwheat were well above ground and growing fast in the warm, damp conditions.

Two weeks previously I had been so impressed with the delights and contrasts of our journey that I had begun writing each day's events in considerable detail, with the objective of possibly publishing them in book form. It appeared likely that I would continue to have an abundance of writing time in Urkien's village of Khumjung. Early mornings were often under clear skies. Afternoons became cloudy and damp and by three o'clock every monsoon day, at this 4,000-metre altitude, they became cold, with little human activity. No one had good lighting at night, so I tried to put aside two hours each late afternoon for writing, curled up in a down jacket.

I undertook a journey for one week, this time without Urkien. In the company of another of the expedition men I walked for two days to his small house at Gokyo, where his wife and three children lived for the summer. He had 16 yaks and dzum (female crossbred yaks), with about 10 calves requiring daily attention. Each evening they would be brought in for milking and the calves would be kept inside the house at night to protect them from wolves and the occasional snow leopard. They made butter and the yaks were also shorn for their long, strong hair, which was used for making sacks and ropes. I did some milking and offered to assist with the butter, but after a few laughs I was told this was women's work. I joined the children in picking mushrooms and bringing back baskets of dry yak dung. The house and corral were many miles from any forest, so dung was the usual cooking fuel. This concerned me because of the absence of nourishment going back into the pastures.

Gokyo is in a broad ablation valley high above an active rumbling glacier, which descends from Cho Oyu and its neighbours. It is now one of the most favoured of trekking destinations, because the travelling is not difficult, it supports two small lakes and at its head is Gokyo Peak (5,483 metres), from which one can see six of the world's 14 summits of over 8,000 metres.

From Khumjung I made many excursions to interesting places. During one of these I was for five days near the route that leads to the Nangpa La, the one reasonable pass in the district for crossing to Tibet. The Indians at the checkpost asked many questions.

West to the Khumbu

Another journey was with Urkien to Dingboche, where the few hopeful members of the Lhotse expedition were awaiting permission and better weather. Discussions on a wide range of topics continued from our first meeting two months previously. Our hosts were impressed with how far Urkien had advanced in his knowledge of English. A big surprise to the surveyor, Schneider, was the way Urkien followed and commented on our discourses on working at appropriate survey stations. Some 10 years later an Austrian group undertook very detailed mapping of much of the Nepalese mountains, and Urkien was employed by them for several long seasons as the sirdar for the main team. He had learned from me the need to handle the delicate instruments with great care and then be willing to sit on a cold viewpoint for several hours while figures are being recorded in a fieldbook. Sometimes I, too, just sat, hoping an obscuring cloud would move to – well, to anywhere, except where we wanted to look and record.

Norman Dyrenfurth observed that I was making copious notes and when I confessed I was contemplating writing a book, he made supportive comments. A year later I had a contract with the London publisher Allen & Unwin and my book, *In Highest Nepal*, reached sellers' shelves. Two months later the publisher informed me there would be a German edition. Eventually I received my first three copies of this book and was delighted to see that Norman had played a part in the project, assisting the Munich publisher with photographs and advice.

TWELVE

Mapping New Ground

Time was passing. The day was approaching when I would start walking to India to meet Enid and Joe Macdonald for a venture that would have more conversation and a different purpose. With them would come more supplies. I knew when their ship was due at Bombay and added three days for them to reach Raxaul, the nearest rail terminus to Kathmandu. I booked four Sherpas – two women and two men – to walk out to Kathmandu, to be ready to begin walking in with us on the appointed day. I also located a young woman, Kami Doma, who had worked in Calcutta and had been a doctor's receptionist in Darjeeling. She had learned some English, so I arranged for her to work for Enid later in the year when Joe and I were away on our work.

Urkien and I departed on a normal rainy morning. The monsoon would continue for at least another month. We knew that the Jubing bridge, on the usual route, was unlikely to be repaired until the rains ceased, so we took the high route, crossing two passes of over 4,500 metres and then joining the normal route at the prosperous village of Junbesi. Large expeditions took about 14 days for this walk. We had no delays and reached Kathmandu in 10 days.

At the lower altitudes after three months of vigorous growth there was an abundance of food along the way. We bought corn, pumpkins, flour and eggs, and drank a lot of chang. The journey was always interesting – travelling was either up or down, never level, but the mountains were regrettably always hidden. In the city, because my clothes were in a sorry state, I avoided all social life, keeping this for the arrival of the others. Enid was bringing in a few respectable items for me. However, I did have to go to clear all my mail and arrange permission for my new group to be in Nepal for 10 weeks.

After two days Urkien and I repeated the two-day walk to Raxaul that Charles and I had done 14 months previously. In another year walking on this route virtually ceased, but in 1955 there were few flights into Kathmandu and during the monsoon they were most unreliable. For Enid and Joe the walk up to the city would be a good break-in for their boat-softened legs, and if there was any fault in their equipment it could be remedied in Kathmandu.

Amid crates of baggage these two welcome travellers arrived on the railway platform. Dr Strong at the mission hospital kindly gave us guest rooms for one night.

The damp heat of foothill monsoon India was oppressive and we were keen to reach cooler altitudes as soon as possible. A short truck drive and then the walking began. We engaged very cheap porters for the brief walk up to Kathmandu, put our good clothes into storage for our return, and made up and posted loads of mail. Our caravan for the return to Khumjung was now three Kiwis, five Sherpas and three local porters. In case Enid and Joe did not wholeheartedly adapt to local food, we bought a few foreign items – chocolate, barley sugars, coffee, sugar and baking powder. Many good flours are available but the cooked results tended to be very heavy. I had learned that they would respond to baking powder and that one could make quite good scones and steamed puddings from several flour bases.

Our first stage was seven damp days on a track that elicited mixed reactions from the two new members. The general filth near the villages and the leeches were offset by the new birds, butterflies and the abundant flowers. On the sixth day we reached Those. (Today, people walking the track get this far by bus on a tortuous road in just six hours.) Those had a cottage industry from a low-grade local iron ore. In many houses a blacksmith operated a forge and bellows to manufacture knives, tools and most impressive chains, large enough to support footbridges over the considerable river. Altogether we were a happy party. The two Sherpanis, with their laughter and singing, contributed a lightness to the journey.

At Junbesi, because of the absence of the Jubing bridge, we had to climb on the alternative track that Urkien and I had used three weeks previously. Here we changed our Kathmandu porters for better-clad locals, who knew the route and could tolerate the colder temperatures. The exposure at 4,500 metres slowed everyone, but in three days we reached the main Dudh Kosi Valley at Ghat. This is several hours upstream from where the Lukla airstrip is now located. Further up the valley the Namche hill taxes all new arrivals.

On the fourteenth day we reached Khumjung, to a warm welcome and a day of rest. Next, the three of us with two Sherpas went up to Tangboche to see the monastery in its magnificent setting. Enid was the first Western woman to visit this site and later to go through to the Everest base camp. We admired the buildings but still the great peaks were hidden, apart from timid hints at most sunrises.

Two expedition surveyors, beginning from 1921, had recorded nearly all the terrain north of the Everest area, which measures about 80 kilometres by 50. No access south of Everest was permitted until 1950. In 1953 Charles Evans recorded much terrain south-west of the mountain. One significant segment remained, in the south-east, at the Hongu and its adjacent valley systems. Three parties had crossed the Ambu Lapcha, the high pass at the head of the Hongu, and traversed its upper basins to depart over another pass eastwards to the Barun, without recording many details. In 1953 Major Jimmy Roberts crossed a pass close to Lukla and made the first ascent of Mera Peak (6,470 metres). His party then descended to the main Hongu Valley, and walked up it to the Ambu Lapcha and crossed to the Imja. Roberts had earlier escorted a team of porters carrying oxygen cylinders to the Everest base camp. He had negotiated a long leave pass from his Gurkha battalion, so he undertook this interesting diversion from the main routes, after the base camp visit. I intended repeating the Roberts journey but adding side visits to nearby passes and mapping it from a series of theodolite stations.

At the conclusion of the 1954 Barun expedition Bill Beaven and Colin Todd had walked from the head of the Hongu down to the tree line to make the first ascent of Nau Lekh, which was a notable achievement. They did no mapping, however.

We left Enid at Kami Doma's house and Joe and I went down to Lukla with our Sherpa team, crossing the first pass to the northeast. Back then it was quite an adventure, but now it is so near the airport that trekkers cross it frequently and some reach the top of Mera. Arrangements had been made for Enid to buy various food items and, with porters, take them to Lukla for us at a later date.

Urkien had pressed me to bring the rifle on this escapade, as there were bharal in the lower valleys. Early on the second morning six animals were spotted on a slope far above us. Joe set off with the rifle. I was then fully occupied in keeping my excited group from spoiling the visible stalking. Two shots rang out and no animal fell. Joe was too far away. The bharal ran about 200 metres and stopped behind a bluff. Joe approached carefully, saw them and this time he hit one. It rolled far down to scree and into heavy shrubbery. I expected it to be useless for meat after the long fall, but I sent two men with a knife and packs to examine the carcass. An hour later they returned, loaded and delighted. The beast had not been as badly damaged as expected. I watched as they dismembered it. I took two legs and the liver for Joe and me. The Sherpas made sausages from the intestines and ate the lungs and the windpipe, to my amazement.

Aila and I left the others for two days and crossed the high pass to Enid's supplies at Lukla. With these we had all the food necessary for the next two weeks in the Hongu Valley, further to the east.

We reached the two high passes that Charles Evans and Geoff Harrow had crossed the previous year. We examined the approaches to Mt Chamlang itself, forming the opinion that it was so formidable that its ascent would require a competent team with a large amount of specialist climbing equipment to negotiate the ice ribs and buttresses. Still, its height of 7,321 metres meant oxygen assistance would not be necessary for a capable party. The first ascent of Chamlang was made by a Japanese group in 1961.

After the completion of our work, Joe, Urkien and the two porters returned to Khumjung via the Mera La. Meanwhile Aila and I went to the head of the Hongu and crossed Ambu Lapcha (5,787 metres), which I had traversed twice the previous year. We followed down the next valley to the village of Dingboche, where Enid was waiting as arranged. We all then walked slowly up the broad, bare valley to the Everest base camp, where we hoped to see the Dyrenfurth Lhotse expedition, but we missed them, as they were higher on the approaches to the mountain.

Base camp with no one in residence is a bleak place, with high cliffs and bare moraines in most directions. To obtain a view of Everest and Lhotse one must climb the nearby Kala Patar, but even from there the view is restricted to just one valley.

We returned to Khumjung and prepared to depart. There were very liquid farewells and I did not expect to see the village again. Our small party walked all the way to Kathmandu, hastily located the house where our good clothes were stored, and indulged in long-overdue ablutions. This time we stayed at the British Embassy and relaxed in the delightful hospitality provided by Sir Christopher and Lady Summerhayes.

I had by now become deeply involved with the problems of Nepal. In the embassy office I looked into the possibility of work there, using my engineering background for the construction of small suspension bridges, buildings and water-supply schemes. The answers were depressing. In those days there were no funds available for such work in the mountains, and little hope of a salary.

After a week of being tourists in India we caught a liner in Bombay for a restful passage to Sydney and, four days later, to Wellington, New Zealand.

THIRTEEN

Back in New Zealand

Settling back into New Zealand in the last month of 1955 was far from easy. There was my book to complete and a publisher to be found. With three expensive mortgages Enid and I bought a modest house with good views on the Cashmere Hills, Christchurch. I obtained employment with a consulting engineer, Guy Powell, a leader in his field who was designing the structural work for several of the best architects in Christchurch, as well as in other centres. As most of my previous engineering work had been in the hydro-electrical and water-supply fields, I struggled for some time to absorb new structural codes. There was much reading and studying to do.

Enid began teaching English part time at a secondary school. Somehow I managed to work on the plotting of Himalayan survey maps and eventually forwarded them to the draughting office of the Royal Geographical Society in London.

While deep in this situation, which would take years to clear, I received a letter from Sir Edmund Hillary, inviting me to be one of the surveyors for the expedition he would be leading in the Antarctic for the next year and possibly a second year. A base would be built on permanent land, on a site not yet examined. Those in the party who were government employees would be paid normal salaries and their promotions and superannuation would be unaffected. Ed thought I would not be paid unless I obtained a permanent state position. It took very little time to decline this invitation. Access would be by ship, and the route was free of ice only between about mid-January and early April. I would have to tolerate an inactive winter in the new base, and the work would not advance my engineering career, let alone our income.

However, I did follow Antarctic events over the next few years with great interest. Harry Ayres at last had an overseas expedition and he was very successful. Many of the base party were known to me, and later I became close to Peter Mulgrew and Murray Ellis, two of the four who finally accompanied Ed to the South Pole. They did some training with dogs and sledges on the Tasman Glacier, so I was able to see something of the men and their equipment. At the time American activity was increasing in Antarctica and I soon found that two of the 1954 Californian Makalu expedition were involved.

After two years I departed from the large office of my wise employer and joined another engineer in setting up our own business. In my rare spare time I did very little mountaineering, apart from some instructing for the two main climbing clubs. A number of overseas mountaineers stayed a few days with us, and I usually tried to take them to our nearest mountains for a weekend.

Sir Percy Wyn Harris, retired governor of Gambia, was one such guest. He had been over 8,500 metres on Everest in 1933 with L. R. Wager. Now in his mid-fifties, he was still relatively fit and proved amusing company. He was astonished when I told him I had written to the Joint Himalayan Committee in late 1952 suggesting he be the Mt Everest leader when it seemed that Eric Shipton would be dropped. Harris had heard nothing about it. His career had been with West African colonial administration, and after 1933 he had had virtually no contacts with the giants of the Alpine Club. He smiled when I said I had received no reply to my suggestion. I was quite unknown to the committee in those days and my knowledge of Wyn was just from the various Everest books. To me, he looked the best on paper of those still living in 1952. However, John Hunt was appointed leader.

Heinrich Harrer, author of *Seven Years in Tibet*, climbed the Otira face of Mt Rolleston with Bill Beaven, John Harrison and me, and complained about the looseness of the rocks. This was a surprising comment from a man who had made the first ascent of the north face of the Eiger, where falling rocks are quite menacing. Back in Christchurch at a function we had arranged, he was a great social success with one of our neighbouring widows. I also introduced him to Philip Temple, and soon those two joined forces for a very fruitful expedition to New Guinea. Philip's writing career began from that enterprise.

The most special events of those years were the births of our two daughters – Sarah Jane in early 1958 and Ruth in late 1959. Of course for some time Enid reduced her teaching involvement. My head was down in my engineering work, but I was also listening to what was happening in the mountain world.

Many people were finding the limited access to Antarctica severely proscribed the type of activities that could be undertaken in that continent. The US Navy brought large planes to Christchurch and, with some caution, began direct flights to the south. Bulldozers and graders were placed on the Barrier Icefield and a runway was cleared. In case conditions meant landing on the ice was not possible, the aircraft needed to have enough fuel to return all the way to Christchurch, a distance of about 3,500 kilometres each way. In the 1950s there were few aircraft with the ability to land on ice and also carry so much fuel. A small American support station was established temporarily at Invercargill, at New Zealand's southernmost airport. Large supplies and a small station were landed by icebreaker on the Antarctic mainland at Cape Hallett, about 500 kilometres north of the final destination. With these emergency landing strips on solid land, flights began from Christchurch. Smaller aircraft, such as adapted DC3s, were able to be sent south by ship, and short-term support staff could fly on a Super Constellation, known as 'Connie'.

Some 8 kilometres from the Barrier strip the American base at McMurdo was begun, adjacent to Captain Scott's 'Hut Point'. Four kilometres away New Zealand's Scott Base had been ideally situated so that the two countries could share sea and air landing facilities. Before long, experiments were made with landing large aircraft on thick sea ice. This proved to be successful and the Barrier strip is now used only when the sea connection is unsatisfactory. Thus, within two years the one-ship-a-year access was replaced by an air service that could operate for the five warmer months. Very soon a permanent station was placed for American scientists at the South Pole itself, a further 1,400 kilometres inland, with all supplies being delivered by air.

From Scott Base the Hillary party reached South Pole overland in 1958, and three weeks later Vivian Fuchs and his team arrived there, having come from the Atlantic side. Fuchs drove on, following the Hillary party's tracks and depots to reach the sea at Scott Base, completing the first land crossing of Antarctica.

One sunny Christchurch day I was pouring concrete on a retaining wall at our steep hillside property when Dr Griff Pugh (or 'Doctor Pug', as the checkpost officer had called him in 1955) rang from the local airport. He desperately wanted a long conversation with me, so I invited him to stay with us for a couple of days. I abandoned my concreting and thought about the meetings I had had with him on oxygen developments at Yeovil and all he had done for high-altitude physiology.

Griff arrived and typically took half an hour to get to the point. He explained that he had arranged a small project, assisted by the American Deep Freeze programme, which had flown him to McMurdo in Antarctica. While there he ran tests on members of the Fuchs party as they arrived after their polar traverse. I had not seen him since early 1955, so he also asked for all sorts of details about Kangchenjunga – the medical, food and oxygen titbits that had not been in Evans's official record.

Then he changed tack. 'Norman, several countries are considering artificial earth satellites. Manned space flights will occur in our generation.'

This was 1958 and to me it seemed a little far-fetched.

'Be serious,' he went on. 'You mountaineers get to great heights and then descend and immediately go back home. Doctors have been with expeditions and have done tests, but little is known about the longer exposure to high altitude. What foods can be absorbed, does the brain deteriorate, are there psychological problems?

Back in New Zealand

What is a reasonable maximum long-term altitude for the human body?'

'There are miners who work at about 17,000 feet in the Andes,' I said. 'Can't they be tested?'

Pugh explained that they had been looked at, but there were language problems and they had not been tested before they went up there, so the results were not very helpful. The miners did not want to undergo dietary changes or psychological tests, nor have instruments attached to them for hours. Scientists considering space travel were becoming concerned about the effects of long, inactive flights. Could the crew be supplied with oxygen at the equivalent of, say, 6,000 metres for months at a time without deteriorating? When they approach a landing place or encounter a problem, could they have the oxygen flow rate increased and thereby perform complex tasks with the same skill they had at sea level?

If the oxygen could be reduced, then so could the cargo load, with many obvious benefits. Could their outward breath be passed through soda lime containers to absorb carbon dioxide and the unused oxygen be fed back, as in the closed-circuit system? Breathing apparatus would not be attached to the pilot – it would be put in a locker, like a fan installation. Yes, I could see the need for this research.

Among the many others interested was the Indian Army. If India had to defend itself, much action would be in the Himalayas and the ground troops would have considerable altitude problems. Some Indian doctors might join a testing team. In various parts of the world there were also mining companies that would appreciate such research.

At Scott Base, Griff had talked to Ed Hillary and some of the American doctors. He told me: 'We can't get British funds, but there is strong American interest. We need a living laboratory at about [6,000 metres], where test subjects will live for most of a year. Ed is keen, and he says you're needed to help put up the testing hut. I agree that with your oxygen background you'd be of great assistance to the testing team. At the end of the long experiments there would be a proving exercise, involving climbing one of the highest mountains without carrying oxygen, probably Makalu. Ed wants you for that part too.'

My first contribution was: 'I think the money will be difficult to raise. I doubt Ed's enthusiasm for another long expedition after just having an Antarctic winter. In the previous southern summer he went to the Antarctic on the Atlantic side. He'll be under family pressure if he is pushed for yet another year of absence.'

Griff had clearly given considerable thought to all aspects. 'Ed is the only one who could put on the pressure in America to raise the money. The expedition would cost twice as much as the Everest climb and it could not be funded from Britain. He wouldn't have to stay the whole year, but be there at the beginning and end. Some doctors and young mountaineers would be the ones for the long-term testing. Ed is clearly a man with an unusual record. He's already done a lecture tour in America and goes down well there. He does not have to be one of the guinea pigs. He'd go in to get everything started, then and go home for the winter, reappearing towards the end when results are being assessed, perhaps leading the final climbing expedition.'

I explained my situation – new business, young family and no wish to be away long from my slender list of clients. Griff returned to England. Ed rang me some weeks later, and I gave the same response to him.

One day in April 1960 Ed came to our house and addressed us – Enid more than me. He had been to America and the basic finances were assured for a medical research expedition. The main sponsors were Field Enterprises Corporation, which had associations with *World Book Encyclopaedia* and World Books. The US Air Force had agreed to supply some instruments and was sending a doctor, Tom Nevison, who was also a climber. Ed would be there for the beginning and conclusion of the venture. He really wanted me for the construction part and for controlling the porter caravan of over 300 loads, which had to go up to the laboratory site – a 20-day walk – during the monsoon. There were now air links through to Kathmandu – no one needed to waste five weeks aboard ship. We succumbed for the construction of the laboratory part of the project.

Ed also wanted me for the Makalu climb, to prove the acclimatisation at the end of the long experiment. I firmly declined that invitation. If those who spent the winter in the high huts were fully acclimatised, they would be in better condition for the climb than Ed or me. He countered that they were good men, but only Mike Ward in the party had Himalayan experience. In my earlier climbs I had seldom given much thought to the risks of high climbing, but in 1960, with a family, I saw things differently. Besides, I was very conscious of how slowly one's brain reacts at high altitudes. I had no desire to attempt one of the highest peaks without oxygen.

Ed revealed that an order had been placed in England for a specially designed prefabricated building for the highest laboratory. He had several good mountaineers and doctors who were available to spend the full time at the experimental altitude. He intended the hut to be near a high col some 3 kilometres from the Ambu Lapcha. I had already made that crossing three times, and I expressed doubts about locating a safe site at 6,000 metres in that area, but I thought that a little lower would be possible.

At about this time I attended a conference in Wellington for engineers considering earthquake problems. On one occasion I found I was sitting beside two Japanese men, while a New Zealander was holding forth from the stage about the different effects on a building depending on whether it is built on rock or on shingle.

The Japanese whispered to each other and thumbed through a small book. A note was pushed to me: 'What is a shingle? Dictionary says try medical section.'

I wrote: 'Try gravels.'

Great smiles. They understood. Afterwards I was talking to them and we exchanged cards. One was the manager of one of the biggest Tokyo construction companies and the other was his consulting engineer. They were to have a week in the South Island, and I arranged to meet them at Christchurch airport. I showed them many local buildings and some of the earthquake research projects being undertaken at the university engineering school. I was invited to see their work should I ever visit Tokyo. They had a meal in our house.

I was the secretary of the New Zealand Alpine Club when we received a letter from a group of five Japanese women who were determined to climb Mt Cook. They were seeking some sponsorship, access to club huts and information on costs in general. I replied with most of what they wanted, and asked about their experience with crevasses, crampons on hard ice and avalanches. I asked whether they wanted a local guide.

Their reply was strongly worded. As they had already climbed Mt Fuji, 22 metres higher than Cook, they thought they would have no problems. They represented a major early feminist wave in Japan and a sponsoring newspaper had already announced this all-women's ascent of Mt Cook. They did not want a man in their party – as guide or anything else. I checked with people in New Zealand who had climbed Fuji and they confirmed that the two mountains were hugely different undertakings. Mt Cook posed far more difficulties and risks.

I suggested a partial solution. I would go on the medical research expedition for the first three months only. I approached John Harrison and it seemed likely he would take my place for the later climbing. On the way back I would have a week in Japan, to include three winter days with the women on Fuji, giving some instruction, and four days looking at Tokyo construction projects. All parties agreed and I made the necessary air bookings.

About two months before we departed for Nepal, Ed Hillary rang me. The sponsors considered that the medical aspect had very little publicity impact, so they had asked that a search for the yeti, or 'abominable snowman', be added to the expedition's objectives. The firm's public relations officer, reporters and some zoologists would be added to the party. Ed accepted these additions and it seemed he even originally encouraged them. He decided to lead a group, including some of the doctors, to the Rolwaling district, where Eric Shipton had seen unexplained tracks in 1951. I would go with the large caravan of equipment and building materials, with three climbers in my team, to the previously chosen valley and erect the laboratory and hut. We would be completely separate from the yeti searchers. Some of the men to be tested would be with Ed. They would still begin their long acclimatisation period, but in another valley. The yeti-searching add-ons to the project would leave the expedition within three months and return to America.

Two weeks before we were to leave I was approached by Keith Marshall, a young architect in Christchurch, informing me that he wished to join me in Japan, but wanted to stay longer than I was intending. With the chance of such good company I changed my bookings to stay for 17 days in Japan instead of seven. I took out an extra life insurance policy for twice the value of the mortgage we had remaining on our house.

FOURTEEN

The Silver Hut Expedition

Six of us flew, with several stops, from Auckland to Calcutta. It was the first time most of us had been in a large aircraft – a Boeing 707 – and I was most impressed. I had never been to an Indian city with Ed. At Calcutta airport hundreds seemed to be pursuing us and there were a dozen or so reporters at the front of the crowd.

All was soon revealed. Desmond Doig, on the staff of the *Calcutta Statesman*, was to be with us for the first three months and it was he who had been inserting much of the promotional information in the paper. This had been distributed to many other news sources in India. I took an immediate liking to Desmond. He had been an officer in a British Gurkha unit and could therefore speak Nepali. He calmly steered us through the official airport facilities and placed Ed and the reporters in a private room, explaining that the rest of us should have a drink and then go to the bus that would take us to our hotel. He explained that the crowds just wanted to see 'Sir Hillary', as he was known in India.

The drive from the airport into Calcutta is one of the most depressing in India. Then, on the third day, we were all in a DC3 with great amounts of accumulated baggage, destined for Kathmandu. After half an hour in the air we were turned back because the pilot had been told there was fog at our intended landing airport. Back in the hotel the curious flocked to see Ed once more. Next day the fog vanished and the view of the main ranges was brilliant when we flew over the passes for the entry to Nepal.

The Silver Hut Expedition

In Kathmandu our accommodation for a week was the Royal Hotel, which boasted that it had been newly converted from a maharajah's palace. It had large rooms and grounds, but was deficient in plumbing. However, the broad, open spaces made the sorting of our hundreds of loads easier. Most of our gear had already arrived in the city.

In the first stage of the expedition there were to be 13 Westerners, and seven more joined some months later. Some of the Americans had brought their wives this far, and there always seemed to be numerous other women about, from the American Embassy and news media. Suddenly the publicity and razzamatazz was almost overwhelming. John Dienhart, the sponsor's public relations man, was clearly pushing his influence in all departments. He looked flabby and unfit, and I guessed the weeks of approach walking to the main ranges would be an effort for him. John went into lengthy huddles with Ed and frequently inserted various media gurus and odd characters into the planning sessions. The rest of us were trying to get our own departments into action, but it was difficult to get access to our leader.

Among many other duties, I was asked to arrange trucks and buses to take the whole party and the freight to the beginning of the walking track, where we would meet the porters. I spent half a day in meetings with representatives of the bigger firms, and we were far apart in negotiating the charge for this small journey of about 30 kilometres, as it was in those days (today a road goes in much further). I said we would have to call in 'Sir Hillary' and his word would be final. I dragged Ed away from another obligatory social event and explained the transport situation. When he appeared, the hagglers were wide-eyed and silent. When Ed stated the rates I had suggested, they agreed immediately and several asked for his autograph. We dispersed and Ed said, 'That was easy. What was the problem?' Like so many people, they had wanted to see Hillary and had hoped the first negotiations would be with him.

From my contact with the Americans it was soon evident that the yeti was the important objective for them. Very seldom was there any mention of medical research. I admired the way

Ed calmly tolerated the pressures and let the media steam blast off. He and I did manage to have a private meeting. It had been decided we would set out in two groups. The yeti-searchers would be heading to a different area, and I was happy not to have the media people in my group. I was to go ahead as planned and carry the building materials and supplies to the proposed medical research site. His team would set out a day ahead of ours, and our routes would diverge after three days.

We arranged to have a mail runner to travel twice between our two groups – Ed wanted to be certain that I was still making progress. Because he had to feed information to the media men travelling with him, he wanted contributions from me, to reduce the yeti monopoly in news despatches. As my three companions were to be in the wintering group and then attempt Mt Makalu, he also wanted my assessment of them after two or so weeks. We did have radios, but contact from deep in the approach gorges would be unreliable until both parties were on big mountains.

Dawa Tenzing was to be my sirdar. At that time he was the best man for the job. Among many other features in his career, Dawa Tenzing had been to the South Col on Everest in 1953, and was sirdar to our 1954 Barun expedition. On Kangchenjunga he was sirdar for Charles Evans and carried a load to the top camp. Urkien was to lead Ed's porters and Sherpas. For the first time Urkien would not be with me. I explained to him that we would be together in about two months. He was concerned about those in Ed's party who had no mountain experience, and also that Doig, George Lowe and Ed were the only ones with even minimal language ability for communicating on the journey. I tried to reassure him and emphasised the importance of the media people for the yeti stage of the expedition. I forecasted that Mike Gill, a newly graduated doctor, would soon be an asset to the party, although on his first Himalayan visit.

The Hillary team departed from Kathmandu amid much camera flashing and well-wishing. We called them 'the playboys'. There were nine of them, but their total caravan numbered 160 men. Besides all the usual climbing equipment, radios, food and tents, this time there was more than the usual volume of medical

The Silver Hut Expedition

supplies. For the yeti search there were telescopes, 'captur' guns and an impressive array of movie cameras. One small tube held a horn to be blown – allegedly a mating caller. We were unsure which lucky person would use it. Over 50 people drove out to the track where the walking began.

A day after the yeti party's departure we were on our way, with a total of 310 loads and having no boisterous cheering party, just two wives to the end of the road. I was happy with my team, although none had been to the Himalayas previously. Barry Bishop was a *National Geographic* photographer who had done some mountaineering in America. Wally Romanes, a carpenter, was among the top ranks of New Zealand climbers. Jim Milledge was an English doctor who had worked in a mission hospital in Madras and done some climbing in Switzerland.

The usual approach-march problems burst out immediately, with loads being dropped while their carriers went seeking food or footwear for the obstacles ahead. Dawa and I stayed at the tail for three days to keep everyone moving, but we needed someone to be several hours ahead, recruiting new carriers to replace the daily deserters. Dawa was later given that job while I wagged the tail. Both his job and mine needed men with some local language and at this stage my fellow mountaineers could not help much in that regard.

Each evening we would discuss the day's progress and the hopes for the following day. Barry would invariably ask what our destination was next day. I had to explain that it depended on the weather and the rear porters. 'Whatever you do,' I said, 'don't keep walking in any afternoon if the cook's boys have not passed you.'

'Why on earth not?'

'The cook and two or three senior Sherpas assess progress each afternoon and they select a campsite. If you go past that point your food and sleeping kit will stop behind you.'

With these big parties it was normal for a Sherpa cook to be employed for the whole journey, and he would have two or three young assistants. While we left camp each morning and everything was packed and moving, the boys would be scrubbing porridge pots and putting away the last items we had used. At some stage during the day the cook would pass us, often unnoticed because he would have a modest pack on his back. Then the boys would pass, loaded with enormous baskets containing all our kitchen equipment, the small items of pepper, jam, coffee and any other containers that had been opened and, on top the giant cooking pots, water-carrying vessels and fire-support steel pieces. Invariably their loads rattled with all the metal pieces clanging together, so they were easily identified. They would have to reach the next campsite and be expected to have drinks available as we arrived. I encouraged my trio to take photographs and wash their 'smalls' on the way, and not to put pressure on the hardworking cooking staff, who had to be the fastest travellers – last to start and first to arrive.

Each evening I encouraged the others to learn a few words of Hindi. I started with some frequently used nouns and counting to 10, which are virtually the same in Nepali and Hindi. I had found that mastering the ability to count made it possible to establish the local price for items for sale, and then the vital words for any transaction soon became known. Soon Jim and Wally had become useful at checking loads as they arrived each day.

The monsoon poured on for two more weeks. As expected, we heard that the Jubing bridge was still out of action and there was no option but to take everyone over the three-day high route, as Enid, Joe and I had done in 1955. Then we would cross the Dudh Kosi at the next upstream bridge. It was very cold and wet at Junbesi, where we paid off 160 barefoot, freezing foothills porters. The payment process went on late into the night. Loads had to be identified and matched to their carrier, and names and thumbprints recorded in a large book I carried. The process was not helped by having 12 named Lal Bahdru and 11 Ram Bhadrus! Before cash was handed over each departing man had his personal kit examined by some of the permanent Sherpas. From this inspection several tent pegs, plates and discarded batteries reappeared. Meanwhile Dawa Tenzing was out in the night appealing to the Junbesi population for replacements to join our well-paid caravan.

We climbed the spurs behind Junbesi in ghastly weather and I dreaded the situation ahead on the passes, which I had crossed

The Silver Hut Expedition

on three previous occasions. In failing light I reached the campsite where our two two-man tents had been erected. There were three miserable animal shelters, which now were crammed with humans. Outside were over a hundred more people, squatted under the expedition's tarpaulins. It was not a happy night.

With the dawn came driving sleet that made me fear snow on the passes 600 metres above us. More than a hundred of the train were still barefoot. I announced that we would wait for a day. Several porters asked to be paid and promptly vanished. Many ran back to Junbesi for food and footwear, and fortunately a large number of locals arrived as replacements for those who did not return. These latter did have reasonable clothing and were aware of the likely problems on the passes.

For the first time I had some idle hours. In the tent I wrote a report to Ed, telling him we would soon be moving again, and no loads had been lost. I recorded a few notes on my companions, as requested.

The next day dawned slightly better but the weather soon deteriorated again. However, I decided to push for the pass. Wally, Barry and a strong Sherpa group set off to stamp a route through the snow while I waited to sign on the last likely stragglers to carry the remaining loads. By 2 p.m. the last porters had departed, so I began my journey for the day. Soon I passed about 40 men and women who were moving very slowly. Many of the loads were extremely difficult to carry on forested routes. The hut sections, although not heavy, frequently extended over a metre above the porter's head. When the load hit a projecting branch the carrier's head would be jerked back, as all the weight was suspended by a headband. Such loads could be nearly lethal in the wind on a high pass. Also being carried were long floor beams, which were awkward on a tight corner or a narrow footbridge.

In driving sleet and with an hour of daylight remaining, I was at the last slopes of the first pass. Just below the summit I found a boy of about 15 curled up in the snow, whimpering and soaked. He could not lift his awkward load, nor would he desert it. I helped him get it to the top. There he called out and was answered by an even smaller boy. Neither was able to traverse the glazed rocks in the driving wind. I escorted them down to easier ground on the other side where there was less wind, and soon they were warm and moving a little better. About two hours after dark I joined the main party and had another anxious night.

The next day was again cold and wet, but not so exposed. By its end we were at the main Dudh Kosi again and on a good track. A load count revealed there were 40 missing. I talked to Dawa Tenzing about this and suggested sending men back for them. He advised waiting and, sure enough, everything appeared. At this stage the first of Ed's mail runners arrived, handing me a small canvas bag and escorted by a very concerned Dawa, who said, 'This man says Hillary Sahib has fired Urkien.'

I opened Ed's package and read his short letter. His yeti party had not made any great discoveries, but at least they were becoming acclimatised to the altitude. Two who had never done any substantial walking were struggling with blisters and culture shock. He considered that some would retreat to Kathmandu and avoid crossing the high Tesi Lapcha, which separated his party from mine. One, John Dienhart, had already left. Then he mentioned a drink problem, and that Urkien had beaten up one of their employees, a man from the local village. He said Urkien was rather out of favour with the media members of the expedition and with the holy men of the village, but did not state that he had been fired.

Urkien had been my special trainee. I had lived in his house and admired him greatly. Dawa Tenzing had recently married his widowed mother, so Urkien had become Dawa's stepson.

I finished my notes to Ed about our progress and sent the runner back to the Rolwaling base. Occasionally, as we were getting nearer, we picked up radio signals from each other, but they were generally poor in reception and of course not wholly private. There was distinctive jamming with extraordinary scratchy noises, and often I would just have started a conversation with Ed's party when Chinese opera would drown our conversation.

On the second-to-last day of the approach walk a garbled radio message from Ed indicated that his party would be short of porters to carry their loads over the Tesi Lapcha pass when they were ready to join my group. With Dawa Tenzing I put out requests for a team to undertake the 5,800-metre crossing, without weakening my own team. An extraordinary assembly of ill-clad Sherpas was rounded up. Few had boots, goggles or ice axes, but all claimed to have made the crossing previously. There were numerous unemployed Tibetan refugees at the villages, but Dawa and my senior Sherpas strongly opposed giving them work while their own relatives, no matter how frail, were available.

At Tangboche the remaining Kathmandu porters were thanked and paid. As none of them would be able to fulfil Ed's porter needs, I let them depart for home. I engaged a small number of local Sherpas to help with the higher lifts to the proposed hut sites. Wally, who was to build the lower 'Green Hut', disappeared into a well-organised series of events. He had long lengths of local pine logs pit-sawn to specified sizes, then began despatching them on Sherpa backs to the chosen site, in the Mingbo Valley, by the foot of Ama Dablam, a great mountain that was still unclimbed at that time.

Wintering food and medical testing crates were stored in a local house and my team was assembled to take the first loads to the proposed top hut site. The outer covering of this hut was a silver-coloured material with some insulation and waterproofing qualities. It had been designed in England and the prefabricated sections manufactured there. The curved segments were hollow, sheathed with treated plywood. They had well-shaped pegged joints and I had been careful, on the approach climb, to avoid any damage to these important joints. At about this time it began to be known as the 'Silver Hut'. Among these first carriers were six of the better Sherpa climbers. We ascended the rarely visited glacial valley. For a time the Mingbo had easy ablation gully pastures and these continued to near where the decision was made to build the Green Hut, at a little above the requested 5,200-metre altitude. Higher up, the valley merged into heavy moraine rocks and then active glacier ice and moraine. At this time the upper valley was covered in new snow, which added to the transport problems.

Not far ahead was the steep enclosing wall at the head of the valley, where we could see the pass, Ama Dablam Col, at just under 6,000 metres, that Shipton and Hillary had crossed in 1952. I knew it was climbable by competent people with good equipment but I confirmed my earlier doubts about building the Silver Hut in such a position, on or above the summit of the pass, as originally requested. The final slopes were about 150 metres of fluted ice in steep avalanche runnels. There would be severe winds on the pass and, as it was meant to house eight men throughout the winter, I was greatly concerned. If things got bad during this long-term experiment, the retreat route might not be feasible throughout the winter. Also it might not be possible for re-supply people to climb up to them in all conditions, unless some mountain experts were stationed all the time in support at the Green Hut. In addition, it seemed likely that some of the wintering men might not be competent climbers.

In anticipation of problems in getting loads up the final fluted ice we had a light winch and steel cable to assist the lifting process. Some of us cramponed our way to the top and wound up the first loads. The cableway had a small steel frame at each end, about 2 metres high. Loads were dragged up the slope, not freely suspended. The back anchors for the winch frames had to be very firmly placed. The big panels for the hut easily snagged on ice pinnacles and soon the top steel frame had broken. Before descending I searched for a feasible location for the hut but found nothing I considered safe for secure anchoring against the wind. The man access problems on the approach slopes looked just as bad from the top. It was a bleak place for contemplating a winter's residence. We carried the winch frame down to the nearest toolkit for repairs.

I was quite disturbed about all this. I chose a temporary safe location at 5,800 metres and had the next loads dumped there. The team went back down to Tangboche and began the relaying of loads to my depot. No construction took place and the large but light panels had rocks placed on them so they would not be blown into the jaws of a rather open adjacent glacier. At least the Green Hut was completed satisfactorily, by Wally Romanes.

I wrote to Ed about my concerns and sent this letter with the next mail runner, after his man had come back to me. Ed's news confirmed that the yeti search was winding down. He and his doctors would cross the pass and be with us within a week. I therefore kept the hut loads going to the selected dump site while I left my group and walked down to Namche Bazar and then up the next valley towards Thame to meet the others from the Rolwaling.

This was late 1960 and the Sherpas had told us that Chinese pressure had increased in Tibet. They were horrified that the monastery at Rongbuk, at the north foot of Everest, had been burned down. The Dalai Lama was by then in India and thousands of Tibetans were crossing the passes to the south and west of their land. The route to Thame is on one of the main high crossings of the Himalayan Range. Although I had been warned about the fleeing Tibetans, the shock was worse than all the rumours.

Vultures are rare in the higher Sherpa lands, but I could see about 50 circling in the main valley, which meant there could be dozens more on the ground. At most open spaces there were large colourful Tibetan tents made from yak hair, and numerous ragged people were sitting around their temporary residences. Scores of children rushed to me to stare at probably the first Westerner they had sighted. The skins of slaughtered yaks were drying in the sun, as were large slabs of meat.

The world's media had been reporting thousands of Tibetans crossing the frontiers, but little was said about the fact that many were bringing animals with them. Hundreds of yaks and some sheep were for sale at giveaway prices, and Sherpas who had access to pastures were becoming overloaded with new healthy herds. The Sherpas know how much hay they can cut each summer, and this governs the size of the herd they can support over the next winter. Soon the market was saturated and surplus animals were being killed. The vultures were doing much tidying. The few Tibetans who had relatives in Sherpa villages stayed for a time, but the majority went down into the foothills without their yaks. Few were welcomed in Nepal, a country that was already crowded, and its government feared offending the Chinese occupiers of Tibet. It was all very sad.

A little before Thame I saw Peter Mulgrew and two Sherpas

coming towards me. We sat in the sun and talked for an hour or so. He said Ed's party was held up in Thame and we might not see him for another day. I enjoyed catching up on the activities of Ed's yeti group, described in Peter's colourful naval language.

'The Americans adored your letters to us,' he said.

'What? They were personal communications to the leader!' I protested.

'Well, we weren't getting much from the outside. The Americans specially liked your assessment of Barry Bishop. You had sorted him out and wrote about him so accurately.'

In response to Ed's request for my assessment of my companions I had written that Barry was the only person I knew who put on weight during an expedition – and he was heavy before we started. I also said I had not known him to use one word of Hindi. However, Barry went on to last the winter in the Silver Hut, and was one of those who made the first ascent of Ama Dablam. Four years later he climbed Everest, but after a night out just below the south summit he lost some toes to frostbite. He died in a car accident in the US in 1994, after a career with *National Geographic*.

I asked about Urkien. The expedition still employed him, but he was rather under a cloud, in Ed's eyes. John Dienhart, the sponsor's PR man, had gone to Calcutta to clear some items through customs. There were rumours that he would not return. He did not.

The radio contacts? The yeti party radio had been purposely jammed by the Chinese, who believed they were spying. Hillary's party and mine had seen aircraft flying right around Everest. Peter confirmed that they were MIGs.

Then Peter told me that Ed was far from pleased that I had not taken all the Silver Hut loads to the top of Ama Dablam Col. I explained the hazards, but though Peter was very experienced with Antarctic conditions, he was new to the Himalayas. He was one of the four who drove tractors to the South Pole with Ed, but he had never been on large, steep fluted ice slopes.

At about the same time Griff Pugh, the scientific leader, arrived from Kathmandu and it was refreshing to know that the medical work would start to receive a push. Griff had not wanted to participate in the construction of the high huts and was even less interested in the yeti search. He had, however, been involved with the design of the higher hut, and wisely timed his arrival for when his particular expertise would be needed. Ed and I had discussed the proposed height of the Silver Hut. He still thought we could build it above the col, at nearly 6,000 metres, but Griff said he would not mind if it was at about 5,800 metres. To him it was vital to have safe access to the hut throughout the winter. He was not going to live up there all the time, but he wanted to be able to visit and be assured that its occupants were well supplied and totally safe. Griff had hired a house near the top tree level, at Changmatang, and acclimatised there for a few days. He also had a large dome tent placed in the Mingbo, down the valley from the Green Hut. This meant the wintering group would have four places to live and work, all above 4,250 metres.

Griff also told me that two Indian doctors would be arriving in a few weeks and the interest from their country was substantial. I never met Larry Lahari and Captain Motwani, who stayed for several winter months, usually living in the lower temporary bases. However, I did later meet two other researchers, Mike Ward and John West, who walked in from Kathmandu, arriving about three weeks after Griff.

At this stage I had an opportunity to hear more about the yeti-seeking party. They had found nothing of great significance, but through Desmond Doig's ability with language and his reporter's talent for locating a good story, they did send out despatches about various alleged yeti samples. A 'yeti hide' was later proved to be that of a bear. Some verbal reports from residents described animals similar to three species of bear. A 'yeti scalp' worn over the head at certain religious ceremonies was shown to be from a deer, stretched on a wood block to fit a human head. Mike Gill and Pat Barcham followed tracks in soft snow that appeared to be from a large animal, but when they reached a firmer surface they proved to be from something much smaller, like a fox. When in deep snow it had leapt, with four feet coming together, making one large footprint. Apparently the American sponsors were happy with these findings – and with the coverage from hundreds of newspapers – and they arranged for Ed, Dienhart, a Sherpa and the zoologist, Marlin Perkins, to do a three-week tour to Europe and America with the so-called samples. The tour would not begin until the Silver Hut was erected.

I had always thought it unlikely that any large new animal would be found. For nearly 200 years numerous British employees in India had been serious hunters in the Himalayan foothills, travelling there when long leave was given, as England was too far away. Many recorded their findings, and before long reasonably complete lists were made of birds and animals. They usually employed trackers, and most footprints were identified by men who were familiar with local animals. It was not until mountaineers came, inexperienced in tracking, that reports of a large mysterious animal began to appear. These received boosts from local legends, as unicorns and lake monsters have had in Western mythology.

At an early stage in the Rolwaling, a group was to leave with Dienhart and mail despatches. Some advance pay had been given to the escorting local men. Most then got drunk – Urkien also apparently had more than was desirable. When he found a mail dispatcher on the ground by the gompa, unable to begin the walk, he took a piece of wood and hit him rather vigorously. A denial was followed by a confession. Urkien remained employed, but he was never again engaged by Ed. The incident had earned newspaper headlines such as 'Blood on the Gompa Steps'. Still, Urkien went on to have a successful career working for Austrian surveyors and then German climbers who sought him out after reading my book.

By now Ed himself had arrived back and we all had a day together, washing clothes, writing, talking about our various exploits, and eating and drinking. Then, leaving the yeti party remnants behind, the climbers set out with more loads to the Mingbo Valley. The Green Hut received much well-earned praise for all that Wally had done, and a strong group cut its way up to the col. Ed admitted that the slopes to the col were more severe than he had remembered from 1952 with Shipton. At the summit there was a fearful wind. We erected the repaired winch and struggled all afternoon to get just four loads up the face. Again loads jammed on minor ice lumps. Putting up the tents was extremely difficult and the noise of the wind prevented much sleeping that night.

At the first hint of daylight our leader announced a retreat. We would seek a site near where the loads were already stacked. The whole party applauded the decision. We descended with the pieces that had previously been lifted, and soon located a position that would satisfy all the requirements of research and safety. While the ferrying of loads continued, a work party dug deep holes in the glacier ice to bury kitbags full of ice and rocks, about 1.5 metres below floor level. Ropes attached to them would go over the top of the structure, to help hold it down during violent winds. Next came the floor and the most interesting part, the assembling of the wall rings. The Sherpas who had been with the party for so many weeks suddenly realised the scale of the building. It was 6.7 metres long and 3 metres in diameter, with windows at each end. When completed it had eight bunks, a dining table, a work table and space around a bicycle-style ergometer. Most food, spare equipment and fuel were stored in exterior snow caves.

When it was evident the rings were going together satisfactorily my role in the expedition began to wind down. There would be joints to seal, doors and windows to place, and then the internal benches and equipment to install, but the materials were all available and the remaining team had everything under control. I did a quick journey up the Imja Glacier with Mike Gill, Wally Romanes and eight Sherpas for a look at the formidable slopes of Lhotse 2. This was a pleasant interlude with a small party, and it was a relief to be away from the responsibilities of large numbers, often including media people seeking an exciting story.

⁌⁌⁌

It was time for me to leave. Winter was approaching and many others were departing also in their various groups. The overall project was an interesting one and I was sad to say goodbye, but I did not want to stay for seven more months, knowing all I had to do back in Christchurch. Ed's yeti party left for their overseas tour, and Griff Pugh became leader until Ed returned in March 1961.

I managed to orchestrate my own journey to the foothills, on the grounds that I was in a great hurry for a plane connection. With two Sherpas I completed the walk to Kathmandu in eight days, a journey that normally took 15. In the city I rang home and learned that Keith Marshall would be leaving for Hong Kong next day. I freighted most of my equipment back to Christchurch but took a windproof jacket, crampons and my boots to the aircraft, as I knew I would be in snow on Mt Fuji.

Keith kept to his appointed timetable. At Tokyo airport we were amazed to see five Japanese women with great smiles who had ignored all barriers and were out on the tarmac to meet us. I was handed a floral bouquet over a metre long. We were escorted past all customs and immigration authorities and before long we were seated in a comfortable hotel for a luxurious meal and an agenda meeting.

I was given a formidable list of engineering projects to visit, and Keith was also invited if he wished. I found that he had just one introduction, and that was to the secretary of the Japanese equivalent of the Institute of Architects. Within a day he joined me on my tour. My guides were the senior staff of the two men I had befriended in Wellington earlier in the year, both having very senior positions with Shimizu, one of the largest and most progressive construction companies. Keith was delighted with the arrangements. The firm had its own architects so he was able to view aspects of construction and planning, which were of more interest to him. I was to talk to the Japanese Alpine Club and be on mountains with the women for two weekends.

I revealed that I had boots, crampons and a windproof. They insisted that I also have a down jacket, gloves, overboots and double-layer trousers. I had not thought these necessary for the lower altitudes of Japan, but within an hour one of the women had checked my sizes, disappeared and borrowed all this gear and an ice axe from a tall Japanese man.

The visit was highly successful socially, and eye-opening from an engineering point of view. The intended instruction on the mountain was less successful. On a Friday night Keith and I went by train to a village near Mt Fuji. He was no mountaineer but was keen to immerse himself in a village that was distant from Western influence.

The five women collected me in a large stationwagon and took me to a spacious mountain hut where there were five newspaper reporters waiting. After a pleasant meal there was much chatter – in Japanese, totally lost on me of course.

By early morning there were about 30 more media people out on the parking area. Part of the fuss was that three Japanese men had made the first ascent of Manaslu five years previously, and I was the first visitor to Japan who had been higher than these men. Manaslu is one of the 14 peaks in the world of more than 8,000 metres. I learned that Mt Fuji in those days was closed for five months a year. During the open summer season there could be up to 20,000 on the mountain in one day, and patrolling it was impossible. My companions had negotiated special permission for a winter ascent, and the media had got wind of this fact.

I fielded questions about Kangchenjunga and the yeti expedition. More difficult were queries about how successful my new friends would be on Mt Cook. I was dubious but made hopeful comments, along with the statement that I had not yet seen them on snow. Eventually we shook clear of most of the entourage, but five seemed to be permanently attached. Mrs Satow, our leader, had no idea how long they would stay. Sometimes one would pull out a small portable radio, talk into it, and then run to catch us again.

We started at about 900 metres and were in soft snow straight away. The slopes were easy but it was very cold. It was mid-December, so I had known the days would be short and the temperatures at least chilly. In the early afternoon our media escort was down to just two. The slopes had steepened slightly but still the snow was soft. I had hoped to find some short, steep, hard sections where I could demonstrate prodding with an axe to locate imaginary crevasses, then rescue techniques and the appropriate rope-handling methods. But that terrain was no good for such instruction. I hoped it would be harder and steeper higher on the mountain.

Twice we passed curious shapes in the snow. I scraped one of these with an ice axe and found I was standing on the roof of a building! The snow must have been about 3 metres deep. Nearby was a cone that stood about 60 centimetres above the snow. A scrape at this revealed mainly food scraps, plastic wrappers and orange skins. It was explained to me that before the season opened, late in the spring, the rubbish would be carried down to trucks on the road. I commented on what an enormous heap it must be, down at ground level. I was told that all hut users are encouraged to put out their rubbish in just one place. If such a system were tried in New Zealand winds, the debris would be all over the mountain in a week.

All five women carried wide and heavy packs, considerably larger than mine. I had been told we would be stopping at a hut some 900 metres below the summit. I was curious about the accommodation and what would be revealed as the packs were opened. The slopes were gentle and the snow too soft to justify the use of crampons. Although the sun was shining, it was wintery cold, and the haze in all directions spoiled most distant views. One woman, Keiko Kawai, a newspaper man and I did all the step-kicking, then we had to stop frequently to allow the others to catch up.

On a smooth white slope another small hump indicated a hut roof. At one edge of it, after five minutes of digging, a shovel was found, tied to the spouting, available for searchers for the hut. After much energetic work we found a door and eventually were excavating at floor level. We entered the small two-room, rather dark hut, which would be brighter in summer in the absence of snow and with the shutters opened.

From their packs came a large range of spare clothing, more cameras, a songbook, a cooker and an incredible selection of small saucer-like dishes and cutlery. Seven courses were served, each about enough for a pigeon. The containers and serving dishes must have weighed twice as much as the food they carried. There was a broad array of sushi food, at sample size. Top marks for presentation but a lean pass for nourishment.

Mrs Satow suggested that three who had been in front should go to the top next day while the others carried their big packs down the mountain. My justification for being there had been to give instruction on conditions similar to what they would encounter on Mt Cook, but what we had outside the door was so easy; it was another world. I offered to take them to the Arthur's Pass area as soon as they arrived in New Zealand, where I would give more relevant instruction.

At dawn the sky was clear but the wind was cold. Keiko Kawai, the strongest of the group, the remaining reporter and I set out for the 900-metre climb to the crater rim. I wore all the protective clothing their friend had lent me. There was a constant northwest wind at this greater height, coming all the way from Siberia.

As we approached the top, some steel towers came into sight. Otherwise the view did not change at all until suddenly we mounted the crest and could see into the broad crater. Although there was a thick coating of snow we saw the tops of many shrines scattered below the skyline, and other roofs that, I was told, were shops for the summer hordes. On the crater rim there were numerous towers for telephone, radio and television relaying purposes. These were a surprise on a summit, which is so sacred. I walked a short distance along the crater rim towards the highest point, which is just higher than Mt Cook. At a large white bump a door suddenly opened and a man emerged in the gap. He said in English, 'Welcome, Mr Hardie. Come in for a coffee.'

'Happily,' I replied. 'But how did you know my name?'

'Your party was on live television for a national hook-up yesterday morning as you started. There have been radio reports on the hour on your progress for two days.'

Inside there were large comfortable rooms and tons of electronic equipment, very like a permanent Antarctic base. Apparently many technicians spend the whole winter at the summit, attending to this substantial communication establishment. Being by far the highest mountain in the country, and quite isolated from its lesser rivals, Mt Fuji is an outstanding relay station. I was asked to wave a Japanese flag in front of a camera and then the television transmission would cease. I obliged and went onto the summit, where the view was extensive. There were many small volcanic cones and it appeared that a large amount of the surrounding countryside was well forested. Towards the cities a brown haze hid all man-made structures.

We descended our deep tracks to the hut, intending to pick up our overnight equipment, but it had all gone down and the hut had been tidied. An hour before the road end we overtook the others, who were very tired, heavily laden and in deep snow. They had to be pressured to unload a few pounds. Then I went ahead to compact the route a certain amount.

We drove to Keith Marshall's inn and separated there. Later that night the manager called me to his office. He had his chef with him. The manager said they knew Englishmen liked a fried egg for breakfast, so the chef had looked up a book on how to fry an egg. A covered plate was shown to me. I was shown a large plate. The lid was lifted and one very symmetrical fried egg lay in the middle. I told them it looked great and the chap should get a job in an English hotel.

In the morning I went to my breakfast table and there was a large covered plate. I lifted the lid and beheld the same egg I had seen eight hours ago, stone cold, staring up at me. The chef was standing beaming by the kitchen door. I had no option but to eat it. Actually it was no great hardship as I had been underfed for the previous two days.

I had found that Mrs Satow's best friend was the wife of Katsuro Ohara, a Tokyo architect who had been on two Manaslu expeditions. Keith spent a day with him and then it was time to leave.

On the last day our engineering and architect friends had asked if there was anything else we wished to see. Keith said he had never been in a Japanese house. This drew anxious looks and indecipherable whispers. It was clearly an unusual request. There had been much entertaining, but all in hotels or the Shimizu clients' meeting rooms, never near anyone's personal quarters. There followed two telephone calls and, after some delay, we were put into a car for a long drive through residential suburbs.

We entered the house of one of the directors of the firm. The owner and his wife were very shy about having Westerners in their small abode. Keith asked a few questions, which seemed quite simple to me, but there was much consultation between the

The Silver Hut Expedition

three people present before an answer was given. Keith was dying to look into cupboards to see the amount of space, see the plumbing below the kitchen bench and enter the bathroom, but every move seemed to be a problem for our hosts. We thanked them and made the visit rather brief. The men had been so open and generous about their firm's operations and techniques. but their houses were very private. I should note that two of the men had been in my house in Christchurch.

The Tokyo kitchen was tiny. The house had just two bedrooms, and few bookshelves or cupboards. The beds folded vertically each day into narrow compartments and were concealed by a sliding screen. With the beds down there would have been very little floor space. Play areas for children, inside or out, were minimal.

One of the reasons for my being in Japan was to publicise my 1957 book, which had just been translated into Japanese. I met the translator and was given three copies of the book, but all attempts to meet the publishers met with imponderable barriers. My London publisher, Allen & Unwin, had never heard from them. The German edition was handled tidily and I received royalties from it, but I saw no money from the Japanese edition. I heard later that the publishers had closed down, but I did meet a Japanese climber in Kathmandu some years later who said most trekkers who went to Nepal carried my book in paperback form. He thought about 10,000 copies had been sold.

Back in Christchurch I worked frantically for three weeks before again taking time from my job to instruct Mrs Satow's team when they arrived. Their large stationwagon was full of floppy bags, including a tent, which they were to put on our lawn. I recall great giggles and shrieks in the first few minutes, and five cameras appeared. They could not believe their eyes when they saw me pushing a lawnmower. I was far too exalted in their eyes for such a lowly task. It reminded me how they had been worried about me carrying a pack on Mt Fuji.

The four younger women – in their early twenties, I think – all gave short bows if I spoke to them, even at a shouted instruction on a mountain. Mrs Satow, who had lived in the US for some years, told them to stop all that stuff, but they were from a polite generation ingrained that way. Their leader, I recently calculated, was 57 at that time. The deduction came from a card she sent recently, which said she turned 100 in 2004. She had worked in the offices of one of the large car manufacturers in Detroit in the early 1930s, so her English was good. Back in Japan she married the owner of a bicycle-manufacturing factory. He was a reserve officer in the engineering side of submarines. When the Japanese navy began building its only submarine-repair depot on the east side of their country, he was very critical as it would be within range of American bombers. He went public, requesting construction on the west side. When war came he was imprisoned for his dissent. The American occupation forces seemed to be aware of these matters, and after the war Mr Satow was released and immediately went back to bicycle manufacturing. Mrs Satow became a court translator for the war crimes trials, so good was her English.

Some friends at Arthur's Pass gave me access to a fine large house for five days. I arranged to take several assistants. Margaret Clark and Beverley Tweedie, both about as tall as the Japanese, had climbed Mt Cook the previous year. John Morris, a forestry scientist, had climbed in several countries. For a few days we were joined by Doug Macdonald, then Philip Temple.

The weather was kind and the event was a brilliant social success, but it was hard work making the women reduce their heavy packs and move with more authority. A mountaineer must kick firmly into snow slopes to gain a secure footing. They alighted on hard slopes with ballerina steps. We did exercises in modest crevasses and tried some elementary crevasse rescue work. The example shown by the New Zealand women was invaluable.

The five Japanese had two weeks in the Mt Cook area but wisely kept away from that mountain once they saw it. They climbed some much more modest summits near the Tasman Glacier, then returned to Christchurch for a week. There they unpacked their gorgeous kimonos and, through the Japan Society, organised a series of tea and flower arrangement shows in various parts of the country. Enid and I kept in touch with them and each returned to New Zealand in later years for non-mountaineering purposes.

The Silver Hut Expedition

While I was enjoying a New Zealand summer my friends were still based at the Silver Hut at 5,800 metres. John Harrison was preparing to leave Christchurch to join them for an attempt on Makalu. John had many talks with me, and I was certain he would fit into the programme with ease. He had already been to over 7,300 metres on Masherbrum and he had a wide range of interests and a sparkling sense of humour.

Sir Edmund Hillary, Peter Mulgrew and Tom Nevison had all been away from the expedition, but were going back again in February to reach the others late in March. The intention was that all would be very high in May 1961, along with eight from the Silver Hut who had been acclimatising since September 1960. Medical tests would continue on the mountain with both groups. Leigh Ortenberger, another American, joined the party for the Makalu attempt.

At the Silver Hut the wintering group had kept in good health. They sometimes skied on nearby slopes and often walked down to the Green Hut at 5,200 metres for a change of scene and company. Every fine day they could see the great unclimbed peak of Ama Dablam (6,826 metres), just 5 kilometres away. Before long they were discussing ways of breaching its considerable defences, and in March they did reach the top. That party consisted of Mike Ward, from two Everest expeditions, New Zealanders Mike Gill and Wally Romanes, and American Barry Bishop. They put in four camps on Ama Dablam and ascended some very difficult lower rock buttresses before managing the ice face, which is so prominent from the main trekking route in the Dudh Kosi Valley. They handled extreme problems at up to 6,800 metres, which indicated that at that stage they had undergone no deterioration after their long time at the Silver Hut. Previously most major climbs in the area were timed so that summits were reached in the calm late May conditions, just before the monsoon begins. Their climb was in early March.

Messages were sent to various media about the successful climb while John Harrison was walking in from Kathmandu. At

Namche Bazar he was told by the commander of the checkpost that he was to go no further and the whole Makalu expedition had to withdraw, because there had been no government permission to climb Ama Dablam. Ed by this time was in the Mingbo Valley, near the small landing strip used a few times for urgent transport problems. Because of the absence of radios on his walk from Kathmandu, he had not heard of the Ama Dablam climb. Meanwhile, Griff Pugh had flown to Kathmandu with a Sherpa who had a broken leg, and in that city he was told of the problem. Griff flew back to Mingbo with this serious news, and Ed immediately flew down to Kathmandu to sort things out.

It was a delicate situation. The expedition had had written permission to operate everywhere in the Mingbo Valley, and Ama Dablam is the highest peak on the rim of that valley. However, the mountain had not been specifically named in the permit documents. After days of looking at maps, arguments, face saving and long lunches, the expedition was allowed to resume. A small fine had to be paid, along with a peak fee. Meanwhile, preparations had been made for climbers, Sherpas and all the appropriate equipment to cross Ama Dablam Col and head for Makalu via the broad Hongu basins, which I had mapped in 1955, but no forward movement was taken. When the message to proceed was sent at last from Kathmandu, the high crossings began. After several days a Makalu base camp was established and the normal build-up of supplies began. The medical researchers had much of their equipment carried forward to the new site, and the Silver Hut was now nearly empty. Most of those who had wintered there were sent a short distance down the Barun for a rest at about top tree line.

Ed Hillary joined them after a flight to the Mingbo strip. The placing of camps on Makalu began, but at a relatively low altitude Ed collapsed with major breathing problems, described as a small stroke. He had to be supported down to the base camp. With him were five doctors who were by then extremely well qualified in high-altitude symptoms. They agreed that Ed must drop altitude and rest for several days. He must not return via the high passes, which had been his route of entry. They were so concerned that it was decided one of the doctors should accompany him on a low-altitude journey back to the Sherpa villages, with instructions that he not go above 4,500 metres.

Jim Milledge, the nominated doctor, left the climbers and descended with Ed and several Sherpas to the 1954 base camp. They walked out in 15 days, mostly on the route I had taken during the 1955 monsoon. Ed had been carried down to base from a similar position on Makalu in 1954. On this later occasion it was thought that his visit to Kathmandu had reduced the acclimatisation he had gained in the earlier walk up to Mingbo at 5,200 metres. He had rejoined the climbers too soon.

Climbing camps were erected substantially on the route used by the French in 1955. To the height of about 7,300 metres progress was good. Three possible summit parties were formed, and even non-climbing doctors went to that altitude to continue testing the long-term guinea-pigs, who by then had been at considerable heights for eight months. Climbers were not carrying oxygen sets but there were some at an intermediate camp for emergencies.

On the upper part of the mountain the winds were very severe, possibly worse than in a normal season. Above 7,600 metres many problems set in. All the men who had wintered in the Silver Hut suffered a variety of severe high-altitude problems. In fact the three who were best at those heights were Nevison, Ortenberger and Harrison, who had joined the group just six weeks previously. Looking back now, I wonder if the rest period down to the tree line in the Barun had caused the wintering members to lose some acclimatisation.

At one stage six Sherpas, with small loads, were all linked on one rope. One man slipped and they all slid about 200 metres. Some loads were lost and one man broke a leg. This greatly reduced the support situation on the whole enterprise, as a carrying party had to leave to support the man down to base camp. In retrospect I was critical of the circumstances dictating that six Sherpas be on one rope. On Kangchenjunga there had been only two occasions where Sherpas travelled between camps without a climber escort, and we never had more that four in total on one rope (one climber and two or three Sherpas). In those days Sherpas had no mountain training.

No one reached the summit. At 120 metres short of the peak Peter Mulgrew collapsed and was unable to walk, even to move down to the top camp. The retreat was extremely difficult, especially with the reduced Sherpa numbers, and they did well to survive the many hazards. Peter had severe frostbite in both feet and a collapsed lung. He was carried to a lower camp from which a helicopter evacuated him and the injured Sherpa to Kathmandu. The others walked back to the Silver Hut and then down to the Sherpa villages.

The experiments were over and the final tidying had to be done. The Silver Hut was donated to the Himalayan Mountaineering Institute in far-off Darjeeling. Jim Milledge and a Sherpa group dismantled it and carried sections down to the first village. From there Tenzing Norgay (the Everest one) was engaged to employ a team to carry the sections all the way out to Kathmandu. Then the hut was freighted to its new destination, for continuing medical work by Indian researchers.

There had been much Sherpa pressure for a school for their largest village. After many discussions, and an approach to the American sponsors, the remaining expedition members procured a small prefabricated building from India and had it flown to the precarious Mingbo landing strip. A good Sherpa teacher was located and the first school came to life in Khumjung. This later led to the formation of the Sherpa Trust, which would become the Himalayan Trust.

Learning of these events in the comfort of my house in New Zealand, I wondered if Griff Pugh was satisfied with the medical results of the expedition and whether he still had concerns that we had not placed the Silver Hut at 6,000 metres, as he had originally requested. He wrote to me that a lot had been learned. He considered 7,300 metres to be the limit for the short-term existence of the human body, and that rapid deterioration occurs above that height. The men who spent so long at the Silver Hut, at 5,800 metres, had not got enough exercise to keep up their body toughness. They each lost about 7 kilograms in weight and therefore had fewer body reserves. If they had been at 6,000 metres they would have had even less exercise and been exposed to a risky situation for rescue purposes. No problems had been noticed in terms of slackening of their brain responses. On their return to sea level all had recovered fully from their chest and frostbite problems. Peter Mulgrew, who suffered permanent frostbite damage, had not been in the wintering party.

Some years later I was present when Jim McFarlane and Peter Mulgrew met for the first time. Both had been frostbitten severely on Makalu expeditions. Jim had had all his toes and the transverse arches removed, leaving short stumpy feet. He had about 12 months of hospital treatment involving not very successful skin-grafting attempts. Skin from his stomach was attached to his wrist for three weeks and then transferred to his feet, which involved his being continuously tied in most awkward body situations. Every few years the flesh contracted a little and he had to have more foot bones trimmed back behind the line of shrinking skin. In small boots he had to walk with a stick and took generally short steps – no more tramping or skiing for him.

Peter suffered less initial damage, but he had his lower legs removed halfway up his shin and artificial feet were made for him. With much practice and determination he managed to walk reasonably well. High-quality artificial feet had not been available six years previously when Jim had his accident. Peter went on one of the Sherpa school construction projects five years later.

Several learned medical reports were written. Both Griff Pugh and John West had later involvements with space-travel research. John's expertise was used by Russian as well as American scientists.

FIFTEEN

Instructing in Antarctica

In the early 1960s the adjacent Antarctica bases of McMurdo and Scott had settled into regular work and transport patterns. A small group of men occupied each base during the winter for minor scientific duties, but mainly to protect the installations against fire or blizzard.

At the beginning of each October, replacement teams would be flown south, along with scientists who would undertake projects lasting anything from four weeks to five months. There were usually two direct flights a week from Christchurch in good weather, so fresh supplies, mail and personnel could be flown in at regular intervals. These flights made it possible for university students and staff to join others in research teams after annual examinations had ended.

Bulk supplies, such as building materials, fuel oil and next year's canned and frozen food, would be taken down in large ships in early February, when the sea ice broke up or melted. Three or so ships usually travelled one day apart, with an icebreaker to open the channel for them. In the first few years, unloading the ships to the shore was a great problem without a landing wharf.

Much scientific fieldwork was done by small 'traverse' parties. Both New Zealand and the US arranged for teams of usually four men to be flown several hundred kilometres from base and landed from a ski-equipped aircraft. They unloaded sledges and supplies to begin travelling huge distances doing geological and surveying work. Radio contact with the bases was essential. At the end of the 'traverse' they would locate a good site for an aircraft to land and then call to be lifted out for transport back to base. In those days New Zealand sledges were normally pulled by dogs, and the Americans had motorised toboggans.

Early in 1962 Bill Bridge, the Scott Base leader for that year, had a discussion with the rear admiral at McMurdo, the American base. Bill told me it went something like this:

'Why is it your Kiwi men never call us for aircraft help halfway through their long field journeys? Our groups will see a crevassed area ahead, sit for a day and then radio us to land and lift them over it. But there are risks in landing in these unknown sites and then taking off again fully loaded. Not to mention costs.'

Bill explained: 'All the New Zealanders have to spend a week at a ski ground in winter, learning basic mountaincraft and how to work as a team. At least one of each team is a mountaineer who can generally handle the route-finding.'

'We could never do that, with people scattered from Florida to Alaska to Hawaii. We have some here from Texas who have never seen snow.'

'Could you give them courses in Antarctica when they arrive?' Bill asked.

'The costs of bringing down professional guides would be prohibitive.'

Then Bill, off the top of his head, announced, 'New Zealand could supply you with free instructors, if you fly them down and provide accommodation.'

The rear admiral leapt at the suggestion. The upshot was that Wynne Croll and I were invited to spend five weeks at McMurdo at the beginning of the 1962 summer. Wynne was another civil engineer and mountaineer. He had once been high on Mt Cook too late in the day and spent a night just beneath the summit. He was always cheerful and was much more of an extrovert than I was. In Antarctica, with regular flights and with a radio telephone connection, I could keep in touch with family and office. However, the pay was one nominal shilling per week, the amount required to stay in the New Zealand social welfare, health and superannuation schemes.

Our flight south was in an American Constellation aircraft, which flew so high we saw very little. The gentle landing was on a well-graded expanse of the Barrier Ice Shelf. We lived in the scientists' quarters. The other buildings housed mainly naval personnel, numbering about 400 that year, who ran the base, the aircraft, building services, the transport and outside communications. Now there are over a thousand staff at McMurdo each summer.

Scientists, officers and other ranks all shared the same small ablution building (the heads) and the one cafeteria (the galley). The scientists were most unhappy with these arrangements and greatly objected to being under naval authority. The raw effluent from the heads and galley discharged to a frozen mass, to which general rubbish was added. Once a week bulldozers would push this ghastly mess towards the sea ice, in the hope that when the melt occurred in February it would all depart down McMurdo Sound. With temperatures always being below zero the outlet pipes from the heads frequently broke and leaked. The stained areas on the approach paths were known as the 'Piss Glacier'. A few years later these problems were rectified and all rubbish thereafter was removed.

In the season about 120 Americans would pass through our brief courses. To go to a genuinely crevassed area would require several hours of travelling each way, but just 40 minutes from the base there were adequate conditions for our exercises. There are thousands of square kilometres of sea ice that are being pushed by winds and lifted twice a day by tides. Around the edges, especially downwind, are massive features known as pressure ridges, which can be 10 metres or more high and quite steep. On these ridges most of the essential techniques could be demonstrated and the pupils required to repeat them. We worked our way through these complex mazes and staged mock slips and rescues.

We had the use of a slow, heavy four-wheel-drive vehicle that held 12 passengers. Each night an engine cable had to be plugged into an electrical outlet to keep the battery charged and the engine maintained above freezing point. If we were away for a long day we had to start up the engine every four hours or it might not fire up when we needed it.

Instruction in Antarctica

It was a new enterprise to almost all our pupils. Some had been on traverses but had left ropes, crampons and ice axes tied to the floors of their sledges because they did not know what to do with them. Wynne and I brought our own ice axes from New Zealand. In the first week the handles of three American axes broke in easy terrain, and two crampon straps parted when men were attaching them to their boots. I complained at the store and found that these items had been there for three years and had never been oiled. The atmosphere is actually very dry in most parts of Antarctica, despite the endless amounts of ice and snow, and the equipment was in urgent need of lubrication. The storeman arranged for the appropriate oils to be flown south on the next plane.

Most of the trainees were very soft, having come straight from university examination rooms, after a few days in Hawaii and then in Christchurch. After just three hours they would want a long rest or even for the day's instruction to finish. However, some pilots asked to come on our courses, as did four men who were part of a parachute rescue team. They had not been allowed to jump in Antarctica because they had no idea what to do when they reached the frozen ground. We had a general feeling that our courses were appreciated. The conversations in the mess, during evening meals, was dominated by those who had been out on the ice with us. To their associates they naturally grossly exaggerated the size and angle of the slopes they had ascended.

In 1962 there was no bar at McMurdo, although spirits and beer could be bought at a shop. Each scientist was issued with one bottle of spirits per week. They decided to save most of it and have a party every Wednesday after work. In cold conditions I enjoy black rum mixed into a hot toddy.

As we were usually back from work first, I was asked to prepare the drinks for the first Wednesday. I asked what that entailed. Easy, I was told. Get some glasses, some nibbles and be sure the bottles are cold. I dug a groove in the ice under our hut and buried 10 bottles. In the late afternoon I had everything on tables when the men appeared, but no one started drinking. I asked what the problem was.

'We sent someone to the galley to bring ice cubes.'

I pointed out that the liquor must already be at about zero degrees.

'Ah, but we like the ice chinking around the top of the glass.'

The cubes arrived. I had several short drinks, which were so cold they were virtually odourless and tasteless, but I soon found them warming inside. After an hour we decided to go to the galley, via the heads. We donned outside protective clothing and in the first minute two men fell on the ice. We were a very noisy group as our gear came off at our destination, by which time three more had dropped out when the liquor hit them in the cold atmosphere. To my taste all the buildings were greatly overheated, so the contrast between inside and outside temperatures was extreme. Wynne and I soon worked out our own system for having a hot toddy each day after work and joining the Wednesday parties for just one drink.

My close friend Harry Gair rang me one evening from Scott Base. A qualified geologist and a capable skier, Harry had been with me at high school in Timaru and at university. He explained he was the leader of a four-man traverse party soon to leave for an 80-day journey of about 600 kilometres. He asked Wynne and me to assist him by loading his dog team into an aircraft, fly with them and unload them up on the interior plateau. We would need a two-hour practice that night, meeting the dogs and learning the ropes.

'Why don't the others in your party do this?' I asked.

'We'll all be flat out at the other end of the plane, getting off the sledge and two tons of gear. Nearly half of it is dogfood. The plane waits just a few minutes with its engines running and the crew of two sit at the controls.'

'Okay, we're coming. We'll see you in 20 minutes.' I told Wynne and we were off, madly enthusiastic. We arrived and were met by Harry and his dog man in the lovely colourful light of the Antarctic late spring.

The dog lines were just behind Scott Base. One steel flexible cable about 100 metres long was firmly anchored at each end. On the cable were steel rings about 8 metres apart. Each dog had a chain 3 metres long attached to its collar and clipped to the main cable. This way the dogs could not reach each other. The lead dog was at one end and the others were tied in a precise order, with the youngest untrained ones at the far end. When they were attached to a sledge, the lead dog was alone and the others followed in pairs, usually with male and female together, a combination that reduced the tendency to snarl and fight.

We walked along the dog line, said hello to each occupant and then we had to unclip one and carry it up a steep pile of logs and down again, holding the chain so that the dog could not take off when it reached the ground. This was a rehearsal for the entry to the Dakota deck, two days hence, when we would have to go up a steep set of narrow steps. Most of the dogs weighed 30–35 kilograms; the leader was 42 kilograms.

Next we attached the team of nine to the sledge and, with a few spectators, set off for a 7-kilometre run on the sea ice. After the first mile, when the dogs had settled to a uniform trot, it was a delightful way to travel.

We duly juggled our course times to have the necessary day with the Gair group.

Early on the appropriate morning Wynne and I were driven over the rough terrain for 10 kilometres to the main runway. Harry and the dog expert drove the team on a 17-kilometre route so they would be tired by the time they reached the plane, and also to keep them away from the unfamiliar planes, tractors, graders and photographic hordes at the landing site. Our Dakota was parked at the remote end of the runway.

The sledge was anchored and Wynne and I carried the dogs up the steps. On the steel floor were ring bolts in pairs, each having a very short chain. The still puffing dogs were clipped to the chains in the same order they were in on the sledge. Meanwhile the other men were loading cargo – and then the sledges – through the rear door of the plane. Loads were tied down, doors closed and we rattled down the runway. There were not enough seats, let alone safety belts, for all of us. I sat on the floor holding a dog chain.

After the plane settled into a smooth flight we moved around to watch the spectacular scenery. The flight went north-west for some 160 kilometres and then turned inland. We climbed to about 4,000 metres, so we had wonderful views. We were told to hold tight for landing, and at high speed the plane descended and its skis just touched the surface. Then the pilot took us quickly back up, banked steeply and turned to look at the marks made by the skis. These told him how soft the snow was and if there was much wind at ground level. He was satisfied, dropped speed and we made a comfortable landing.

Doors were opened, our stairs put in place and we ran out with the dog line and two steel bars to anchor the ends. We were under strict instructions to set the line away from the aircraft take-off path and under no circumstances to let a dog loose with propellers turning and with the bags of dogfood being unloaded! Each dog was carried down to the snow. Then, by holding its collar so its front legs were off the ground, we rushed it to its appointed place on the line. The dogs were surprisingly quiet and co-operative.

By this time the cargo was on the ground. We said a few niceties, shook hands and climbed back on board. I wished I had been able to join such a traverse party. The pilot twice took the plane back and forth along the tracks made on landing, to compact the surface. Then he revved it and after a short run we lifted off. In a very brief time we were back at McMurdo. The party succeeded in all their objectives. Harry went on to earn a doctorate, then worked in Western Australia, the US and Thailand. He now lives in Cromwell.

I had been asked to take some Himalayan slides to Antarctica, and on two Saturday nights I gave lectures to the scientists and pilots. This resulted in invitations to various interesting escapades. One pilot offered us a flight to make an air-drop over the South Pole. He pointed out that we would be in the main fuselage, with a specialist cargo-handling crew of four men. An immense door had to be opened in the floor for the drop, meaning the fuselage would not be pressurised, and he considered that because we were mountaineers we would be able to tolerate the cold, thin-air conditions. We would be flying in one of the new C130 (Hercules) aircraft. The Pole Station had been in existence for five years. Planes landed there only occasionally – for changing personnel or the carriage of delicate cargo and fuel. Most bulky supplies were then dropped by parachute.

After take-off the master 'dropper' gave his briefing. We could see 10 great pallets, loaded with supplies and attached to parachutes. Below the pallets were small wheels that ran in grooves in the aircraft floor. He explained that as we approached the Pole the belly door would hinge open and three or four loads would roll down to the hole. We must not go near the hole ourselves. We had to wear a harness and, when near the dropping zone, we were to clip it to a steel ring on the fuselage wall. The Pole is 2,800 metres above sea level but they would be dropping from 4,500 metres, for several reasons. One was that parachutes require time to open and free fall. Also the spotters on the ground wanted to have a clear sight of them in the air to take bearings on the arrival location. The plane itself would buck up and down with several tonnes rolling back to the hatch and suddenly dropping, so the plane had to be well clear of the ground to tolerate these balancing problems.

We flew over the flat expanse of the Ross Ice Shelf and then the Beardmore Glacier appeared ahead. On our right we could see many glaciers that descend from the Polar Plateau to the shelf. Several looked easier to ascend with sledges than the Beardmore, which had been Scott's choice and was followed by Shackleton. However, the side glaciers do not point directly to the South Pole, meaning their routes may be easier but would be longer. We flew low over the Beardmore to limit altitude stress. The thought of man-hauling sledges up that glacier, week after week, as early parties had done, was appalling. To try to get the scale of what we were seeing I observed the time it took to pass one unnamed tributary glacier. Knowing our speed, I calculated it was almost 10 kilometres wide.

Eventually, near the top of the glacier, gigantic crevasses could be seen, and then some nunataks (mountain peaks) peering above the Polar Plateau. Over this vast emptiness the plane slowly climbed to its operating height. The crew released the webbing strops and the chief talked by phone to the pilot. When the belly door opened the temperature dropped rapidly. The pilot put the plane into a climb, so the floor tracks were sloping. With the Pole just ahead, three loads rolled along their tracks and vanished. As warned, the plane jumped all over the place. Wynne and I stayed well clear of the action. Beside each safety clip on the wall was an oxygen mask at head height. If anyone had a problems at 4,500 metres it would have been easy apply a boost to the lungs.

The plane made two more runs, the last being most vigorous, as the pallets had to roll further to the open door. From our altitude we could see three small buildings and many vehicle track marks. It looked so bleak and remote. With the cargo safely departed the yawning hatch was closed, we turned and headed back to McMurdo, some 1,400 kilometres to the north – a six-hour round trip. I tried to imagine walking the distance, without dogs or motors, as the first two British parties had done.

One by one the flight crew went to the rear of the aircraft and stayed for a few minutes. Then the drop crew did the same and the smell of cooked meat wafted past. When they had settled back on their seats I walked back and found a small galley, with standing room for one. On a short bench was a gas ring and below it a carton of thawing steaks. I cooked myself a big one and moved away to give Wynne a turn. I became converted to eating steaks rare when the meat is of high quality. While walking around the aircraft on the return journey I made sure I avoided walking on the trapdoor.

With a vehicle at our disposal and the sea ice still in evidence, we visited penguin rookeries, Shackleton's and Scott's huts and many lesser-known sites. Having daylight all the time meant it was tempting to not stop for a rest. The American base galley provided three main meals a day at normal mealtimes, but then opened each midnight to cater for those who were on shift work. We would sometimes get back at about that time and call in for a warming coffee. Inevitably we would see the plates of beautiful food and end up having four meals a day.

All too soon the last of the scientific field parties had passed through and our training work was over. It was time to return to Christchurch. I recall how green the ground appeared as we crossed the New Zealand coast at the Rakaia mouth, after being away just five weeks.

Other mountaineers from New Zealand continued this instruction for another 10 seasons before the Americans began training their own instructors. They and the specialist staff at Scott Base also combine forces on occasion to make a very strong joint rescue team if there is a major emergency within the range of the available aircraft.

SIXTEEN

The Mt Rolleston Rescue

Bill Beaven arranged four enjoyable climbing trips in the 1960s to the harder areas of South Westland and Otago, similar in location to those we had undertaken as students, 15 years previously. Earle Riddiford joined three of these ventures, but we regretted the enforced absence of Jim McFarlane. The parties were made up to six, so we climbed as three pairs. On these occasions we had better and lighter food than had been possible during the war years. Twice we arranged access by jetboat, which was capable of travelling a long way up a turbulent river. For one other journey Jock Montgomery, who had his own plane, made a well-placed initial air-drop of supplies, which fortunately landed undamaged. Derek Cook was another regular member of this group of six, who climbed Brewster, Aspiring, Pollux, Huxley and many smaller summits. On one of these trips John Harrison joined us, giving us many opportunities for post-mortems on the Silver Hut and Makalu expedition. Enid and I had been to John's wedding two years after that expedition, and we became very close.

During the 1960s to 1980s we took regular summer holidays with two other families. Through a good farmer friend I arranged access to a private beach in a remote part of the Marlborough Sounds, some six hours' drive from Christchurch. We set up our own campsite and walked on the local hills, kayaked at sea, fished with lines from a dinghy and played a lot of not very good tennis. We had no electricity, motors, telephones or refrigerators. These holidays were so successful that the same three families kept returning to that particular secluded beach year after year. Our climbing friends from student days, Ken and Isabel Tocker, were one parent pair. The others were Norman and Marion Macbeth. Norman was editor of the Christchurch *Press* for some years. Our farmer friends were the Webbers, the Hopes and the Wells.

Before long we found ourselves getting to know many of the local landowners and being invited to many of their social events. We took some of them, and particularly their children, on most of our adventures. The three families' friendship was so strong that even the third generation from the originals is still happy to arrange joint projects. Our daughter Ruth later married Richard Wells, the son of one of the farmers, and they are now based in Nelson. Not surprisingly, they have a second house in the mountains.

Our two daughters thoroughly enjoyed these outdoor holidays. Each winter we took them on ski weekends, from when they were aged just four and five. I had skied a little when I lived at Pukaki in 1948, but was far from expert. I launched Sarah Jane and Ruth on tiny edgeless boards with rather unsafe bindings to their boots. In just a few years, with better equipment and better tutors, they soon passed my mediocre standard.

I was often called out on mountain searches. Enid was more concerned about my presence on these than when I was away with the Beaven parties. On a search one was often working in atrocious weather to save a life, or climbing with people whose ability and stamina were unknown. With the pressure of family and my work I tried to avoid searches unless there was a call for special skills or the missing person was a close associate. Such accidents most often happened during weekends. I dreaded receiving calls from the police at about 4 a.m. on a Monday.

Search and Rescue in New Zealand is under the control of the Police Department, which co-opts local experts in sailing, flying, mountaineering or whatever field the mishap occurs. Wynne Croll proved to be a highly skilled search controller on mountain rescues, enjoying the confidence of both police and mountaineers.

Just before the shortest day in 1966 Wynne rang me at night from Arthur's Pass, stating that there was a serious problem with four young climbers missing on the Otira face of Mt Rolleston.

A first group of searchers was proceeding to the mountain, but there might be a need for more in two or three days. I had climbed the face five times, once with Heinrich Harrer as mentioned earlier. The beginning of the climb is about two hours' walking time from the main road to the West Coast, mostly on a track. The climbing route involves a steep rock face with occasional ice gullies.

The four had been seen progressing on the face on a Sunday afternoon in deteriorating weather. As Monday was a dreadful day and they had not appeared, police were notified and a search put into action. The first searchers climbed to the skyline ridge by an easier route and attempted to lower a cable towards where the men might be located. Bad visibility, driving wind and snow made movement nearly impossible. The face is quite broad, with many options of difficult routes. No one was found, but twice someone thought they heard calls from the face. The searchers retreated to spend the night near the foot of the face.

Police asked me to lead another group to strengthen those already on the ground. John Harrison and I went in his car to Arthur's Pass and reported to Wynne. Six more men were to join us. We were told that there were three tents near the foot of the Bealey Slide, and some of us could stay there. Those initial searchers who seemed most tired should come back to Arthur's Pass village. Attempts were to be made to put a camp near the summit, or at least past the low peak, and to try the cable again on the ice-plastered rock face.

The next day was as bad as its predecessors. We struggled through to the camp and had a general discussion. Some went upwards, some returned to Arthur's Pass, while John Harrison and I went along the foot of the face, looking upwards at any hint of clearing weather and calling and listening. Through the shrieking wind we heard no human sounds. We returned to the tents in the declining light of late afternoon Wednesday. Our campsite was far from ideal, but there was no other place within reasonable access. I did not expect the snow would slide. A platform had been dug and one tent was hard against the inside face. I put my gear into it. The two other tents were side by side, further out on the debris created by the previous party's excavation.

The Mt Rolleston Rescue

Inside these tents we cooked, talked and retired early, with bleak thoughts about those on the face. We hoped the other searchers higher up in their tents were securely placed. I had my own large-framed pack, from the Kangchenjunga expedition, and I placed it upright behind my head. In our three-man tent John Harrison was on one side with his head away from us. John Wilson was in the middle, and we talked for a few minutes. One month previously I had been nominated for a position on the Canterbury University Council. There were three candidates for one seat. John told me that his father, Reverend Malcolm Wilson, had just heard that he had beaten me by two votes. I was not greatly disappointed. Mac Wilson would do a good job.

We fell asleep quite early. The weather seemed to be slightly better, but colder.

I woke suddenly to hear desperate noises coming from John Harrison. I tried to move but from my hips down I was pinned by an incredible weight of snow. Clearly we were under a large avalanche, our tent flattened on our chests. Being protected by the upright pack frame, I had some free arm movement and air, which would not last long. I turned John Wilson's head to share my air and found that he, too, was securely pinned. I could not reach John Harrison and very quickly he fell silent. We shouted and got no response from the other tents. I knew that sound did not travel well under snow, but their tents were quite close. Perhaps the avalanche was very big and they had been swept further down the face.

I suggested tearing a hole in the roof of the collapsed tent, just above our faces, as an air hole. My left hand and John's right joined to make a broad hole, but the snow on top was heavy – for it to be so unmoveable on our legs it must have been very deep. Our hands did not reach the surface.

I told John Wilson it was vital we remain calm and go off to sleep. At high altitude, half a litre a minute of oxygen was adequate for sleeping, but movement required about three litres or more. Panic would use even more. I suggested we should just try to sleep so there would be less brain damage when we were dug out. Powdered snow contains a small amount of air and some might enter through the hole we made. I loosened the top of my sleeping bag to enable the air trapped inside to circulate. With some very private thoughts I quickly drifted away. John, too, became unconscious.

Some time later I slowly became conscious with a crushing headache. I realised I was still in my sleeping bag, but out in the open, with occasional snowflakes drifting onto my face. Someone had made a big groove in the snow and I was in it. My vision was blurred on my right side, but I could hear murmurings and, in the pitch dark, recognised John Wilson's voice. Thank goodness at least he was alive. Behind were more complex noises, which I gradually identified. Someone was applying artificial respiration to John Harrison, and another voice said he was stone cold. There was a three-voice conference, with the sound of bags being packed and best wishes called out in the dark.

Hans Bohny, one of the three, checked that I was comfortable and then looked at John and two others who were unwell but had not been wholly unconscious. Hans was fully clad, including boots. He stood upright all night, usually looking upwards for the next avalanche, being ready to take action if the worst happened. Gradually my mind grasped his explanation of what had occurred in the early night.

Peter Squires and Ian Gardiner had been sitting in their tent working on a radio when the avalanche struck the site. Being upright and further out on the slope, they were covered by a smaller depth of snow. They made a difficult exit and were horrified to see no other tents. With a plate as digging tool and gloved hands they identified one tent site by the faint glimmer of torchlight inside the collapsed, snow-covered frame. They pulled out Hans, Nick von Tunzelmann and Roy Yates. Next they looked for the third tent. which was considerably further under the snow, with no sign of poles or guy ropes. After a very long time they eventually dug to two white hands poking through a hole. We were cleared and lifted, and as we were warm in our chests, we were placed on a snow shelf while the search went on for John Harrison. They worked on him, in turns, for about 20 minutes, but tragically he was dead. They thought John Wilson and I had been unconscious for a little over two hours. Ian and Peter were now walking down to Arthur's Pass in the dark to inform Wynne, as search controller. The walk right through to the township took five black hours. Many more searchers were expected next day, including some from Invercargill.

Hans talked to me most of the night and he made such a lot of noise with his stamping feet, to keep them warm, that sleep would have been difficult anyway. The horror of John's death weighed heavily and I did not want to sleep. Hans told me of his troubles in Arthur's Pass. I was aware of most of these, but having them confirmed made me forget my headache for a while. He had recently built a fine restaurant and was greatly in debt. Slips on the highway had meant that the roading authorities had banned buses on that route. The restriction lasted about three years, on and off, and this was disastrous for the only restaurant owner. The ban on buses also put off many private motorists who might have driven that way. Hans also complained that the National Park Board was giving him very little building work, although I knew him to be an accomplished stonemason and carpenter.

I had time to reflect with gratitude on the brilliant work of Peter and Ian in digging for us, nonstop, when another avalanche might have been on the way. Then they had persevered with respiration treatment in trying to bring John Harrison back to life, before walking out during a miserable night on fresh snow with no visible track. How fortunate we were that they were in the party and that they had been sitting upright when the slide struck. The casualty list could have been far worse.

Dawn came slowly. We could find no food in the avalanche and digging debris, but no one seemed very hungry anyway. The weather was a little better and eventually our shouts up the Bealey Slide were heard, so the higher party packed up for their withdrawal. Soon a large group came up from the road. Those of us who had been under the snow felt we were able to walk out rather than being carried. Wynne was expecting this, and there would be vehicles at the highway to drive us to Arthur's Pass township. I looked into the snowy mess for the rest of my gear. It seemed we had been under three metres of snow. The opinion of Brian Hearfield and Jim Wilson, who had been near the summit, was that late the previous day the wind had changed to southerly and a large volume of more powdery snow had fallen on the upper slopes. This was the snow that had slipped, not being bonded to the lower layer.

I walked out and reported to the doctor, Peter Strang, and to Wynne. I said I was well enough to drive to Christchurch and would take John Harrison's car, calling on his in-laws on the way. Peter gave me dozens of Aspros for my continuing headache. I rang Enid, who was greatly relieved to hear from me. A policeman had rung her at 3 a.m. to say there had been a serious accident to the search party, but had given no details.

As I staggered out from the call I was caught by a large media contingent. I felt dreadful, hungry and not very patient. It may have been due to my confusion and sense of loss at the time I was questioned, or it might have been due to editing, but the published accounts differed sharply from my intentions and my later recollections.

I was reported as saying a lot about Hans and little about the two who did all the digging. I was also critical, apparently, of the original four, who were rather inexperienced for a midwinter climb in failing weather. It was stated that I approved of putting restrictions on future climbers.

However, the country's emotions were so stirred that a fund was established for the support of John's widow and two daughters. It grew relatively large and was well invested, affording them a considerable amount of help for 20 years, but not a fraction of what it was to lose a man as special as John Harrison.

In the afternoon as I drove to Christchurch the weather cleared enough for a helicopter to make two sweeps across the Otira face. No sign of movement was seen and everything was under deep icy bulges. The search was abandoned. When summer came, two bodies were located, one tied to the face and one near the ridge, near where a search group had been struggling at one stage. A year later the other two were found on the Bealey face below the low peak of Rolleston.

I was more than welcome when I reached home that time, and I never went on another high mountain search.

The Mt Rolleston Rescue

My headache lasted for about five days and I had much trouble with double vision, which alarmed my optometrist. He arranged scans for cancer but found nothing. He decided some brain cells directing the muscles near the right eye had been oxygen-starved. I had a correcting addition to a lens, and with this assistance my vision returned to nearly normal.

SEVENTEEN

The Himalayan Trust

The school built in Khumjung in 1961 was a great success and soon pupil numbers became too large for the sole teacher to manage. Children from other villages were walking incredible distances each day to receive education. Others were moved by their parents to live with relatives in Khumjung, to enable them to attend. By late 1961 Sir Edmund Hillary had already received many complimentary letters about the school, along with requests for other villages to receive the same assistance.

Ed approached the sponsors of the 1960 medical research expedition, who agreed to help build two more schools and include teachers' salaries for three years. The main sponsor was Field Enterprises Corporation Ltd, which, among other activities, publishes the *World Book Encyclopedia*. A little later Ed became the camping equipment adviser to Sears Roebuck, and much of that firm's outdoor goods were used in the building work.

Two schools were built in 1963. For these buildings the only major imported material was corrugated aluminium roof sheeting. The walls were made of rock, supplied and broken to the desired shapes by local Sherpa residents. Timber from pine trees three days down the valley was pit sawn in the forest and carried to the site. When the schools were finished, the mountaineers, in a brief sortie, climbed one of the most prominent unclimbed peaks in the immediate area – and declined the risks on another, just 90 metres from the summit. They had been thoroughly acclimatised through their work at the school sites.

In my book I had written about the problems of the village water supply in Khumjung in 1955. Nearly a kilometre above the village was a small spring that gave a regular output of good-quality water. Several times a day most women walked up to this source and returned with a wooden cask full of water. The cask was supported by a headband and, when full, weighed 30–40 kilograms. Enid had also witnessed the hardships involved and the consequent limitation of household water, and she had strong views on the subject. The 1963 expedition placed a long plastic pipe to bring the water to the outskirts of Khumjung. Village women were spared the long walk but still had to carry the water from the pipe terminal to their houses, and there was still no water for irrigation purposes.

During the early 1960s Chinese forces were extending their influences into the furthest corners of Tibet and there were soon problems in defining the southern boundaries of that country. In some places the assumed frontier was along the crest of the main range, but often it was down into gorges, where the headwaters of some Indian rivers were inside Tibet. Very few of the assumed boundaries had been surveyed on the ground.

There were many incursions by armed Chinese into what Indian and Nepalese regarded as their territory. Some of these in the Indian sector escalated into considerable exchanges of gunfire and there was a real concern in India that the Chinese might be considering extending their occupation further. The Indian Army moved several large units into its northern provinces, and for a number of years an 80 kilometres wide area on the south side of the Himalayas was declared out of bounds to all who were not Indians. The various checkposts in Nepal that I had visited previously had Indian officers controlling them. By the early 1960s there were enough trained Nepalese Army officers to take over the equipment and duties of these Nepalese posts.

One day in 1964 I received a telegram from the Indian High Commission in Wellington. It was addressed to 'Major Hardie', instructing him to report to a military survey unit near Darjeeling and to obtain transport and engagement details from the Wellington military attaché. I rang the High Commission, stating that

I had never had any connection with any army and that they must have made a mistake. I was told that they had received a cable from Delhi stating that there was a general mobilisation of mountain units and they believed I was in New Zealand. I had to be found and told to travel. My address had been obtained through the New Zealand Alpine Club.

I declined firmly and heard no more. I suppose I must have been mentioned in reports by Indian officers at the three checkposts, where I accepted hospitality in 1955. It was so rare for them to see a Western visitor. Also my name has appeared on some published maps and on sketch maps for mountaineering journals.

In 1966 the Indians reduced some of the access restrictions for outsiders on portions of their lands, and the Nepalese authorities' half-hearted restrictions were also lifted. By this time Ed had a flood of requests for more schools to be built. There were many problems arising in organising the construction of more buildings, including the payment of staff and the selection of suitable sites. Villages needed to have a substantial number of supporting adult residents. Also, the government of Nepal was seeking to establish a few conditions about the education of its young citizens. The personal pressures on Ed were becoming a burden.

Ed's father-in-law, Jim Rose, suggested that a trust be set up to share some of these problems and to give continuity and authority when approaching sponsors and government departments. He advised Ed to invite a number of people who had been with him on expeditions to be on such a trust board. Rose visualised having some teachers, doctors, an engineer, an architect and others. A deed was written and the resulting body was called the Sherpa Trust.

I have not recorded here all of those who served on the trust board, but I mention a few with whom I had been associated on other expeditions. Mike Gill was the first doctor appointed to the board. He and Wally Romanes, a builder, had been to the top of Ama Dablam in 1961 and went high on Makalu, so I was very close to them.

Murray Ellis and Peter Mulgrew had been with Ed to the South Pole. Another was Jim Wilson, the brother of John, who was under the 1966 avalanche with me. Murray had been the main builder for the two schools in 1963. Jim had completed a doctorate in philosophy and religion at an Indian university. I was also invited to join the initial board.

Board members and their spouses held quite successful fundraising ventures in the form of 'Kathmandu bazaars', where a broad range of Nepalese goods were sold during a weekend in a New Zealand city. Most of the articles had been brought back by expedition members or by workers on school-building projects. Some articles, such as printed prayer flags, were made in New Zealand from wooden blocks bought in a Sherpa village. Trust members dressed in Sherpa clothing and the building schemes received useful publicity but not large amounts of money. Many businesses supplied building materials at a reduced price, but there was generally a shortfall in terms of the bigger items, such as airfares and Sherpa and teacher wages. As for Ed himself, though he was becoming absorbed almost full time in this work, he received no monetary remuneration from it, earning his living from book royalties and his work as equipment adviser for Sears Roebuck.

After a few years Trade Aid and other similar organisations established shops in various cities and they did not welcome the alleged undercutting of prices by the bazaars. Fundraising was not easy and it was evident that ongoing American support would be necessary to continue the project.

The absence of communication within Nepal was another source of difficulties for the board. For instance, Ed and a work party could be walking in towards a project and be met en route by a delegation presenting a strong case for assistance at another village. The lengthy process of referring back to a New Zealand board for authorisation purposes was absurdly cumbersome. It was thought better for Ed to have a large sum of money with him and to have the power to make decisions after discussions with his building party on site. Thus the board annual meetings tended to be poorly documented accounts of what happened the previous year. The board did very little forward planning and had little say in developments.

The projects received generous American and then Canadian assistance, but put a stop to the building parties extending their time in the mountains to include climbing nearby summits.

The government of Nepal expressed some concerns, requiring that teachers be Nepalese citizens and that the teaching language in the schools be Nepali. They also ordered that each school have a maximum of five years of trust operation and then be handed free to the government. They disliked the name 'Sherpa' in the title and insisted on a change to the Himalayan Trust.

In the early years of the trust Elizabeth Hawley, an American journalist living in Kathmandu, took a great deal of interest in the aid work being done in the Khumbu. She began to act as an agent for work parties, handling their mail and arranging local supplies, and before long became most helpful in advising trust representatives in their contacts with senior Nepalese officials. Her interest and industry was extended to other aid groups who were active in Nepal. Although not a mountaineer, Hawley kept records of the ascents of most of the higher mountains of Nepal. In 2006 she has retired but is still in Kathmandu, advising groups on the complications of travelling in Nepal.

Each early building party included a doctor, and the medical needs of Sherpas were being vigorously discussed. On one early visit, Dr Max Pearl, from Auckland, accompanied Ed, as did Ed's brother, Rex Hillary. Max and Rex were added to the board, and discussion began on the desirability of setting up a small hospital in one of the higher villages. The need was obvious, even to an amateur like me. Goitre was prevalent and some children suffered brain damage through lack of iodine in their' mothers' diet during pregnancy. People in a mountain country handling big animals such as yaks also suffer broken limbs that need setting. Sherpa houses had no chimneys, so smoke was the cause of many eye complaints.

No village had electricity, so there would be limitations on the type of medical equipment used and therefore the work done. A small basic hospital was built at Khunde, the twin village adjacent to Khumjung. A New Zealand doctor was appointed sole charge for two years. It was a very isolated situation, initially with a time lapse of three weeks before any backup advice or opinion could be obtained, even from Kathmandu. However, a succession of young

The Himalayan Trust

doctors took up this appointment and made big improvements to the lives of hundreds of Sherpas. Two of the first, John McKinnon and Lindsay Strang, joined the trust board and their experience proved invaluable.

Back in New Zealand in 1973 Norman Kirk was prime minister. His Labour Party had made an electoral promise of large increases in overseas aid, mainly to the Pacific Islands. The World Wildlife Fund and some high officials in Nepal had suggested that a national park be established in the Mt Everest area. The idea was drawn to the attention of the New Zealand government, which decided to send a deputation to Nepal to assess the situation and make recommendations.

I was asked to be one of the three in the group. The leader, Bing Lucas, was the senior executive in national park administration, and I knew him well through my five years on the Arthur's Pass Park Board. The third, Ross Hodder, was from the New Zealand Forest Service. As the other two had not been to Nepal I was to look after the transport and engage Sherpas for portering, interpretation and cooking duties.

In Kathmandu we were joined by Hementa Mishra, who had a forestry degree from Glasgow and was employed by the Nepalese Forestry Department. Also attached to our party was Melvin Bolton, an Englishman who had worked on a new national park in Ethiopia.

We flew to the recently built Lukla airport, enjoying a spectacular trip in clear weather, then walked gently up to Khunde, where Hillary and five other New Zealanders were involved in another project. Immediately the pressure was on us to explain to Sherpa residents what would be involved in a national park. On our second day there was a meeting of most of the village, with our team and Ed's, at the Khumjung gompa. Language was a problem at the outset. Ed and I had been able to converse with expedition Sherpas about mountain matters and food, and John McKinnon was adequate on medical themes and knew some basic Nepali. However, it was not easy to explain the administration, restrictions, benefits and tourist controls of a national park. We were asked some basic questions that we were unable to answer without direction from the two main governments involved. Would high-altitude grazing still continue? Would there be restrictions on tree felling, fire lighting and building more houses?

I encouraged Bing to visit the Khumjung school and other points of interest at that altitude and, as we were acclimatising satisfactorily, move higher to other valleys and avoid large meetings until we had a better feel for the nature of the land, its vegetation and climate. We should obtain individual feedback but avoid making promises, as detailed agreements between the relevant governments could be years in the future.

Furthermore, it became clear that the five of us held divergent views on the purpose of a park. The concept in 1974 New Zealand was that national parks were for the total protection of native birds, forests and plants. Because no mammal is native to our country, any found in a park should be shot. Melvin, with his African background, regarded parks as game reserves, where all species would be protected. Hementa seemed to be in sympathy with that view, although there were few indigenous animals in that part of Nepal. We needed to walk through some of the huge pasture areas where yaks were taken for high-altitude summer grazing to see their effects on the forests. Humans tending the yaks had to be allowed to have simple houses for summer use. Sherpa houses, especially in their main villages lower down, have timber in their roof and floor structures, and the occupants burn much wood for cooking, heating and lighting. The wood is obtained from areas that may be recommended for park protection. Some forest management would have to be included in any park proposal.

I had the impression that the area of forest had declined since I first saw them 20 years previously. Inside the forests the emergent regrowth appeared less healthy, with many replacement seedlings being nipped off just above ground level by yaks. The forests' future survival looked doubtful. Ross observed this with me, but because it was all new to him he did not express firm views. In the past 20 years many Sherpas had received money from expeditions and bought yaks, particularly when they were being sold cheaply by Tibetan refugees. Thus overgrazing was a likely cause of nursery degeneration.

The Himalayan Trust

Our group went to the Everest base camp, which had few residents at the time because most mountaineers were higher, above the icefall. We visited many adjacent valleys and lived in comfort, helped by the eight competent Sherpas who were our escorts. Hementa was pleased with his personal performance. He told us that two years previously he and a Kathmandu servant had flown to Lukla and walked upwards for four days. At Dingboche he had become so ill he thought there was something badly wrong with him. He staggered back to Lukla, flew out and made an immediate recovery at home. It turned out he had not known anything about acclimatisation, nor about the new hospital at Khunde. He said he was the first person from Kathmandu to reach the Everest base camp.

On Hementa's early sortie he had not spoken to any Sherpas, but his servant had leaked rumours of future game reserves and Sherpas being removed from the higher grazing grounds. I had heard this also, from an old Khumjung friend on our first day at Khunde. This restriction would be a severe alteration to local lifestyles and would be extremely difficult to control. I wanted our team to realise the special features of the land and its peoples.

There were by then about 7,000 trekkers each year arriving up the track at Namche Bazar. Twenty years later the number had doubled. Our opinion was that restrictions should be put on trekker numbers, and that they should carry their own cooking fuel, to save local forests. Sherpas should be able to continue their past lifestyles, but be encouraged not to increase their yak herds and to consider other sources of fuel and building materials. Simple solar panels for water heating would be useful for most of the year. Roof sheeting, although visually out of place, would be more efficient and would save hundreds of mature trees. They also needed instruction on fire prevention and fire-fighting.

We returned to the main track and approached Khunde again. The valley echoed with the chopping of axes, and dozens of loaded yaks were carrying split timber to the villages. It appeared that after the earlier big meeting, the rumour of impending cutting restrictions had spread, so residents were stocking up. We saw at night that trekker sites had two fires operating – one small one under the control of the Sherpa cook, and the other a large one to keep paying groups warm. Did they need that big blaze?

Discussions went long into many nights. Bing Lucas and I wrote copious notes. We interviewed numerous residents and looked at the schools and the new hospital. I noted that walls were made of rocks with no mortar. In some circumstances an external plaster of clay, water and yak dung was applied. The plaster on one face reduced the passage of cold air through the walls but did not add to the structural strength as a cement mortar would have done. In a recent minor earthquake a portion of the hospital wall had collapsed, luckily without dropping the roof rafters, and was replaced in just a few hours. It concerned me that the collapse of a trust building would generate negative publicity that would affect fundraising.

No country that has a building code for seismic areas allows stone residences or hospitals to be built with totally unreinforced supporting walls. Nepal, however, had no codes for mountain structures.

School roofs were corrugated iron or aluminium with no insulation of any kind. Pupils, and particularly teachers from the warmer Kathmandu Valley, were obviously cold and wore an extensive range of colourful clothing. I resolved to raise these matters at a trust meeting.

Our reporting group returned to Kathmandu, where we dispersed. Bing and I spent several days seeing various government officials and recording our discussions. But not one senior official we met had been to the remote Khumbu area and we did not appear to be taken seriously. There were much larger social and political problems in the valleys closer to the national capital. Bing and I thought that a high-level New Zealand offer of financial support might draw some response from Nepalese officials. We praised our colleague Hementa Mishra and hoped that after our departure he would be consulted, especially for the interpretation of suggestions that might come from Wellington.

We returned to New Zealand and the bureaucratic wheels turned slowly in the formulation of reports and the establishing of Cabinet priorities. Then Prime Minister Norman Kirk died unexpectedly. His replacement, Bill Rowling, was burdened with weighty problems and did not attend to the Nepalese issues in detail, but indicated that there could be favourable outcome for an Everest national park. Then the Rowling-led Labour government lost power and the National Party under Robert Muldoon took office.

The New Zealand High Commission in New Delhi was closed, but a diluted version of our report was accepted and the government undertook to finance the establishment of the Mt Everest National Park. Bing and I were no longer involved, but it was announced that New Zealand park staff would go to Nepal as advisers for a maximum of six years. Money would be provided for some buildings, information centres and transport. Young Sherpas who reached a certain educational standard would be brought to New Zealand to attend the park rangers' diploma course that had recently begun at Lincoln College.

Details between Wellington and Kathmandu took months to finalise. The park name, Mt Everest, was to change to Sagarmatha, the Nepali name for the mountain. The free courses at Lincoln were to be for all Nepalese citizens, not just Sherpas. After six years the New Zealand government ceased all support apart from the educational assistance at Lincoln. Enid and I lived just 14 kilometres from Lincoln, and for the first five years we had frequent requests for assistance. Pupils were encouraged by the staff to write projects about their own home districts. Nothing was available about Nepal in the college library in those years, so I was often asked for my books or diary extracts to assist in their assignments.

Other Himalayan Trust board members who lived in Christchurch also gave occasional assistance with students. Some official Nepalese material has now arrived and earlier theses are available. I am no longer involved, but Enid and I are still invited to Nepalese New Year celebrations at Lincoln.

I did raise my concerns about the school and hospital construction with Ed and his brother Rex, who by then was the main builder for the trust. They argued in favour of their methods on several grounds. The Nepalese government would take over all the schools in five years, so why build to higher standards than they would? I replied that the low-country schools built by the government did not get so cold, being in a warmer climate, so insulation was not so important to them.

I pressed for even just one reinforcing bar along the tops of rock walls, with a cement mortar around it, to add some structural integrity during an earthquake. Here their defence was that Sherpas knew about rock walls so they could easily repair any damage. A reinforcing rod would be difficult to transport and would be beyond the Sherpas' range of skills to repair if there was a collapse. But what if a roof collapsed over a trust hospital? I countered.

I also requested that less wood be used in trust buildings. A concrete floor at ground level would mean fewer trees being cut, and the base of the rock walls would be more stable with concrete poured against them. They felt that the costs of transporting cement were too great, and said that in such a steep country there were not many deposits of gravel and sand suitable for making concrete. I argued that small amounts could be found. We agreed to differ. Building continued as it had, but after the trust's construction of the Lukla airport small quantities of cement and insulating materials were included.

·ǁ·

At Christmas 1974 I was back in Nepal, this time leading a trekking party of 12. They were Enid and our two daughters, Sarah Jane and Ruth; two Tockers and Macbeths from our regular holiday group; David Hughes; Frank Davie; and two teenage boys. One of these became Ruth's brother-in-law seven years later. The other was Sam Mahon, an accomplished artist and son of Peter Mahon, who later wrote the courageous report on the Mt Erebus aircraft disaster in Antarctica.

Because of fog at Kathmandu airport we were delayed one day at Bangkok. On arrival for the beginning of the walk I found our local agent had bought all our food and sent it one day ahead with the porter group. We caught them on the first day, but I had not been able to add some interest and variety into the menu for the next 30 days. There were frequent complaints from my party as the monotonous Spam appeared every day. We were driven along the tortuous new road to Jiri and then walked for seven days to Khumjung. At least the agent had selected a good Sherpa team. The two cook's boys were a great social success with our daughters and with Sam and Marty. The sirdar was Ang Temba, who had been with me on three previous occasions and had carried a load to the top tent on Kangchenjunga 19 years earlier. In the meantime he had married Dawa Tenzing's daughter.

I appreciated seeing the country again, this time through the eyes of our daughters. Being midwinter it was extremely cold and the light faded at about 5 p.m. each day. I found that at the higher camps I had to do what I had condemned in the park report, lighting a fire to keep the party warm. We had down jackets, but no one wanted to go to bed before 10 p.m. I made the fires in modest proportions and thought about the problem. Practically no trekkers go there in midwinter, so perhaps rules could be stretched for that period.

We walked to Tangboche and then went up the spectacular Gokyo Valley, where I had spent time with yak herds in 1955. Here it was even colder, with no fuel to burn apart from small amounts carried for cooking purposes. Seven of us reached the summit of Gokyo Peak, which at 5,483 metres is higher than Everest base camp. I was particularly pleased that Sarah Jane and Ruth, aged 16 and 14, were among the party. It is one of the few reasonably accessible places from which one can see six of the 14 peaks over 8,000 metres. The sky was brilliantly clear but clouds gathered in the late afternoon.

That night there was a very heavy fall of snow – more than 60 centimetres. Some of the party were worried about the return down the valley, but the Sherpas loaded the yaks as usual and put a large, strong one in front. They called and whistled to him from time to time to keep him moving and forming a route. We followed behind the yak train, full of admiration for the experience of such travel and scenery.

We walked to the Lukla airport and, as it was midwinter, it was rare for us to see other tourists. The flight to Kathmandu, at low levels, made our upwards walk of three weeks previously, seem very short and simple. To the others the city had many delights, but to me it had lost much of the charm it had in 1954, and I remembered Charles Evans saying then that it was not as good as it had been in 1950. The city was losing its isolation.

We flew to Singapore and were invited to attend a reception at the New Zealand Embassy. We were happy to see that the Hillary family was also there, on their way to Nepal, intending to spend much of the year in the mountains during the construction of a second hospital and airstrip, this time at Paphlu. Just a few days later we heard of their terrible tragedy. Lady Hillary and her younger daughter, Belinda, were killed in an unsuccessful aircraft take-off from Kathmandu airport. The two Hillary girls had been very close to ours, and Louise had been a valued friend to Enid and to me. We had shared family holidays, bazaars and trust meetings in each other's homes. It was a tragic loss.

The Paphlu buildings were duly constructed and soon put to full use. Meanwhile, calls came from the Khumjung for the establishment of a high school. Many talented pupils were completing studies at the age of 12 and had the ability to go higher, or even to university, but few parents could afford to send their children to Kathmandu. There were other problems. Some of the trust's early schools had by now been handed to the Nepalese government, which appointed teachers from Kathmandu. The new teachers invariably were inadequately clad for the colder climate, and were also Hindus going to a Buddhist village. Some would visit home for a festival and never return. As a result a few schools remained closed for two or three years. Then the trust would receive requests for work parties to return from New Zealand to do maintenance work on the buildings so the schools could open for a further five years. This had happened several times.

In 1980 Max Pearl, chairman of the medical committee of the Himalayan Trust, was drowned in a New Zealand river. This was a huge loss. The trust had many difficulties and a lot of work to accomplish. John McKinnon, who had been the first doctor in residence at Khunde, became the next medical chairman. Ed himself was very depressed after the deaths of Louise and Belinda, and his positive influence was lacking for two or three years.

The New Zealand government began giving a small annual grant to the trust, but donations to the trust by business firms remained non-tax-deductible. In the US and Canada certain donations could be partially deducted, and contributions to the Canadian arm of the trust also attracted governmental subsidies.

The Himalayan Trust did build two high schools and, rather than more hospitals, several medical clinics, which would have a resident nurse and be visited two or three times a year by the nearest doctor.

Peter Mulgrew had been unhappy with some of the directions the trust was taking and he had resigned from the board in 1974. Then in 1979 he was killed in the Erebus crash. Peter was on the flight deck at the time, explaining through the speaker system the features of the visible terrain.

I remained on the Himalayan Trust board and supported most of its diverse undertakings, but I was still uneasy about the amount of timber being used. This was not just a local problem: it was occurring in all the other Himalayan valleys. I thought the situation should be examined by a professional forester with a conservation background. Perhaps something could be begun in the Khumbu province, which could be extended by example to other aid schemes. In 1986 I was in a party of five that went to the Khumbu with a brief to report on the state of the forests and to make recommendations for their future care.

In the group also was Udo Bennecke, a New Zealander with an Austrian background and forestry qualifications. Most of his working life he had devoted to the protection of indigenous forests in heavily eroded mountains north-west of Christchurch. He had travelled in many parts of the world, examining and speaking on forest and land protection in mountain environments.

By this time Sir Edmund was the New Zealand High Commissioner in New Delhi. A Labour government had restored New Zealand's diplomatic contacts with India and a new embassy was being built. Ed flew in to Kathmandu to brief us at the beginning of the project.

We flew to Lukla and travelled a route similar to that used for the national park survey. By 1986 there were even more tourist trekkers on the tracks and in new hotels and lodges. Most groups were carrying their own gas or liquid fuels. Sherpas on the whole seemed more prosperous and better clad. Much English language was being spoken and the brilliant mountains were still there.

Five small tree nurseries were being attended sporadically, but we saw little evidence of successful replanting. While I lived there in 1955 most children went up to the high pastures with their parents when the yaks were driven up in the summer. The bigger children would spend most of their time with the animals, keeping them within reasonable boundaries, away from neighbours and from certain forests. Children became experts at throwing stones and using slings to direct their shaggy charges.

But in 1986 we were told that the young children were attending school, and, on leaving, finding paid employment escorting trekkers. During the winter, when back near the home villages, the yaks wandered about in the trees and nibbled anything that extended a shoot above the snow. There were few fences to contain them and the animal numbers were high.

The national park had eventually been established, in 1978, so we noticed a few changes. With animal protection and some prosecutions of poachers, the few musk deer, previously in a small Tangboche herd, had expanded. Himalayan tahr, which had been rare, were now common and would sometimes appear in the villages. We saw signs of the mountain fox and the woolly hare. High up, near the moraines, there were numerous marmots and mouse hares scurrying under protective rocks.

There was evidence of much tree-cutting near tourist routes and fires still being lit. Sherpas were permitted to burn modest fires for their own use. The land areas are so large and the park staff so few that controls were hard to apply. Enterprising Sherpas, keen for business, set up primitive hot showers for walkers and had a boiler near the track with a set of pipes to a partly secluded wall. For about 15 hours a day they would feed wood onto a fire to keep the water hot for showers. This used many yak-loads of wood.

Udo considered that the existing tree species were adequate for a general-use forest, but long-term management was essential. He suggested that larger villages have a small fenced enclosure nearby where residents could see how well tree recovery could proceed in fully protected circumstances. Nurseries needed expansion and more care. Sherpas should be encouraged to use more efficient wood-burning devices in their houses. Leaf mulch from forest floors was had always been dug into the ground in the home fields to rejuvenate ground that produced potatoes or buckwheat. With more open areas they now had to travel further to obtain leaf mulch, but this needed to be encouraged.

Our lengthy report has been substantially adopted and brought much positive assistance from Canadian sources. Forest recovery, education and new animal-management methods take years to develop. A professional forester now visits the area each year and keeps a watch on progress, advising the various workers involved.

In 1988 I retired from the Himalayan Trust board. There had been differences but they were not serious and things were getting better. I had been on the board for 22 years and was now 62 years old. There were two others older than me, and about four in their fifties. The trust needed new blood – people who were in touch with current developments and able to go to Nepal.

I have kept in touch with most of the trust members and it is gratifying to observe that more schools and clinics have been built, extending into new foothill areas. Better buildings are being constructed and special courses are being run by Jim Strang for advanced training for school teachers. Forests in most of the Khumbu area are gradually improving.

EIGHTEEN

Mt Herschel, Antarctica

I now jump back in time to 1967 to pick up the Antarctic story.
Louise Hillary's brother-in-law Larry Harrington, a distinguished geologist, had already led a geological party to the southwest of Cape Hallett. It had been a versatile and strong expedition, but because they had relied totally on man-hauling of sledges, they had not covered much ground. Larry, a convincing character attached to Armidale University in New South Wales, put up a strong case to Ed for further survey work north of Cape Hallett. The mountains in this area are spectacularly steep, as they rise from the frozen coastline. Distances from the sea and air landing locations are not great, so a plan took shape to combine mapping, geology and climbing for the beginning of the 1967–68 summer season.

The New Zealand government's formal plans for that southern season appeared to have been finalised already, including all of the transport aspects. Sir Edmund, who is a member of the Explorers' Club in New York, was introduced to a senior admiral who had the controlling authority in flight planning in the US Antarctic programme. He kindly oiled the wheels to make a Hercules C130 plane available to us, enabling us to fly from the Barrier Ice Shelf near the McMurdo Base the 500 kilometres to Cape Hallett. To be able to get to Antarctica at all, we had to be added to the official New Zealand programme, which was achieved, but with some reluctance from Wellington. It was the inclusion of geological and surveying objectives that made the difference in our favour.

Mt Herschel, Antarctica

We were a party of nine. Ed was the leader and I was his deputy. Mike Gill and Murray Ellis were included again, with Peter Strang, the doctor who had attended the debriefing after the Mt Rolleston search. Larry Harrington was to arrive one week late, with an assistant geologist, Graham Hancox. Strengthening the climbing talents were Bruce Jenkinson and Mike White.

The flight to the main landing strip in sight of McMurdo and Scott Bases was uneventful. We were driven to Scott Base, allocated beds and almost immediately went off to a reception at McMurdo by the American leader, Rear Admiral Abbott. McMurdo VIPs and media representatives as always focused on Ed. After a while I was able slip away to have a look at the changes at McMurdo since my previous visit, five years earlier.

The rubbish dump had disappeared and there was a short-term disposal depot in a hidden valley, from where trash was transported to a ship once a year. Very prominent on the hill was a nuclear reactor, which supplied power for the whole base. This came in for so much criticism that it was later removed, along with about 8,000 tonnes of adjacent rock, following an amendment of the Antarctic Treaty. Very little had changed at Scott Base in the 11 years since it was built, other than the aircraft hangar becoming a store shed.

Admiral Abbott was our pilot next morning for the flight to Cape Hallett. He kindly took us on a wide circuit past the landing location, so we had a close view of our intended mountain. Herschel is 3,335 metres high and it presented a uniform steep slope on the top half. Through the misty small side-ports of the cargo bay I saw pale green ice in flutings, which appeared to be avalanche chutes. Nearer the sea, great cones of avalanche debris confirmed the origin of the upper gullies. No intermediate shelves were visible for safe camps on the upper face, and the access from the frozen sea looked hazardous. The scenery was spectacular but the shortest route on our nominated objective looked most forbidding.

We landed by the cape and walked out on the frozen snow. When the engine noise stopped I saw that the party looked rather glum. Ed, who had been up on the flight deck and saw more than I did, fortunately dismissed the originally proposed face climb, mentioning that a target about 7 kilometres to the north looked better. There was not a dissenting voice. I was greatly relieved.

The Hallett Base commander, an experienced chief petty officer known as Chief, met us then spent some time with his admiral while we unloaded our sledges and two motorised toboggans. Soon the plane departed and we walked the short distance to the base, observing the brilliant scenery in all directions. To the west was a continuous range of high icy mountains. To the east a broad bay was covered in ice, with many grounded icebergs. Far to the north were lower mountains shrouded with haze and patches of low clouds. We were to travel in that direction for the start of our programme.

Cape Hallett was initially a joint American and New Zealand base for scientific work and to enable possible emergency landings if aircraft had problems on the long flights between Christchurch and McMurdo. From 1967 the New Zealand occupancy lapsed for several years. The American team now numbered about 20, who were there for the period when flights were operating. They undertook weather observations and had few other duties, but of course would be more than fully occupied if an air emergency occurred. There were several small buildings and dozens of containers of spare food informally sited on what had been penguin nesting grounds. Because of the low temperatures and the absence of large storage warehouses, the emergency containers were never unpacked. Around each structure were the remains of a rookery, and a few fat, clean birds were noisily appraising possible laying locations. For about a mile to the south there was a broad beach and terraces on which more birds were foraging and awaiting the arrival of their mates. At this time of the year the open sea was some 15 kilometres away. From a small rise behind the base one could see distant thin black lines, slowly moving. These were penguins approaching the breeding grounds. On a long journey they lie on their stomachs and paddle forwards with their flippers and feet, stopping to get up on their feet if they see an obstacle ahead. When they arrived they were full of fish and shiny clean from sliding on miles of sea ice.

Chief indicated he wanted a meeting with us. I presumed this would be about our programme, radio procedures for assistance and our return date and so on. Instead we spent 20 minutes on his problems in keeping his idle men contented, when all were new to Antarctica and not interested in its terrain or history. He issued each of us with a small cotton towel, explaining that it was not for drying us, but to wipe handbasins and showers after we had finished our shared ablutions. The point came clearer later when we visited the small bathroom – facilities were very basic.

Our two snowmobiles were unpacked and we loaded the sledges for a one-month journey. The machines looked small and cold. I would gladly have exchanged mine for a dog team if one had been within range. There was quite an amount of equipment provided from the Sears Roebuck selection of polar goods. We pored over these items, wondering how they would perform.

We farewelled Chief, sat on the loaded sledges and the drivers started the motors. With some reluctance we moved, a little faster than a snail, following where the plane had been the previous day. At the end of the plane's ski tracks our machines were immediately bogged in about 20 centimetres of snow. All passengers dismounted and pushed for about 3 kilometres in deepening snow. With our starting point still visible in the rear, across the level terrain, we were all aware that the snowmobile motors were grossly underpowered for the task. They were light two-stroke machines that were popular in America for pulling skiers on frozen lakes, but quite unsuitable for low-speed heavy haulage. From the motor to the track mechanism there were belts that heated rapidly and then kept slipping, while the engine raced and overheated.

We tried halving the loads and putting both machines on one lightened sledge, but had the same problems. Eventually, those of us who could ski went in front to compact a route. Behind came a snowmobile with an empty sledge to further compact the snow. This returned and picked up a partial load. We travelled some 17 kilometres in this way and set up a camp, not far from the first cliffs of the main range. From there, relays with the vehicles finally brought along more supplies. One party walked ahead to find a safe route off the ice on to solid land.

Apart from the snowmobile problems we were quite cheerful.

Ed and Murray were surprised at the conditions. They told us of the easy driving, day after day, up on the plateau on the way to the South Pole 10 years previously. The snow in Hallett Bay was warmer and wetter than they had seen, and the sledge runners would not ride on top of it. The ominous clouds to the north indicated likely fogs near the vigorous sea currents by Cape Adare, and the snow there might be worse.

A reconnaissance party did find a way off the sea ice onto solid land, and another was hopeful that the next glacier to the north would be climbable and reveal a way to the top of Mt Herschel via a side route, avoiding that glistening face. Getting off the sea ice was quite an epic achievement and some parties have had big problems in locating a suitable place. The ice rises and falls three or so metres twice daily with the tides, and with an offshore wind the gap can widen; later in the season the ice departs from the land.

We carried two long sheets of thick plywood, normally tied across the front of the snowmobiles in such a way that they would jam and stop a fall if a hidden crevasse opened during the journey. The plywood was untied and placed over the tide crack. Vehicles and lightened sledges were then relayed onto solid land, which was still covered in ice. The bridge boards had been chosen to be wide enough for the sledge runners.

It was time to get serious about the mountain. Supplies and tents were sorted for four men away five days, with two high camps. As soon as we began to rise up a gentle slope the deeper snow put the snowmobiles out of action. All eight of us put the supplies on our backs and worked our way up a snow-covered glacier, amid occasional mutterings about the deep snow and the absence of Sherpas and dogs. They, too, would have had troubles in these conditions. We decided the most hopeful route was up a tributary arm of the Ironside Glacier. After a lift of about 900 metres all loads were dumped. The route ahead for the climbers looked hopeful and with any luck there might be wind-swept ridges higher up, where the depressing snow had been blown away. All but the four who were aiming at the summit descended to the camp on the sea ice. Going down with empty packs, the snow was so thick and damp we found we could not turn on our skis, so we ended up carrying them much of the way to our base tents.

While we awaited the climbers we undertook various other parts of the programme. I set up the theodolite to begin surveying work, and joined Murray and Ed for a look at the country to the north. Graham and Ed drove back to Hallett to collect more food and vehicle fuel. The journey was timed to pick up Larry Harrington, who had by then arrived. In the baggage they included a large bag of American steaks. One of the emergency containers was open and they were invited to help themselves. By the dates on the packages they were six years old but we decided they were excellent.

At Hallett, Chief was told the sorry tale of our underpowered snowmobiles. He very generously offered us the use of an old army weasel, which had been written off some years ago. He towed it to his garage and ran hot air through it to clear away years of ice, then put ether in the system and it started with a roar. He allowed us to use it to assist our next stage of hauling the main baggage northwards on the sea, but advised us not to risk taking it up the next glacier, the Moubray. Instead we were to leave it out on the sea ice to await our return journey. That was fine by us, and for the first time we had our party, now nine, and all our remaining supplies in one depot.

The four climbers returned with success stories, but quite different from what was intended. Camp 1, which we had all placed, was a long way from the summit and they had a tent and cooking gear for placing at Camp 2. However, the upward plodding with big loads to Camp 1 had been so arduous that they decided to undertake a very long climb, as there would be light throughout the night. They chose not to place a second camp, but to climb with one-day loads and, if possible, go right onto the summit. The first to attempt this marathon were Mike Gill and Bruce Jenkinson, who began their effort at six o'clock on a fine, calm morning.

They had to gain some 2,500 metres in height. Before long the deep snow gave way to very brittle ice, which crampons would not penetrate. There were crevasses to avoid and some short ice walls. They reached a minor bump on the far north ridge of Herschel and then saw a way to a large plateau that linked to a vast névé behind the ridge visible from the sea. In a very cold wind they found the plateau was covered in deep, soft snow and progress was tiring and slow. To avoid these conditions they went to the main ridge, which was clearer and had occasional rock outcrops, but the extremely steep drop down to the eastern side meant any turning of obstacles was slow and exposed.

They stayed with the north ridge for three-quarters of its distance, crossing mixed ice and rock obstacles. Just below the final pyramid a reasonable access to the upper névé was found on their right. Being tired from a very long day, they made two dumps of surplus clothes and finally, under what looked like a wholly rock rib, they left ice axes. The hand-holds, obscured from below, often had ice on them. Eventually they reached the cold and exposed summit at 7 p.m. By then a northerly was blowing and they were keen to get down to the protection of their jackets. They bypassed the long north ridge in favour of a convenient glacial plateau that had a steep ice traverse at its lower end, and reached their camp after being away for 19 hours.

On the following day Mike White and Peter Strang repeated the climb but avoided the long north ridge altogether, staying out on the glacier and the plateau. Snow had blown in to cover the first party's steps, so much cutting and anchoring had to be done. They, too, reached the top of Herschel, and their overall time was 25 hours. Four very tired men picked up their total camp and struggled down to join the others at sea level.

Next we travelled north, sometimes on land but more often on the sea. At a secure position near the beginning of the Moubray Glacier we were held back by bad weather for three days, securely camped on the stable side of an active tidal crack. Here Peter and I shared a tent. I remember hearing much splashing and bubbly breathing on our first night there. After some time I looked out and saw a Weddell seal had given birth to a furry pup on the land side of the tidal water. Soon they were joined by a very pregnant companion.

Seals after a long swim underwater make heavy breathing noises for two or three minutes as they blow out the carbon dioxide from

Mt Herschel, Antarctica

their system and take in a new store of oxygen. They are unlike dolphins, which can take in air in less than a second. In such a remote place we saw no predatory skuas or leopard seals. Seals can swim up to about 8 kilometres nonstop under sea ice. Here, with the open sea perhaps 25 kilometres away, they had to follow tidal cracks to where they could emerge for air.

During the bad weather we sometimes emerged to admire the fascinating seals. Mothers and pups spent much time lying in the weak, intermittent sun, and are quite mobile on the ice. Mothers did a lot of gnawing at the edges of thinner expanses of ice to make holes. In some tides and onshore winds the tidal crack could close, and enlarging the hole meant the adults always had access to the water and their next meal. We soon found that they were making easier passages for their young, for the time when they were introduced to the water.

We lived in Sears polar tents, which were conical, with central long poles. With two to a tent and one small cooking stove per pair we could warm our dwelling and, if need be, partially dry any damp garment. In the Himalayas most afternoons are warm and clothing can be aired and dried, but in Antarctic locations the temperatures seldom made zero, so natural drying is nearly impossible. Ed occupied one larger tent that also served as a meeting place, radio room and writing office.

With Larry's arrival, science raised its head and there was more purpose in our enterprise. I asked him if Chief had given him a lecture and a small towel. He had, and offered an explanation. On Larry's previous visit his party of nine had all been taken south from New Zealand in a US icebreaker, which had spent at least a week in opening shipping channels. Larry's team was twice transferred to other ships before going ashore at Hallett. In New Zealand they had all been told to take clothing for extreme Antarctic conditions. They had not been told that in the icebreakers the heat is turned up so high that the crew wear T-shirts. With continual sweating in their woollen shirts the New Zealanders got the reputation for being – well, odorous. Chief, at Hallett, wanted be certain that we all washed. Or that was Harrington's story.

Larry talked about the new concept of continental drift, which was far from receiving general acceptance in 1967. He said that there was a likelihood that part of New Zealand, Tasmania and the Robertson Bay area, just ahead of us, had all been in close contact, perhaps 80 million years ago. Sir Raymond Priestly, the geologist to Scott's second expedition had been ashore at Robertson Bay and reported structures quite unlike anything in Tasmania. Larry wished to have his own look and see some base rocks in this land, which appeared to be 99 per cent covered in ice. Rocks could be difficult to find.

Cape Adare, to the east of Robertson Bay, projects about 30 kilometres into the Ross Sea. Because it separates that sea from the very active Southern Ocean, it is subject to vigorous tidal action and strong wet winds. This accounts for the frequent bad weather and the deep, damp snow in the whole area.

We worked our way up the Moubray Glacier to Adare Saddle at its head and obtained the view of the bay and some islands in it. For me there was little purpose in going further north. The geologists should proceed to their chosen objective, but I had passed several surveying points where mapping observations could be made. We decided to divide the party at that stage. I set up a surveying station at the turning point and, with three others, went back to the foot of a mountain called Crash and camped near it

No one moved during one day of bad weather. When the weather improved, the four of us set off at 3.30 a.m. and ascended a long ridge with rotten rock sections, then ice and more rock. One of the summits was reached at 10 a.m. and, as this had a good view, Peter Strang and I stopped there with the theodolite. It was helpful having someone who could read and write on a mountain summit. In Nepal with a Sherpa companion, I always had to write down the various bearings and descriptions, linking them to the exposures of the camera part of the instrument. There would be hassles with gloves and pencils to enable the accurate use of the telescope, while the Sherpa would become bored and chilled. I would get cold hands and take a long time at each station. With Peter I explained what was required when we were in our tent. At each survey site he lay down below me, curled up to keep out of the wind, and wrote down the figures I called to him.

Mt Herschel, Antarctica

The views inland were most complex. Many icy ranges reared their heads. Two of the larger peaks, Minto and Sabine, had been seen and named from the sea many years previously. While being absorbed in that direction we were suddenly hidden in wispy clouds rising from the Ross Sea side. Murray and Bruce had gone to another summit and fortunately were returning. We packed the instruments and set off down the route we had climbed.

We faced a driving wind and thickening wet clouds. I was roped to Peter and for much of the way I could not see him ahead. The two in front were able to identify our ascending steps. It was vital to keep to them, knowing that our tents were in open country, miles from any clear fixed point, and could be hard to find. When we had been on more level ground for a while, all the time looking ahead, we saw shapes, and then five tents instead of two. Ed's party had also retreated in the bad weather and erected their tents beside our pair. Ed had been most concerned when he found our tents empty. The conditions down at his level were very miserable, while we had had some clear sunshine on our summit.

The geologists had been unable to descend a major line of steep bluffs above Robertson Bay, but they had picked up rock samples and examined strata through binoculars. Larry saw enough to decide that Priestly had made a mistake in the small portion he saw. The base formations had some conformity with those in Southland and Tasmania. He mentioned basalt outcrops also. These were more recent volcanic ridges, which often occur near the earth's crust, where one continent is grinding against another. Larry was expecting these, especially as there are a number of volcanic cones in the main Royal Society Range not far away. In New Zealand the granites and basalts of Fiordland also occur near the great faultline that is believed to exist under the sea between Antarctica and south-western New Zealand.

We sat out more bad weather and, as time was running out, headed south towards Cape Hallett to conclude the expedition. Loads were taken forward in relays by the two suffering vehicles. Suddenly the main axle of the rear snowmobile broke. There was no possibility of repairing it. For two days some of us put on waist harnesses and pulled a sledge while the surviving snowmobile did light relays with the remaining gear, after abandoning quite an amount of it, as well as some rock samples.

When we sighted the final, longest stretch of sea ice, it was with great relief that we observed that the ice was still there and the weasel could be seen some distance away, with much wind-blown snow nearly hiding one side. It was then late November and during that month the ice often moves, widening the tide cracks, and later breaks up and floats out of the bay. Larry told gruesome tales of orcas swimming with a dorsal fin protruding a metre above the water. The weasel started easily so we sent a radio message to Chief to say we would be with him the next day and could he notify McMurdo to place us on a waiting list for a flight back to base and then on to New Zealand.

What a joy it was to travel behind a caravan that had power. Four of us fixed climbing ropes to a sledge and were happily pulled on skis across the patchy ice at about 9 kph. It was not all easy. Although the motor performed admirably, the tracks and their runner wheels were working loose. Some bolts fell off, then a roller wheel. The Hallett Base was in sight when a second wheel departed. Chief on the radio said he was going to leave it to drift out with the sea ice and we were not to bother repairing it. We reached our destination amid desperate mechanical noises.

Fortunately we arrived at a time when the existing staff were not wanting the washing facilities. We cleaned ourselves and some clothing and enjoyed many cans of American beer. We had a day to spend at Hallett until a plane could come for us.

Peter and I went to solid land about a mile to the west and completed another round of mapping observations. The geologists were nearby, scratching at the rocks that were abundant at that location. In the afternoon most of us walked among the penguins. During our absence the extensive beach had nearly filled with birds. An estimate that year put the numbers at 18,000 Adélies. The open sea was by then quite close so the birds did not have to travel far. There were thousands of nests, each with one egg on it, or by then sometimes a chick. The noise and smell were unforgettable. Skuas stood nearby, awaiting a chance to raid an unprotected nest. White Arctic terns occasionally circled overhead. They were nesting in cliffs close to our survey station after their flights from the Arctic.

We flew south and had another night in the relaxed comfort of Scott Base. There I was surprised to see Bob Norman, who had been three years ahead of me at the School of Engineering. Bob had been the senior design engineer in the Ministry of Works and had just been appointed to the State Services Commission, which was unusual for an engineer. Among his duties was the inspection of all the facilities of the Department of Scientific and Industrial Research.

It had been an interesting expedition. We left feeling very grateful for the generous assistance given by our American colleagues at both bases. Without them we would have achieved much less and had to work much harder.

NINETEEN

Back at Home Base

After the Mt Herschel expedition I spent many good years based in Christchurch. My engineering flourished, with many interesting projects. Several organisations wanted my services on their local committees, and I was able to spend much time with family and friends. I regarded myself as having retired from large expeditions, although I did go to the Himalayas for several short visits on behalf of Hillary's trust.

John Harrison, who was killed in the Mt Rolleston avalanche, had been married to Annie, the daughter of David McLeod. David had a Cambridge history degree and was the doyen of Canterbury high-country farmers. He lived at Grasmere Station and also owned the neighbouring Cora Lynn. Much of the latter land had been absorbed into Arthur's Pass National Park and its high country had been retired from domestic animal grazing, in an attempt to reduce erosion. The house on the Cora Lynn land was vacant and John Harrison had been interested in obtaining it. As none of the family wanted the house after John's death, and I had been so close to John, David asked if Enid and I would like to buy it, with a pocket of land beside it.

We, with our girls, then aged seven and nine, drove to Cora Lynn and, after a one-hour inspection, our answer was yes. Birds flew from two rooms, the verandah had fallen down, the minimal kitchen drain was blocked and the wood stove needed a re-fit. There was no electricity or telephone, and water came from a rusty roof to an underground storage tank. The place had been built many years before timber treatment was invented, so there were signs of borer in every room. The roof was supported by mountain beech limbs cut from the nearby bush. The lavatory, of long-drop type, was 30 metres away in a gorse field that had not been trimmed for 40 years. No family had lived there since 1915, although two rooms had been used by deer shooters, who left their marks on walls. They had cooked on an open fire so stalactites of soot decorated one of the rooms and there were wire hooks hanging over the fireplace for holding billies.

It would be a challenging project, but the situation was ideal. It was less than two hours' drive from Christchurch and there were no other buildings within 2 kilometres. Substantial mountains stood on all sides, many of them bush-clad on their lower slopes. Not far away was the Waimakariri River for fishing and kayaking. Arthur's Pass and four ski grounds were not far away.

With the assistance of many friends, the interior cleaning and sealing the roof took place quite rapidly, but rebuilding the verandah and installing a windmill waited for two years. The gorse was removed totally and a boundary fence built. Accomplishing all this without electricity for vacuum cleaners and saws was daunting, but soon we were entertaining our friends there and taking our daughters' young friends out for weekends.

I was on the Arthur's Pass National Park Board and I had some work in Westland. The mountain house was a happy stopping place on the way to meetings of these groups. One of the most memorable times at Cora Lynn was when we used it as a base for teaching outdoor pursuits to senior girls at two schools where Enid was teaching. The staff would live inside the house with us while the girls were in tents among the trees 50 metres away. We walked over many of the local mountains, undertook big river-crossing exercises and learned much about living in the bush. On these occasions I usually brought along two young male students to assist with the instruction.

During the first winter we drove there one Friday night, just ahead of 25 girls, and found that the water in the pipes was a dreadful brown colour. When the house warmed, there was also a smell. I investigated the underground water tank, which had a corrugated-iron cover. The iron was bent and the framing that held it had collapsed. Nothing could be done about it in the dark, so we carried good water in buckets from a creek 200 metres away.

Next day I found that one of David McLeod's cows had stood on the iron and fallen into the metre-deep water. A passing hunter had seen her and each day he cut grass and fed it to her, until he eventually found the owner, who lifted her out with a front-end loader and rope slings. No one had thought to ring us. The following weekend I took up a hired sludge pump to clear the tank, then worked for two days cleaning all the pipes and our hand pump. Next I built a cattle-proof steel cover.

When Sarah Jane and Ruth were teenagers we bought kayaks and I put a frame on my trailer, enabling it to carry eight of these craft. During some summers our girls and their friends had numerous adventures in the river, and sometimes we took the trailer over Arthur's Pass to the challenges of Westland torrents. On many occasions we went through the Waimakariri Gorge – a spectacular journey of about 80 kilometres. We made these into festive events and stayed together to assist anyone who rolled over in the turbulent pools. The journey took four to six hours. Now that stretch of river is well known as part of the Coast to Coast triathlon. The best kayakers cover the gorge section in less than three hours, but there was nothing competitive in our forays on the river.

Passengers in the TranzAlpine Express see part of the gorge on their rail trip to the West Coast, but we saw much more, including salmon swimming up to their spawning pools, two overhanging caves where there were rare bats, and we always saw a few paradise ducks. Our ventures down the river would be done on a Sunday, when Enid would drive the car and trailer to our exit point, collect the tired, dripping participants and drive on to Christchurch.

We were happy that our daughters fitted into our outdoor activities so easily. I encouraged them with tramping, water activities and skiing, but I never pressed them to begin high mountaineering.

For many years Enid had taught English, but she felt that there was a need for more counselling for students, and decided to move into that field. She took a year off teaching and completed a university diploma in counselling. After that she was in demand at schools in this new and challenging territory.

Eventually all good things must slow down, but not be allowed to stop. Our daughters moved away from Christchurch. A government regulation was announced limiting the maximum service on a park board to nine years. As I was in my thirteenth year on the Arthur's Pass Park Board, I had to depart. Some aspects of my business also declined. Keith Marshall, in his forties, had a serious stroke and had to retire, which reduced some of our better work from architects. My engineering partner, Peter Anderson, died of cancer when he was 48. He had been wonderfully tolerant of my absences in Antarctica, at Himalayan Trust meetings and on construction enterprises. He was keen on big ocean yacht racing and during his absences I attempted to cover his work. But I was in my late fifties and found it increasingly difficult to keep abreast of the ever-changing, highly technical demands of modern engineering design. I began vaguely considering a change.

One day in May 1983 I was walking in central Christchurch when I bumped into Colin Monteath. He said, 'The DSIR has been advertising for a leader at Scott Base for next summer season and no one has applied. Why don't you try?' Colin for a few years had been employed by the Antarctic Division of the Department of Scientific and Industrial Research in assisting the large range of scientific enterprises taking place each year.

I discussed this with Enid and my business associates. Next morning I filled in the application forms and the same afternoon I was interviewed for the position in the office of the Antarctic Division.

The meeting lasted half an hour and I do not recall being asked one question. The director spoke at great length about the need for discipline among the base staff, good relations with the American neighbours and the need to entertain government guests. Two other staff men walked in and out of the meeting and said very little. No indication was given as to whether I was likely to be accepted or if I should return for a further interview. I went back to my office. Six weeks later, on a Friday, a DSIR receptionist rang me to say I had the job and I had to start the following Monday in the Christchurch office.

I moved mountains at work and arrived as requested. One of the DSIR office assistants told me the department had re-advertised in all the army officers' and police gazettes and still had no response. The director really wanted someone trained in leadership and able to discipline a possibly unruly team. I was amazed to hear that all the others who were to occupy Scott Base for the next summer and winter seasons had already been interviewed and appointed. I had expected that as leader for the season I would be part of the interviewing committee and would have some input into the selection process.

There would be few responsibilities for me for several weeks. I was to get to know the DSIR administrators and make myself familiar with the files and the library. I had to study the written submissions of the 25 mainly scientific projects that would be on the ice for the next season. Most of the staff had previously handled similar pre-season preparations. The field leaders who made their submissions were generally very experienced. Their documents summarised past progress and the intended programme for the coming season. Costs, weights, dates, numbers, food requirements and helicopter flight requests were all set out in fine detail.

When Scott Base was first built, some air support was given to field parties by two fixed-wing aircraft flown by New Zealand pilots. However, for several years before the 1983–84 season there were no New Zealand planes in Antarctica for internal flights, and this would continue for my time in charge. There were six American helicopters at McMurdo and 250 hours of their flying time had been allocated free to the whole New Zealand programme. There would be astronomical charges if those hours were exceeded.

It was a big job collating all the field-group requirements to work out the most desirable and economical flight schedule. The helicopters were quite large so three or four parties could be resupplied in one flight, so long as precise locations and requirements were known. Colin Monteath and Hugh Logan had good relations with the diverse group of scientific leaders and they did an outstanding job in establishing a workable programme.

I was told to use files in the library to seek information on any of the scientific work being organised. I soon found that there was an embargo on the Mt Erebus air accident file. This did not surprise me as it was, and still is, a very sensitive topic for both the government and Air New Zealand. I also found that the final reports of previous base leaders were locked in the director's office and I had no access to them.

For an hour each Wednesday the director would shut his door and be unavailable. Apparently he spoke by radio telephone on these occasions to the leader of the wintering party of 11 then in residence at Scott Base. No file notes were made of these discussions and no instructions were given to the office about decisions that might have been made.

I knew one man who had been the base leader on an earlier summer. He explained that this conversation occurred every Wednesday throughout the year. It was usually a repeat of what he had heard at the initial interview. Most leaders wrote strong final reports. As the policy was then to always employ completely new staff every year, the leader would often air his views in his final document. This usually criticised the lack of continuity, and the cost of retraining a whole new team each year, in the knowledge that each leader would not be reappointed.

With my engineering background I was interested to see drawings of Scott Base and familiarise myself with the services of power, water, sewerage, fire-fighting and the workshop. Heavily bearded Garth Varcoe, plant engineer, had a hand in all these matters. The diesel generators and their stand-bys had good records. The Christchurch suppliers sent a maintenance man down south for a week each summer, and each new base mechanic had a preliminary week in the supplier's factory. Water was pumped from the sea, passing through a desalination plant. This worked well but it could not produce the high pressure and large volumes necessary to fight a major fire. Fire-fighting would be done with gases.

Garth was quite open about problems with the electrical and telephone systems. With the policy of changing staff every summer, and sometimes winter also, there had been 22 different electricians so far at Scott Base. Wiring had not been subjected to testing before being sealed under floors or walls. Many an electrician, idle in the winter, had run extra circuits for private lights or telephone extensions. They were not on drawings and sometimes came from American reject stores, so they did not match New Zealand colour codes. The base was being rebuilt: one new structure each second year. Garth was trying to be very particular about wiring circuits in the new buildings, and said he would be visiting about three times when I was in residence to check on all these important services.

Matching accommodation requirements and flight schedules was a complex exercise, but the outlines of this had been done before I was appointed. However, I had to be familiar with its operation in case there were flight delays. That season the base had 92 beds, 48 of which would be occupied most of the season by the operating staff and 15 army tradesmen, who were building the foundations for the next new structure. By 1983 Antarctica was no longer an exclusively male preserve. Women formed part of the Scott Base staff, the scientific teams and the visiting VIP groups.

Altogether 370 people would be passing through the base over the summer. Field scientists on arrival attended a two-day survival and radio course at the base, then went out to their various work locations. Five groups of four VIPS would be there for four nights, and there would be other visitors from time to time. All needed to be assured of a bed, and there had to be contingency plans in place in case of delays or mishaps.

The army group, called engineers, were mostly trained carpenters and welders. The specialist tradesmen required for drains, plumbing, insulation and so on would be flown in to stay for about a week at a time. Some flexibility had to be built into this schedule according to the progress – or lack of progress – of the foundation and floor work. The long-term intention was that Scott Base should have about seven different buildings, connected by closed passages. In each passage would be a fireproof door, so that a fire in one building would not spread to its neighbour.

At the end of August the annual Antarctic training camp was

held at the army camp near Lake Tekapo. All those going south during the season had to attend, apart from the 20 VIPs, in five groups of four, who would have brief escorted tours during November and early December. Even scientific leaders who had been down five or more times before had to participate. I imagined the main purpose would be for snowcraft safety, but there were numerous other activities and lectures.

Instruction covered health, first aid, fire-fighting, radio communication, rescue procedures, vehicle use, helicopter passenger behaviour and many other topics. We gathered at the Tekapo ski grounds, wearing Antarctic clothing, and stayed a night on the snow near the top of the main run. The organisers demonstrated a range of rescue procedures and built igloos and snow caves to show how secure they are. New to me was a demonstration of a signalling mirror, the size of a postcard. It had a viewing gap through which one could see where it was pointing. Someone on a hill behind the army camp, 45 kilometres away, flashed this mirror numerous times, and it was clearly visible to us without binoculars. It was explained that an aircraft searching for a lost party would come over the horizon and an observer in the plane could see the mirror flash from almost 100 kilometres away, a distance at which the lost members would be unable to hear the plane's engines. Pupils were told to sweep the horizon with the mirror if they were expecting a plane.

I found the camp very useful for the chance to meet the various field leaders. I had expected they would be critical of the bureaucratic insistence on the need for precision with weights, dates and locations for the helicopter support flights. But they were not greatly concerned about these issues and co-operated well in the planning of the many complex movements. However, they, too, criticised the system by which the base staff had to change every year, and the consequent lack of continuity of contact with the administrators.

In the month remaining before departure there was still work to do, but things had begun to fall into place now that I had met all the project leaders. The fire crew had a further training week in Christchurch. As the base buildings contain insulation materials that are toxic when burning, all rescue work had to be done using protective clothing and full masks. In this gear the crew had to practice locating and carrying dummy bodies from blacked-out coolstores and from some old underground drains.

Although I was not to be in the fire group, I did join them for two days. They worked well together and I, like them, was keen by now to fly south.

TWENTY

Scott Base Season

Early 1 October 1983, 30 men and women boarded an American Hercules for the flight south, along with much heavy cargo. There were no seats and few windows. As the fuselage was not pressurised we flew at altitudes much lower than is customary for normal passenger planes. Most of us were the nucleus of the Scott Base staff for the five-month season, plus the 11 who would stay on to winter over. This group had been well trained to work together as a team, so that any 'misfits' could be recognised early. Their fire-fighting training had helped this bonding.

Twenty minutes before landing, one of the crew announced that the plane was about to fly lower and he would allow the entry of cold air, to help acclimatise us for when the doors were opened on the sea-ice landing strip. We were prepared with our extra protective clothing in separate bags and soon were waddling around at twice our normal girth. We clipped ourselves to ring bolts for the touchdown, and soon we were out in the bracing clear air. Everything was white except three small green buildings and eight orange graders. If there is a build-up of wind-driven snow on the runway, the graders form a line just before a landing or take-off and make a long sweep of the area.

The wheeled base vehicles were there to meet us, but I was put on a sledge and pulled by dogs via a direct route, avoiding the road through Mactown, as McMurdo was known. The dog man had worked out a route through the tide cracks and we beat the vehicles by about 10 minutes. The buildings were hardly recognisable since my last visit, in 1967. The main accommodation block, containing dining, kitchen and sleeping quarters, looked most comfortable. A few of the original tunnel-shaped rooms still existed, and from the outside the new base looked unimpressive, like a collection of square coolstores. In fact their construction is similar, as the walls are made from two sheets of thin metal separated by 20 centimetres of thick polyurethane foam. There are not many windows, and the floors are high off the ground, to stop wind-blown snow forming solid ice above the foundations.

Nine of the 11 from the previous wintering party were to depart the next morning, but the electrician and mechanic were held back for three days so they could explain changes and maintenance problems to the next operators. I had no opportunity for a private conversation with the winter leader. The cynics said the total changeover policy was to prevent the old hands explaining shortcuts and developing rackets with the nearby Americans. The completely new team would arrive buoyed with enthusiasm and Tekapo camp indoctrination. A few years later some continuity of senior staff was established.

One of the Christchurch staff took me to Mactown for most of the second day to meet the many heads of departments with whom I would be co-operating. Most of them had been there for two or more seasons. Service officers and the scientists had their own separate establishments, drainage and rubbish problems had been substantially resolved and the nuclear generating station had gone. The officer in charge there was Captain Schumacher of the United States Navy.

I had been advised to immediately establish several domestic routines at Scott Base. One of the most important was the management of the bar. At a meeting of all staff, 10 men, mostly the next wintering team, volunteered as barmen. We were not bound by New Zealand licensing laws, so we decided the bar would open each day at 5.30 p.m. and close at 11 p.m. On five special occasions these hours would be extended. The socialising area was relatively small, particularly if all of those from the base's 90-odd beds decided to be thirsty at the same time. To be certain that we would not be swamped by excessive numbers of visitors from the American base, we established that entry would be by invitation only. During the summer McMurdo's numbers would rise to 1,200, but they had three bars of their own. Over a hundred personnel at Mactown were New Zealand citizens employed by catering and transport contractors, but we decided that they, too, would have entry by invitation only.

Back in Christchurch I had looked at the lists of liquor sent south each year and had been surprised by the very large number of liqueurs in each bulk order. When the bar was unlocked for the first time I saw little space for liqueurs on the shelves, and none under the bench. Before the previous mechanic departed I asked about the consumption of the exotic drinks. He said they arrived at wholesale prices and duty-free. Staff would buy the cheap liqueurs and post them home at the modest postal rates available to them. At the base most of them drank bottled beer.

Scientists began arriving, as did the team of army builders who were preparing the foundations for the next new building. The survival team erected their tents out on the ice and all new arrivals underwent a two-day emergency course. Most emerged from these courses feeling much more confident about living in Antarctica.

Every Tuesday morning I attended an administration meeting at McMurdo – for 10 Americans and me. The main purpose was to confirm the flight arrangements for the following week. The first item was always a presentation by the chief meteorologist. He produced photographs from the polar-orbiting satellite, showed weather maps and was generally very accurate in his forecasting for conditions anywhere in Antarctica, right up to the flying routes to Christchurch and Hobart in Tasmania. Most staff and supplies came from Christchurch, but icebreakers sometimes used Hobart as their departure base. Captain Schumacher and the chief American scientist had copies of New Zealand's requested flights. We confirmed the most economical way to distribute the many field parties to their chosen destinations, keeping helicopter hours to a minimum. Very rarely did we have to change the preliminary flight lists drawn up in Christchurch several months previously.

Most of the men at the meeting were senior military officers, and the others were the principal scientists. I was impressed with the captain's calm authority and the fact that all participants had always done their preparatory work. At the end of these meetings Captain Schumacher and I usually had a private session to discuss any relevant matters concerning the two bases. At the first meeting he wanted a long discussion on the American VIPs who would begin arriving in early November. He wished each group to have an afternoon at Scott Base to observe its operations, including a dog-sledge ride and drinks in the bar at the end of the day. He offered a similar afternoon at McMurdo for New Zealand VIPs. They had no dogs, but because of McMurdo's size there were more active science projects to see.

On the third morning at Scott Base I was one of the earliest to breakfast and in the first minute I heard that late the previous night there had been an accident involving one of the base's light trucks. Before I heard half the story there was a phone call from the director in Christchurch, who was furious that the participants had not told me. He demanded that I cancel all driving authorities and order driving tests for all who had access to vehicles.

My enquiries revealed that three Americans had been in the bar very late the previous night and had been too drunk for the 40-minute walk back along the icy 'road'. A New Zealand soldier from the construction team had taken them in a truck and on the way he skidded and rolled the vehicle, fortunately not injuring anyone. I looked at the truck. All the tyres were bald and nowhere near New Zealand standards for reasonable treads. The base mechanic considered he could soon straighten the chassis and order new tyres. He also arranged tighter controls on vehicle keys. I had stern words with the barman and the driver concerned.

The mechanic, postmaster and army officer all insisted they had to have access to motor transport, and I agreed. I did not subject them to driving tests. For the others I tightened some driving and bar rules and there were no further traffic incidents. Deep down I resented the fact that the director had found out about the accident before I had. Someone at the base had been encouraged to go over my head, and it was to happen again.

Each time a plane arrived from Christchurch I would drive

the largest vehicle the 12 kilometres to the airport and collect the scheduled Scott Base personnel and their baggage. Mail and supplies were taken to the American base and distributed from there. I gave each set of new arrivals a half-hour talk on safety matters, their itineraries and the general state of the overall programme. They would be shown their accommodation and then any scientists would be in the hands of the outdoor instructors for their survival course. The VIPs, who came for just four days, would have an experienced Christchurch person with them and so did not undergo the safety course.

Scientists undertaking projects on the sea ice generally arrived first, because the ice became unsafe in late November and could vanish by late December. They would be sent out by helicopter or motorised toboggans. Of the 25 programmes for the season all but one were within helicopter range. That exception was a coal research quartet, who travelled past the South Pole and were landed 1,600 kilometres from base. The two women were geologists and the two men were capable mountaineers and mechanics. Dr Margaret Bradshaw was their leader. They were conducting research on the very thick, high-quality coal that exists in steep country some 200 kilometres beyonf the South Pole.

※

For the first two months I was busy seven days a week. It was not long before nearly all the 92 beds were in use and the place felt crowded. There was much administrative juggling to be done but I had no receptionist or secretarial services available to me. During this busy period I seldom left the buildings except for the meetings at McMurdo or airport duties.

On one occasion I was driving to meet a plane when I heard by radio that it would be two hours late. I drove over the sea to a pair of tiny tents that housed an American seal research programme. They were about 8 km from a point of land where 30 or so seals were basking in the weak sun. Out on the sea two large holes had been drilled in the 3-metre-thick ice. In one hole the scientists had placed a long, thick steel pipe. The bottom 2 metres of pipe were made of glass and contained a chair, connecting to a ladder to the surface. Thus it was possible to climb down the ladder and observe the underside of the ice. I sat there for half an hour, in complete silence. Some light penetrated through the ice so I could see various colours of plankton and occasionally tiny fish. Large jellyfish are fascinating to watch swimming.

Men above pushed two seals down the second hole, which was sloping, not vertical like the observation shaft. They swam about gracefully and poked their noses up the hole for air several times, before going back up to the surface. I went up myself and talked to the team about their work. They were the studying sounds, navigation and endurance of Weddell seals. They would capture one and transport it to a distant hole. The sounds it made on the surface and underwater were recorded, along with replies from others and echoes from the shore. By using other, nearer holes the scientists found that the animals had some range-finding ability that enabled them to tell whether a journey would be too long for their lung capacity. An adult seal could swim about 8 kilometres without a breath.

During the first weeks of October, American aircraft from Christchurch were the main passenger and freight carriers. As the season became busier and the landing conditions more stable, four New Zealand planes joined the fleet. These were equipped with only wheel-landing facilities. Some of the American aircraft had ski-landing equipment added for flights to projects at far inland destinations where no surface grooming could be done.

The crew of one New Zealand Hercules was to participate in a penguin count. For some years there had been concerns about the survival of penguin colonies, particularly those nearest to human activities. The rookery at Cape Royds is the furthest south in the world. A helicopter flying low in the vicinity can scatter thousands of birds from their nests, allowing the predatory skuas to feast on exposed eggs and chicks. Leaving eggs for a brief time in Antarctic temperatures can also rapidly stop the incubation process, and with such short breeding seasons penguins will not lay eggs a second time. Having been scattered, there is no guarantee that returning birds will all go to their correct nests.

Estimates of Adélies at Royds ranged from 4,000 to 6,000 pairs. One serious count had been made and another was required in 1983. It had been found that humans walking quietly among nesting birds would disturb those within 5 or so metres, but they seemed to return to their nest sites all right. It was considered that the most suitable time of the year for the count would be the brief time when the birds were on their nests.

I read how my predecessors had done their count and decided to repeat their methods. Four of us were landed at 2 kilometres from Cape Royds and quietly approached the rookery. From a high ridge I pointed out the territory each was to cover. Then the plan was to attempt to visually divide one's segment into 10, then count the birds in that portion and multiply by 10. Of course there were hundreds of birds moving all the time, wandering back and forth to the beach. Others were involved in noisy territorial squabbles while marauding skuas flew around the fringes. The count could not be accurate, but it was a noisy and interesting problem to attempt to solve. The authorities wanted to know the numbers of breeding pairs, but it was a difficult figure to establish. We took our total number, halved it and made a small deduction for rowdy teenagers, arriving at 2,317 pairs. Most younger penguins stay at sea until they mature at four or five years old.

Another part of the penguin count was a photographic fly-over at high altitude, using good-quality cameras. One of the Hercules crews, after a night at Scott Base, flew a high course to Christchurch to include eight rookeries. In Wellington the photographs were enlarged and students spent many weeks of their vacation in counting the populations of each colony. I heard later that the final count for Cape Royds, two days after our ground efforts, produced a figure 300 pairs higher than ours.

The food at Scott Base was good and creatively prepared. Two chefs with one assistant produced generous dishes, which were always appreciated. Although much of the food had been frozen, there were regular additions of fresh greens and fruit from the aircraft arriving during the busy months. The chefs were most cooperative about providing special treats when they were told of a birthday among the base staff, or when they were notified that we were entertaining American guests. Many people drank wine with dinner, paid through their bar accounts.

As the base population was changing so much with all the coming and going, there were no fixed seating for meals. This fluidity allowed all sorts of exchanges of ideas. It also gave the chance for small field parties, now in a large dining room, to have a break from their constant companions.

There was virtually no library. Ten rare books were locked in a glass box, and the only other books were a few cheap paperbacks, left behind by past occupants. Fortunately many of us had brought reading material, so there was a good supply of books among us.

About 3 km to the north lay an easy snow slope for those who wished to ski. A simple petrol motor drove a rope tow to the top of the run. Instead of pulleys at intermediate points, the rope dragged over empty fuel drums half buried on their sides in the snow. Skiers held the rope and had to go around the end of the drums when ascending, and lower the rope back in its right position after the drum had been passed. I could not get the army men interested in the skiing, nor were they inclined to walk to any of the great viewpoints not far from the base. For recreation they would be transported to McMurdo, where they had access to a good gymnasium. They worked as a team and joined a basketball competition against the Americans.

In early November the first VIPs arrived. Each group of four had a Christchurch DSIR staff member as leader. Before their flight they would be issued with programme sheets, historical information and safety advice. A helicopter was at their disposal for their entire four-day stay, and the DSIR person with them was meant to ensure that the hours used did not exceed 20. The names of those arriving would be posted on the base noticeboard ahead of time. I was surprised to note that many of the initial parties consisted of departmental secretaries and their stores officers, who wanted to see where their materials and staff were being used at McMurdo and Scott Bases. They would also be taken to the historic Scott and Shackleton huts and to some of the more interesting scientific field operations. These latter trips gave me a chance to deliver mail and an occasional bottle to remote groups. Among the early visitors was Michael Cullen, then a new Labour Opposition MP.

As soon as our first party left, a group of American VIPs arrived. I was always asked to sit at Captain Schumacher's table for the first night of each such tour, and I would invite them to see the New Zealand operation. There were a number of senators and senior government appointees. Conversation would initially be very general but somehow always turned to the next American presidential election, which was 18 months away. Of course most of them faced losing their jobs if President Reagan lost. Captain Schumacher and the various serving officers were just spectators to these discussions, and I had little to contribute.

There was always praise for the compactness and tidiness of Scott Base. A few scientists would be assembled to demonstrate their research work. The visitors always wanted a ride on a sledge, so the 'doggo' had been informed and a team made ready. Usually there would be some scrapping of excited dogs for 10 minutes and then a rewarding lengthy run. There were 19 dogs at the base that season, enough for two full teams. All the field parties had snowmobiles or helicopter support rather than dogs, and forward planning indicated there would be no future use for the dogs apart from these one-hour 'jollies'. Most other countries' operations had stopped using dogs several years previously and New Zealand was being criticised for persisting with them, particularly by American conservationists. It was claimed that large numbers of seals were being slaughtered to feed the teams.

Back in the Christchurch office I had read much of the criticism and looked at the response to it. For several years New Zealand had been sending south frozen mutton and old horse carcasses for the dog teams. They lived reasonably well on this food, but for living outside in the dark winter it was found that they needed more fat in their diet. Therefore doggos were permitted to kill 12 seals at the end of each season. The instruction given in my year was that this was to be reduced to 10 seals, all of them old males after the mating season. They were not all to be taken from the same herd. The killing took place after the summer party had returned to New Zealand. I could not see that this policy would harm the seal population. Three years later New Zealand's dog operations in Antarctica ceased. Some animals were brought back to New Zealand and the rest went to enthusiastic purchasers in Alaska.

The captain enquired about the rifle used by our doggo. He said the American base had no firearms, despite being run predominantly by military officers. I explained that the bolt for the rifle was in the postmaster's safe and I had hidden the ammunition separately. The dog man, postmaster and I would all be needed to assemble it.

One VIP party enlivened Scott Base more than others. In it were New Zealand's Governor-General, Sir David Beattie; his son, a solicitor in his late twenties; and two aides. They took a great interest in everything, had read their information sheets and eagerly joined in all events. They were similarly enthusiastic at the American base. A large supply of whisky arrived with them and a bottle was handed out to each field party their helicopter visited.

Another group included Thea Muldoon, wife of Prime Minister Robert Muldoon. When I had seen the VIP lists in Christchurch I had noted that National MP Marilyn Waring was to be in that party. Apparently two days before it left she withdrew, to be able to stay back and cross the floor in Parliament to vote against a controversial item of legislation being promoted furiously by her leader. She was replaced for the Antarctic trip by one of Muldoon's office secretaries, who did not appear at all interested in Antarctica. On the other hand I had many conversations with Thea Muldoon and found her the best informed of all our many visitors. In retrospect, I believe that Marilyn Waring showed a lot of courage and determination. She could have dodged that enormous issue, one of the biggest events of that parliamentary decade, and avoided a lot of trouble. On the other hand I can't help wondering if Muldoon had timed that debate deliberately, thinking that Waring would be out of the country.

Back in August at the Tekapo camp one of the scientists had told me he had heard that some occupants of the South Pole Station had boasted they were growing cannabis. We had laughed about this, considering it an American problem. In early November Captain Schumacher indicated that he wanted a talk with me. He wished to borrow the keys to the three historic huts. There had been so much looting in the early 1960s that they were securely locked and, as they were on land that was informally a New Zealand protectorate, the keys were at Scott Base. I parted with the keys for a day under strict conditions. The other matter he raised was that of the Pole Station cannabis.

'We have been told cannabis has been grown at the Pole. I have hired the Christchurch airport detector dog to be here when we bring out the last year's occupants. Do you want the dog to check any of your staff?'

'I have no suspicions of any of our staff or scientists. I prefer to keep well away from this issue,' I replied.

The South Pole Station had been established in 1957 and rebuilt 1971–74, with all materials being flown to the site. There was space for 50 residents. Sometime in the brief summer it could be full, but generally about 30 wintered over. The average air temperature outside was about −50° Fahrenheit. The ski-landing hydraulics for the Hercules aircraft had to be at temperatures above −48°, which usually meant after early November. From this month there were frequent flights for changes of personnel, food resupplies and the freighting of hundreds of tonnes of diesel for heating, cooking and lighting. The flights would begin soon on the 2,800-kilometre round trip.

I mentioned the detector-dog situation in one of my agony talks to Christchurch on a Wednesday afternoon. As usual, the director was jumps ahead of me: he already knew the dog was going south. He said he would not allow it on a New Zealand plane and I was not to let it near Scott Base. Our sledge dogs were all bred on the ice and had built up no immunity to other animal diseases. If I had any suspects among New Zealand citizens, I was to put them on a New Zealand plane for checking in Christchurch. There were none.

I confirmed to McMurdo that we did not want the dog. I later discovered that three Pole staff were hurried back to America on the first plane and told they would never see Antarctica again, but I heard no more details.

·ıı·

In December the sea ice thins considerably and when it gets to under 2.5 metres thick it becomes dangerous for large loaded aircraft to land on it. Usually another site, further away on higher ground, is chosen and over a period of about five days the whole operation is transferred to this safer location. I had to admire the efficiency of such large-scale changes.

The thinning of the ice saw several of the Scott Base projects conclude and their operators depart. With fewer arrivals and the VIP visits over I began to have some free time. I particularly liked visiting the small hut at Arrival Heights. This involved a two-hour walk and a climb of about 600 metres to where Scott's men in 1904 and Shackleton's in 1915 would climb to look with telescopes over the frozen bay, to see if there was a ship coming for them, out beyond the solid foreground. At such a distance, with the ice so thick, they would have expected to see just masts and perhaps topsails over the curved horizon. How different it was in 1984. In January an icebreaker would clear a passage right through to the shoreline. Two of Shackleton's men in 1916 had been impatient and were lost on fragile ice when trying to walk across that bay between huts before it had completely frozen.

One of our survival team of three was Rob Hall, who was to die near the summit of Everest in 1996. The team worked well during the season and I became very close to Rob. A scientific group was working at about two-thirds of the way up Mt Erebus, examining the gases being emitted from the active volcano and checking the seismometer that had been installed there some years previously. This instrument had a radio connection to a rotating graph in the base laboratory, so the state of the volcano could be read at any time. Rob decided to join the mountain group on a resupply flight and flew up on a Friday afternoon.

On the Sunday morning I received a radio call from him. He had mountain sickness and wanted to be flown back to base. I reminded him that the pilots had Sundays off, and that all but one of them had been in the Scott Base bar on Saturday night. (There were strict rules about no drinking for 36 hours before flying duties, and one pilot was always held back for emergency flights.) Rob said it was an emergency. I knew that the previous year he had climbed Ama Dablam – 6,828 metres high. He and I were the only ones in Antarctica at that time with real altitude experience, and he should know if his problem was genuine at just 2,000 metres on Erebus. But another problem was that two of the VIP visits had used more than their quota of helicopter hours, and calling one out for Rob would force me to ration use for other parties. Rob insisted that he was ill and had to drop altitude.

I rang Captain Schumacher, who told me what I already knew about flights on a Sunday. In the end I gave in and a helicopter brought Rob back that afternoon. I went to meet him at the helipad and he appeared with his normal bright smile. I took him to my room and tore great strips off him. However, this did not spoil our relationship. Enid and I were invited to a number of his parties in Christchurch and on two occasions I talked by telephone to him while he was on Mt Everest.

*

While the main air strips were being moved to an inland site because of the thinning of the sea ice I had the usual nightly call from the long-distant coal research party, but now they were in trouble. The main drive shaft on their one snowmobile had broken and they had no possible way of repairing it. They were among mountains, some days' travelling from the safe terraces where they had been landed and where they were to be lifted out three weeks hence. They needed a spare part to be dropped by parachute.

At the store I found that the right part was in stock. An American Hercules was allocated the job and the pilot asked me to come with him, to talk to the ground party by radio during the location and dropping actions. They were among quite large unmapped mountains and the pilot thought that having a New Zealander on board would be better than having his wireless man try to interpret a radio-modulated Kiwi accent coming from the ground party. I asked a chef to bake a cake for the coal team, sorted their mail and arranged two parachutes. The ground party were told by radio we would come next day. They gave their calculated latitude and longitude positions. The pilot told me to confirm the location and write the figures on a piece of paper to hand to him after we left the Pole. He would feed them into the navigational flight plotter. He intended to land at the Pole, discharge a fuel load into the storage bladders there and then continue for the air-drop.

There was a fall of snow during the night and the grooming graders were not yet at their new location. I was driven to the plane, away out on the endless flat desert. There were five other passengers and a crew of five. Much of the fuselage was taken up by a colossal cylindrical tank, securely strapped to the floor and walls. Fuel in the American services was measured in pounds and we had 28,000 pounds of diesel on board. There were another few hundred pounds of assorted cargo on the floor and no seats for passengers.

The plane taxied to a starting point, warmed up and then roared across the snow, but in an 8-kilometre run the nose ski never lifted. We turned around, went back on the newly formed tracks, turned and tried again, with the same result. We shifted the loose cargo to the rear, strapped it down and we, too, sat at the back. More runs and still the nose ski would not lift above the new snow. After a total of 12 attempts the pilot announced that he was now short of fuel. We were to abandon the attempt and try again the next day.

At the next appointed radio call-up time I told the ground party the drop would be delayed for one day. They had been standing by, ready to light coloured flares when they heard us in the area. They were on a short strip of glacier not large enough to land a plane but had a good drop zone for packages.

Next morning the snow had compacted enough for us to lift off in one long run. This time there were seven passengers. The flight was uneventful. I sat on a box by one of the small windows, gazing at the complex ranges not far below us, a reminder of the air-drop flight with Wynne Croll in 1962.

About 15 minutes before the Pole touchdown one of the crew, a steward I think, came to us. 'The skipper says we'll be on the ground for 20 minutes emptying this tank. There will be no embarking call – he will just take off. The propellers will be turning all the time. You can go to the ground, to the rear only or you'll lose your heads. Do not enter the Pole Station. I'll take your orders for the shop and bring the items to you.'

I wanted to buy a South Pole T-shirt, and I also had a parcel of 1,400 stamped envelopes from the Scott Base postmaster for franking. (Stamp collectors love to have envelopes franked in exotic places.) I handed this parcel to the steward, who was familiar with this type of request. He said the envelopes would re-appear on the next flight north. We put on our protective clothing and got ready to disembark. I had noticed that one man wore bright red clothing, but took no particular notice. Outside he handed me his camera and put on a special hat and beard, stating, 'I promised my son I'd send him a photo of Father Christmas at the South Pole.'

Some of the buildings were below ground. The only one above the surface was a large dome and it, too, was slowly disappearing beneath the build-up of wind-blown snow. There were flags of many countries, fuel pipes, black rubber fuel bladders and weather and radio masts. One separate small tower had an unusual appearance. I was told it was a tracking device for the many satellites that are in polar orbits.

After I had taken photographs and 15 noisy minutes had passed, I climbed back into the plane. The engines had been kept running to prevent the hydraulic oils freezing. The skipper placed me in the co-pilot's seat, which delighted me. I handed him the co-ordinates of the intended air-drop and he fed the figures into the flight plotter. The doors were closed, the engines roared, we rushed down the endless emptiness and were easily airborne with the lightened load.

Just two minutes in the air the steward reported that a man had been left behind. The pilot flew on, talked to the Pole Station by radio and found that the man had entered the station despite instructions to the contrary. He was sent out on the next flight and then straight back to America, having lost his job on the ice.

Ahead, large mountains appeared, with big cumulus clouds looming among them. I located the ground party by radio and was told that although they were in sunshine there were many clouds quite close, without much wind. When the instruments indicated we were close, the pilot began flying figures of eight around the cloud fringes. We understood that those on the ground were at about 3,300 metres above sea level and the neighbouring peaks were estimated to be a further 500 metres above them. We could see occasional ice-covered mountains, steep and spectacular. Once I saw a black shining escarpment several hundred metres high. It must have been coal.

Suddenly the radio on the ground became clear: 'We can hear your motors.'

We circled cautiously some more and heard from the ground that the sound had been lost. The pilot said, 'Tell them to light their flares. We'll get them on the next run.'

Sure enough, we came in lower on a complex course and two coloured flares were suddenly obvious. With great skill, among threatening peaks, our pilot flew us over the tiny group of Margaret Bradshaw's party on the ice. The parachutes were dropped and they were seen to open. Up we climbed above the clouds and circled until the ground party reported they had the packages – nothing had dropped into crevasses.

The co-ordinates of the new runway near Scott Base were put into the computer and we set off for home. The pilot had a few words to the steward, who then brought to each of the six on the flight deck a large plate and spoon. A generous helping of ice-cream was ladled onto the plates. I noticed it was Tip Top, the Christchurch brand. The pilot told me, 'On each flight I always buy a five-gallon package and take the remnants back to the officers' mess. It is so much better that the American stuff we have at McMurdo. Pole Station has a separate catering order.' I went back to the fuselage, giving the co-pilot his rightful seat. I was pleased to see that at least we still had Father Christmas on board.

In mid-January, as the weather near the coast warmed to nearly zero, there were indications of more movement in the sea ice. We were told that an icebreaker was approaching the area and in the next fortnight three ships would arrive, several days apart. Where necessary the icebreaker would remain in the vicinity to clear their entry passages. The Scott Base staff were told to provide storage space for the next season's bulk supplies of food, fuel and building materials. The unloading of ships had to be a precisely controlled performance.

Each ship was about 50 times the weight of Scott's ship *Discovery*, which had wintered in that bay in 1904. No wharves had been constructed and the sea is not deep enough for ships to come right up to the shore, so a device was used that had been successful in Greenland. A large ice mass, perhaps the size of the incoming ship, was floated to the berthing position. It was really like a moderate-sized iceberg. It was tied to the shore and a portable steel bridge put across the gap to allow vehicles onto the iceberg. Gravel was put on the surface to stop slipping. When the ship arrived it was tied to the iceberg and unloading proceeded, using its own jibs to place crates directly onto trucks and trailers. They had to be careful not to place too many heavy items onto the ice at once – partial melting and tidal movements can cause the berg to roll over or tilt at a dangerous angle. Trucks had to be loaded and moved quickly to solid ground. The mooring of the iceberg remained, so it did not depart with the rest of the sea ice later in the season.

Nearly all Scott Base staff were kept busy for two weeks during the unloading period, and soon all freezers and the store were full again. I was invited to the bridge and captain's cabin on two of the cargo ships. The generous accommodation, navigational aids and physical comforts were in sharp contrast to what I recall from my time at sea. The first skipper told of the views he had as they came up the sound. About a dozen orca patrolled the edge of the sea ice until the icebreaker arrived. Then they followed it towards the shore. Great cracks were opened for hundreds of metres, disturbing the small groups of basking seals. The orca took advantage of these suddenly available water routes.

One afternoon there was a general call at Scott Base to see orca nearby. I rushed out. Much sea ice, very near the base, was on the move on an outgoing tide. Clearly visible was an island of ice, some 10 metres square, which was slowly moving. On it were seven Weddell seals – four adults and three pups. The latter would have been about five months old and would not yet be skilful swimmers. Two adult orca and a half-sized one were trying to tip the ice island over. All three leapt on one edge and the ice tilted about 10 degrees. The seals scrambled to the top edge. This was repeated from other approaches, with the same result. Then the young orca went to one side while the two big ones swam to the opposite side. From a distance they swam fast near the surface and just before the ice they dived down together, bringing over their tails in unison. A considerable wave shot across the ice island. On the third such co-ordinated attempt a seal pup was swept into the sea and caught immediately. The orca tossed it into the air from one to the other and soon it was a gory carcass. It was undoubtedly rapidly consumed. In five minutes the three returned to the ice island, which was now becoming more distant. Another pup was seen being thrown into the air.

The island disappeared behind other floating ice and the gruesome show concluded. Although sad for the seals, the display had shown the great skill of the orca. The obvious communication between them was amazing, to achieve what they did. I wondered about the swimming ability of the adult seals. They clearly didn't fancy their chances trying to outswim orca.

Some 300 kilometres north-west of Scott Base is a large area of land that has almost no ice cover. Because of the proximity of protecting mountain ranges, the precipitation is very low. There are small deep lakes and a number of primitive plant forms in this area, known as the Dry Valleys. There have been many research projects in the area, and a small New Zealand base, Vanda Station, was built near one of the lakes. American and New Zealand projects had been active in the vicinity for several summer seasons and it was soon found that there appeared to be no deterioration of human excreta or kitchen waste. Temperatures rarely came up to zero, so no bacteria could act, and there were no coastal scavengers to tidy the sites. The decision was made, before my time, to supply empty fuel drums to campsites. All waste, even urine, was to be placed in the drums, where it froze. One of the duties of helicopter pilots was to pick up the drums if they were returning with a light load. The drums were lowered to sea ice and would float away to the Great Southern Ocean with the next summer melt and offshore winds.

With the scientists having left the Dry Valleys at the end of the season, there were still three full drums to be collected. I joined a pilot as his assistant. We flew to Vanda, then another helicopter arrived, containing Americans – four men and three women. Some of the ice on Lake Vanda had been melting for the previous week and there was a small patch of open water. Over the years the leader of Vanda had issued a certificate to anyone who completely immersed him or herself naked in the lake. Cameras were forbidden. The new arrivals talked us into joining them for the plunge. We all, women too, dropped off gloves, head gear and outer jackets in the hut and walked 50 metres to the water. At the edge we removed our undergarments. Some dived, others stood and vertically dropped to the stony bottom. I dived, turned and took six rapid strokes to the shore. Some kind person lent me a spare towel and I was quickly into my clothes. I signed a book and wrote my address for the posting of the certificate, but it never arrived. We flew back over the ocean and pulled a lever to drop our loaded drums.

Back at Scott Base I checked all my bookwork and watched as most people left. Our helicopter hours were five fewer than the specified maximum – just enough for the doggo to visit some scattered seal colonies and shoot the specified 10 animals to supplement the dogfood supplies.

The season ended in late February. As the wintering party had been there throughout the summer, there was no great changeover ceremony. While I had been there a New Zealand flag had flown all the time. On the last day I was told to take down the flag and keep it. The winter leader was supplied with another one. Since then I have raised that flag once: on a pole in Akaroa for my eightieth birthday.

In 1986, two years after I left Scott Base, Bob Norman was asked to look into the management of the DSIR Antarctic Programme. He had just retired from being the Commissioner of Works. Then he was asked to chair the Ross Dependency Research Committee. At about this time there was much reshuffling going on in government departments. Bob guided in a series of changes that made the Antarctic operations far more efficient, and prevented the exercise of too much power by any one individual. In the Christchurch office of 26 people, six are capable of being base managers and they rotate their positions to ensure continuity.

Building services are properly drawn and records kept by permanent professional staff. Construction contracts are mostly now let to building contractors rather than the army.

It was a great experience to be employed for a season in Antarctica and I enjoyed my time there.

TWENTY-ONE

Reunions

Early in 1984, just back from Antarctica, I began to contemplate where to seek employment. I was 59 years old and I had parted from my engineering office in Christchurch. In very short time I was appointed to the position of supervisor of a large construction project in a secluded valley near Nelson, some five hours' drive from my home. I rented a house in Nelson while Enid retained her position on the staff of Cashmere High School in Christchurch. She planned to join me during school holidays.

My work involved overseeing the construction of a timber mill, which was to cut, treat, dress and package timber, mainly for export to East Asian destinations. The design was Canadian and the timber-handling processes were mostly automated. It was inspirational and rewarding work that kept me occupied for nearly two years.

The countryside in the Nelson area is of great interest to an outdoors person. In weekends I walked on the local hills and kayaked on the many rivers and along the fascinating coastline. Small-scale artistic and musical activities flourish in the city. I went to all sorts of not-very-well-attended functions.

I had been in Nelson about two months when I was invited to a dinner at Government House in Wellington on a Friday night, in appreciation for my hosting the Governor-General in Antarctica. The aide-de-camp's card explained that Enid was also invited to the black-tie occasion. I rang Enid, wrote an acceptance message and made flight, motel and car bookings.

Late on the appointed afternoon I flew to Wellington, collected a car and drove to the motel. I went back to the airport for Enid but her plane did not arrive and little seemed to be happening at the airport, apart from an obvious police presence. After half an hour I enquired and learned that the plane had left Christchurch on time. I rang Government House to explain that we would be late. Lady Beattie came to the phone. After I explained the position, she said, 'You come now and your wife can taxi to us.'

'No, she's bringing my dinner jacket and black shoes from Christchurch. I will have to change in the motel. I expect Enid will also be changing for the occasion.'

'Just come as you are.'

I watched the runway for another half-hour and then several planes landed in quick succession. Enid was on the third of these. As we hurried to the motel she explained that the pilot told passengers there had been a bomb scare at Wellington airport and he had to circle over Marlborough until a clearance was given to land. When we had changed I rang again and explained that we were on the way. The gate guard inspected our invitation and sent us to the parking area. At the main door Lady Beattie stood holding out two large glasses of champagne. As we hurriedly drank them she explained that we had missed the soup course and entrée orders were being taken.

We were seated at a long table with the Beattie family, the American ambassador, the Muldoons, two from the New Zealand Antarctic office and Captain Schumacher. Enid was asked to explain the details of her delay, and one of the Governor-General's aides said bomb scares were not unusual at the airport. The police and flight authorities had a policy of making no announcements in case the perpetrators were just after publicity.

We went on to have a delightful evening, with the conversation centring mainly on Antarctic matters. At the end our hostess expressed sorrow that we had to go to a motel. 'Why not stay here?' she said.

We declined. Among other things was the thought of having to get into my dinner jacket for breakfast. But Lady Beattie was undeterred. 'You come here for breakfast, then,' she said.

We went to our motel and came back for breakfast, at which the American captain was the only other guest. Thus we started the day in a happy, relaxed manner. While the men talked, Lady Beattie took Enid to see some of the private rooms. On one prominent wall was a painting of a clothesline holding very windswept washing, with Wellington hills in the background. It was explained, 'I have that as a reminder of what it will be like next year when our appointment ends and we go back to our house!'

Back in Nelson I bought a small yacht, which was moored at the well-equipped marina in Havelock. It was a broad, sluggish vessel that contained a small galley and a sleeping space for two – or more at a squeeze. I sailed through all the major arms of the complex Pelorus Sound and learned a lot about sailing alone. Sometimes I invited a work colleague to join me, and Enid came for some adventures when she was in the area. On rare occasions I went outside the heads and into the bigger oceans to the French Pass area. I did not join any sailing clubs. From what I heard they seemed to be largely concerned with racing, while I was far more interested in viewing the charming area with its active sea- and birdlife.

When the mill was in full operation I returned to Christchurch and to partial retirement. However, I continued to work on small engineering projects from home. The advances in answerphones, fax and computer technology made a small-scale home office quite feasible. I designed the structural portions of numerous houses and small buildings for architects and draughtsmen. The mill at Nelson consulted me for many of the extensions and alterations they commissioned as their technology advanced.

Having been away so long we found that the house at Cora Lynn was in need of much maintenance. It was still without power, and Enid and I were finding that our visits to the mountains were mainly for work on the house. During my absence in Antarctica and Nelson many of our younger friends had moved to other centres, so there were few we could ask to come and help. After struggling on for six years we sold the house to a group of friends who have extensive mountain interests. For similar reasons we also sold the yacht, Havelock being so far from Christchurch.

Instead, we bought a seaside house in Akaroa with sewerage, electricity, water and telephone connections, and within easy reach of shops and cafés.

In 1974 the Montana Group bought large areas of land near Blenheim with the intention of planting grapes. Most people in those days thought that the South Island of New Zealand was too cold for growing grapes commercially. A group of six Christchurch men looked for a site to set up an experimental vineyard, with the aim to establish which of the main wine-producing grapes would grow best. They found that the property Enid and I owned at Halswell appeared to be ideal. It faced north to the sun on a gentle slope within easy range of the city. Three of the members were my mountaineering friends. Nine varieties were planted on just one acre, so quantities would be too small for wine to be sold to the general public.

Before long I became intrigued by the progress and joined them, while still being one of the two landlords. I learned a lot. All nine grape varieties survived the winter frosts and a few good wines were made. The partners did at least 90 per cent of the work – post and wire erection, winter pruning, spraying, bird protection, weed control and numerous small tasks.

Three initial members went on to become wine writers and judges: Don Beaven, Graham Watson and Ivan Donaldson. Ivan left us early and established his own large family enterprise, Pegasus Bay Winery, near Waipara.

Other intending growers and Lincoln University staff looked at our progress and themselves planted larger areas. Sadly the hardest worker, Brian Hearfield, died at a young age. Allan Cookson, Neville Ackroyd and, later, Terry Hitchings continued the operation for 23 years, long past the intended proving time for a growing experiment. The outdoor work was healthy and the associated social events were often hilarious.

In 1986 two opportunities for travel came our way. A close friend, Ernesto Henriod, who was the chief engineer of the World Bank in Washington, asked if we could exchange houses for six weeks. He had married a New Zealander and they were keen that their children should see something of their grandparents and the country. Ernesto had the responsibility of arranging hundreds of million of dollars annually of civil engineering work in Third World countries. We enjoyed the comforts of a delightful house in Washington and managed to see many parts of North America. It appeared that Ernesto wanted his eventual retirement to be in Christchurch.

While in Washington I was invited to give lectures to a mountaineering convention in Japan. Both Enid and I attended the three-day event and stayed on for four more days, accepting generous hospitality in beautiful mountain surroundings. In their homeland the Japanese look after their forests with great care, despite the clear felling they carry out in other parts of the South-East Asia. We also spent a day with Mrs Satow and her party from the 1960 visits.

·||·

A year later I was climbing a ladder to inspect a problem on my garage roof when the bottom of the ladder slipped on a concrete slab. I fell back and did something serious to my back. Enid ensured that I did not move while she rang for an ambulance. A scan in the hospital revealed there were numerous radial cracks in one vertebra. The experts said if I did not move for six weeks it would heal and I would make a complete recovery. I took this very seriously and did recover. Of course the many hospital visitors had plenty to say about me falling off a low roof. Hearing initially of my injury, they had expected at least some spectacular crash off a great mountain.

In the late 1980s I often reflected on the expeditions of the 1950s. Back then few had given a thought to gathering together again, but in late 1989 a surprise fax arrived from Paris. It explained that in the following year there would be functions at Chamonix to celebrate the fortieth anniversary of the first ascent of Annapurna. A decision had been made to invite all those who were first on the summit of the other 13 of the 8,000-metre peaks as well. All expenses were to be paid. I accepted and said my wife also wished to attend. A polite reply said Enid would be welcome but her airfares would not be paid.

We planned a tour that included seeing most of the 1955 Kangchenjunga expedition members and staying with friends in London. On arrival in Chamonix we heard the background to the planned reunion. The leader of the original expedition had been Mayor of Chamonix and also Minister of Sport in Paris. He and the town citizens wanted to make the gathering an outstanding occasion. Maurice Herzog was the sole survivor of the Annapurna expedition, and no one wanted a festival for just him and eight widows. Originally 41 invitations had been sent out and there were 39 acceptances, including one from Sir Edmund Hillary. When it was found that Ed was willing to make some small television appearances, there was a flurry of interest from the media and from many sponsors. The invitation list was then extended to include some other expedition leaders, such as Lord Hunt (Colonel John) and Chris Bonnington; also Junko Tabei, the first woman to climb Everest, and many others.

We stayed in a luxurious hotel and had vouchers to all the town's restaurants, the equipment hire shops and some of the aerial ropeways. There were four days of 'formal' sessions (which were not very serious) and one when we were able to get onto a mountain. George Band and I headed for Mont Blanc du Tacul, along with the Japanese Manaslu trio and three Americans. We thought we were making good progress out in front when we were passed in complex terrain by four younger Russians who had the previous year traversed the three main peaks of Kangchenjunga.

Most enjoyable were the evening gatherings in restaurants. We usually found ourselves with the other English speakers – the Americans and British. The Americans had brought their wives, but none of the Brits had. I had previously met the three American men as they passed through Christchurch on their way to Antarctica. I had had many discussions with Charles Houston, who led the 1953 K2 attempt. He has kept up with the research on high-altitude physiology and is still consulted on space travel.

Reunions

Ed Hillary was worked very hard. He was on stage for various discussion groups and hundreds of villagers and tourists wanted his autograph. We saw him in a street one morning at about 10 o'clock. He looked grey and was shivering. A television company had helicoptered him to the summit of Mont Blanc and had him addressing a live Paris breakfast programme. He had not been given a jacket, nor any food. They took a very unkind risk. Ed was over 70 and had already been carried out of the Himalayas on three several occasions. With his other obligations he was unable to attend all our restaurant gatherings.

Tenzing Norgay had died two years previously, but four other Sherpas were in Chamonix. They had been attending guiding courses run by their hosts. It was good to see them.

Enid and I had Eurail passes so we took in several days in Spain, Andorra and Austria. The hills behind Salzburg attracted us by day, and at night we absorbed the wonderful music of that beautiful city.

⫘

Although partly retired as an engineer, I kept in touch with a few engineering projects and possible developments. In 1992 there was a serious electric power shortage in New Zealand, at a time when more than half the country's electricity was generated from hydro sources. I decided to express some of my early thoughts about tunnelling through the Southern Alps to bring water to the existing eastern storage lakes. Since my first considerations of this idea at Pukaki in 1948, detailed contour maps had been published. I worked away at several possibilities. As I had no engineering or draughting staff, I approached a South Island firm, Royds Garden, which had already designed hydro-electric schemes. One of the directors was Jim McFarlane, who had visited most of the areas concerned when we were students together. Despite his severe frostbite damage in 1954, Jim had a highly successful engineering career. The other directors were also impressed by my proposal.

Two of us met a delegation of Electricity Corporation of New Zealand (ECNZ) engineers, who allocated money for us to prepare a scoping report, but without doing any river gauging or test bores. The intakes of all the schemes were in national parks or wilderness areas, so it was to be a confidential operation. I explained that any intakes for a tunnel would have a simple gate and a minor weir. There would be no suggestion of storage dams in such sensitive areas. Roads and dwellings would not be necessary either. Each of the rivers considered for diverting was a tributary of a large Westland river that had no highly significant downstream operation on it.

We flew over the possible routes and prepared a report on a scheme that would go a considerable way towards resolving the irrigation and electricity problems on the eastern side of the South Island. It was sent to Wellington. Later a reply came stating that it was of great interest but that the money earmarked for the next three years was all going into gas generation. Then ECNZ vanished and a number of power supply and transmission companies appeared to take its place. Few of them seemed to be considering new large-scale schemes.

In 1993 we made a booking to join a party doing an 18-day walking tour in the mountains of Bavaria and Austria. We found that by travelling early to London we could also attend the Everest fortieth anniversary, and if we stayed on after the tour I could visit some hydro-electric tunnelling schemes in Europe.

Two functions were held in London. One I attended, at the Alpine Club, was for a limited number of members. The other was a lecture by some of the original climbers. While it was good to catch up with several friends from the past, it was a rather low-key affair compared with the Annapurna celebrations at Chamonix. Absent from these happenings was Charles Evans, John Hunt's deputy leader and my leader on Kangchenjunga. We visited him at a rest home in the Lake District, where he was in a wheelchair in an advanced stage of disseminated sclerosis. His brain and sense of humour were as alert as ever, however. It was our farewell to Charles. I did not see him again.

The walking with friends in Europe was relaxed and happy. After a few days our leader agreed that those with more experience could aim at higher objectives. It was early in the season so the huts were not crowded and there were many spring flowers still evident. One day in a higher valley two of us came across the hardly noticeable intake of a tunnel. Inspection of the map showed that it took water 40 kilometres to a power station, and was joined on the way by two other branch tunnels.

Enid and I left the others in Munich and went to Norway by train. I had previously made contact with a Swedish firm drilling a tunnel near the border with Norway, just south of the Arctic Circle. We went to the site and for three days I was able to watch the drilling machine in operation and discuss the many environmental issues around which the scheme had been designed. The excavated rocks from the outlet all went by railway to a crusher for making road foundations and concrete. At the intake end a control gate would divert a fixed flow to the original river. A strict regime of tidying the sites at the project's end seemed reasonably obtainable.

We travelled to Berlin for three days, not very long after the wall had been removed. Then we flew back to our more normal life in New Zealand.

·ǁ·

But not for long. For the fortieth anniversary of the Kangchenjunga climb in 1995 we decided to walk to the base camp for the route to the north of the mountain and also visit the campsite at the start of the Yalung Glacier. This latter place was the nearest reasonable destination for a trekking group. The actual base camp for our original expedition was three hard days further up the glacier and involved specialist skills. From the original party of nine just three of us felt able to undertake the 19-day walk: George Band, Neil Mather and myself. We invited eight others to accompany us, including Bill Packard, Tony Astill and Enid.

In the intervening 40 years several tortuous roads had been built in the Nepalese foothills and some landing strips had been cleared for light aircraft. By using these we could avoid the approach through Darjeeling, which had been the easiest route in 1955. With a small team of porters in an ancient bus we wound through beautiful country, but it was difficult to appreciate from inside the hot vehicle being driven at its maximum speed. On the second day at a very steep location the rear axle broke. To our amazement the driver carried a spare and in an hour we were moving again – just as fast.

Soon after walking began Enid was having difficulties. The heat, the altitude and the stressful approach drive all contributed to her decision to leave us to it. Bill Packard was also having problems from the medication he was using. They decided to go back together, and walked for three days to Sukita, from where an aircraft could take them to Kathmandu. I had mixed feelings about this turn of events, but if I left the main group they might feel there was not much point in continuing the journey.

It all turned out happily in the end. Enid and Bill reached Kathmandu, rested a few days and then joined a New Zealand group travelling by bus to Lhasa in Tibet and, after a week, flew back to Kathmandu. My party walked to the two main objectives and enjoyed the experience. I went up to 6,400 metres and I seemed to acclimatise at about the same rate as I had done 40 years earlier.

Then another reunion was mentioned. Jim Milledge from the 1960 Silver Hut group decided to arrange a gathering from that expedition. The hut itself of course was now in use high in a valley in Sikkim. Jim found that of the original 22, only 11 were still alive, and of these, just four considered themselves well enough to walk for nine days to an altitude of 5,000 metres.

Jim persisted and invited a few others to make a party of 10. Again I asked Bill Packard, who went well this time. We gathered in Darjeeling at the end of November 2000. The town had become very crowded and the smoke haze over the Indian plains on most days had come up to the 1,800-metre altitude of the old shopping area. It had once been a great retreat destination for English families who lived down on the plains. Several high-quality schools were built for the children of the English occupiers of India. The schools are still there and are very popular. The pupils now are mostly Indians from affluent families.

Most of us this time were members of the Alpine Club (UK);

ages ranged from 29 to 75. The other three from the Silver Hut expedition were Jim Milledge, Mike Gill and John West, who was then a professor at an American medical university. We drove through deep gorges in Sikkim and then slowly walked our way up a heavily forested spur towards the Nepalese frontier, some 32 kilometres south of Kangchenjunga. Most of our supplies were being carried by yak, so I missed the joking, singing and chang drinking that accompanied travel with Sherpas. However, yaks have their good points and it was a relief to be carrying very little at my advanced age.

On the fourth day we were above the forest level and for a short period had a clear view of Kangchenjunga, which did not look particularly high because it slotted into a gap between two neighbours of 7,600 metres, which were quite close to us. Finally we came to a large terrace that had 18 buildings of very mixed quality on it. This was one of the principal training bases for Indian army mountain units. It was also the base for the climbers who sign on for the Himalayan Institute courses in Darjeeling.

The Silver Hut stood at the top end of the cluster of buildings and the whole area was temporarily deserted for the winter. We looked inside the hut and there appeared to be no evidence of any further medical research, which was the reason the hut had been given to India 40 years previously. There were cupboards containing everyday medical supplies. The three others from the expedition, all doctors, were a little disappointed that it now appeared to be just a clinic for ailing soldiers.

Socially the trip was a great experience. We had long discussions on a great variety of subjects from our varied backgrounds. Perhaps the most interesting participant was John West, with his accounts of consultations with both American and Russian space travel gurus. He had watched launchings in America and in Russia, and briefed crews for both countries. Griffith Pugh's forecasts to me in 1958 had come true.

We returned by the same route and went our separate ways, thinking we had done quite well, considering the fate of many of those of the 1960 expedition. I imagined I would not be seeing these mountains again.

However, in 2004 a message came from Kathmandu stating that if any of the summit members of the 1955 Kangchenjunga expedition were still alive, they would be invited to a festival and seminar for the fiftieth anniversary of the climb. Fifteen months out from the events two of us replied that we would attend, and the third said he would probably go. Joe Brown, the fourth member, did not want to travel overseas.

Much later in 2004 the Himalayan Club sent invitations for celebrations in Mombai and Kolkata the following February. At about the same time a message from London advised me to go on for events there, just after the Kathmandu celebrations. It would be a busy year.

Enid joined me on these occasions. The Indians at Mombai generously took us for four days to the cooler air of the Ghat mountains, south of their city, to recover from jetlag before facing the traffic hazards and eager audiences at the first big event. John Jackson, also from the Kangchenjunga expedition, was lecturing for the British Council in Mombai, so he and his wife joined the Bands and Hardies for a three-week tour. The lectures seemed to be well received and there was no problem about English being the language on all occasions. We were entertained in the same clubs I had been in half a century earlier. The colonial rulers might have departed but many of the old traditions remained. The well-guarded cricket ground near the centre of the city is a hallowed treasure, regularly used by eager and knowledgeable thousands.

In Kolkata our reception was equally enthusiastic. A special book had been written on the history of Kangchenjunga and there was an issue of postage stamps to mark the anniversary. Again our hosts entertained us at the exclusive clubs and in the grounds of some luxurious residences. Each day we were required to sign hundreds of autographs. Evidence of technical advances in India were all around us. One occurred during a lecture that was frequently interrupted by cellphone conversations. The president stood up and announced that he would charge the next culprit with a fine of 1,000 rupees. This brought much applause.

At the end of our obligations we went to the hill station of Darjeeling. By this time some of us were finding the large numbers of people and the hot seasoning of the local food was causing strains on our elderly bodies. We were glad to get up to the hills after a night train journey with little sleep. We had three nights at an ancient Victorian guesthouse where a fire was lit each night in our rooms and everything was managed in a calm, efficient style. Enid had never seen Kangchenjunga except from the air on her flight from Lhasa in 1995. Each of our daylight ventures was planned to be in sight of the massif if the Indian smog or the high-altitude clouds ever cleared. On the third morning there was a partial clearance for an hour and Enid saw how it towered up, away beyond deep dark foreground gorges.

Many Sherpas live in Darjeeling. Some of them and the staff of the Himalayan Institute looked after us. Just two of the local residents who had been on the 1953 Everest expedition were still alive, but the matronly daughters of some of the others were in attendance, dressed in their best traditional garments. It was comforting to see that they all appeared to have prospered and were no longer the tea plantation coolies of the 1940s.

Finally a farewell party was held for us in Mombai, which went on until 2 a.m. Enid and I staggered exhausted to our plane and it took a few days back in Christchurch for our stomachs to return to normal.

Three months later we landed at Kathmandu airport. Across the main entrance was an enormous white banner: 'Congratulations and felicitations to the first summiteers of Kangchenjunga'. There our hosts were mostly Sherpas, who now owned large trekking companies and some of the city's hotels. I had been on expeditions with the fathers of most of them, and I was very happy to renew links with some who had been children at the Himalayan Trust schools on some of my visits.

Formal invitations had been issued and we were given typed itineraries. On the first evening we gathered in the grounds of the British Embassy, where Enid and I had been entertained in 1955. Nicholas Bloomfield, the ambassador, explained that this was a popular posting and he was the nineteenth to be there since the Summerhayes family we had known.

In the morning there was an opportunity to see part of the central city and then attend a press conference, which lasted for an hour. After about 20 minutes some of the questions became rather political, aimed at city administrators rather than the mountaineers. The language changed from English to Nepali and our chairman handled the questioners with some skill. He was Ang Tsering, son of the man who had accompanied the 'yeti' scalp to America and Paris with Ed Hillary in 1961. George Band was leading a trekking party in East Nepal and had been due in Kathmandu on the day we arrived. Owing to clouds at the Sukita air strip, no plane had come to collect them and they missed the first two days in the city. However, Tony Streather and his son did appear.

Next morning we attended one of the large parade grounds to prepare for a street procession. Our eyes bulged at the sight of three open horse-drawn carriages and hundreds of people in uniform. We found later that there were four marching bands, hundreds of army people, sports teams and city administrators in the slow-moving line. Enid, the ambassador, Tony Streather and I travelled in the first carriage. Behind us were three others who had been on Kangchenjunga expeditions in the 1990s, from Georgia, Slovenia and France. They added a broader feeling of its being a truly international occasion. For over an hour we wound through the city, under more 'summiteers' banners, until we were escorted to an open-air dais for speeches and presentations. Halfway through these George and Susan Band arrived from the airport.

The procession re-formed and we proceeded through more narrow streets. In the afternoon and during the next day there were seminar sessions. One highlight for me was a paper read by one of the Sherpas we had assisted to take a course at Lincoln University. After leaving New Zealand he had worked in Nepalese national parks and then gone on to gain a doctorate. His presentation was on the religious significance of many of the Himalayan sacred summits. During an interval a delegation of three men from Sikkim cornered Tony George and me. Could we attend a similar event in Gangtok in September? It would be timed to coincide with an annual two-day ceremony for the blessing of the gods of Kangchenjunga. Fares would be paid by the Tourist Department of Sikkim and a helicopter would transport us into the remote city, which has no airport.

In Kathmandu we all stayed at the Yak and Yeti Hotel, which has accommodation for 600 guests. One wing was closed for the year. At breakfast about 20 appeared in the dining room. We were told that there had been a substantial decline in tourist and trekker numbers, but no Nepali wanted to suggest a reason. I formed my opinions after talking to some of the few Westerners who had been there in recent years. The so-called 'Maoist Rebellion' is widespread in the country. Walkers have been robbed but not physically harmed. They have seen government buildings burned and schools closed. The fact that the Crown Prince murdered most of the royal family four years ago has added to the impression that Nepal is a land not fully under control. The brother of the murdered king now wears the crown and four months before our visit he had disbanded Parliament and adopted direct rule. There was a strong military presence and our friends were reluctant to discuss the subject.

Some of the seminar sessions were held at the Hyatt Hotel, which was also nearly empty. One series in the conference room was attended by the new crown prince and princess from another branch of the royal family. Security was very tight and there was a prominent military presence. Before the royal party arrived all 400 in the conference room had to go out and then come back in through metal detectors. Most of the audience were Nepalis, with a few from India. There were probably just 10 who were foreign mountaineers.

At the seminars I was nearly always followed by a stream of autograph hunters. They were particularly keen for me to sign programmes or first-day covers with specially issued Kangchenjunga stamps. Some gathered at the Yak and Yeti foyer and sent up messages for me to sign bundles of 50 or so envelopes.

We greatly enjoyed our days in Kathmandu but were sad to see its main industry, tourism, in such a sad state. It is still a charming city with many delights of scenery, buildings, restaurants and tours to sample. The people are helpful and charming. Language is seldom a problem. Yet I had thoughts of what it was like in 1954 when I was there with Charles Evans. Then there were very few motor vehicles, no hotels, little noise and the early Buddhist architecture was prominent. The temples are still there, but they are often in the shadow of a multi-storey tasteless monster. On the better side there is now a water supply and the sewers are piped and do not smell so badly. But still in 2005 in the early evenings the electric lights would be dimmed as the load came on the system, and every hotel room had candles ready for the next blackout.

We flew on to London and then the Lake District for restful days with Mike and Sally Westmacott. They had both been with me at the Silver Hut reunion and had visited us at home. Mike had been on the 1953 Everest expedition and was secretary of the Alpine Club for many years. From them it was not far to an hotel in the mountains of Wales, where all the Kangchenjunga expedition were to gather with their children and grandchildren, making a party of 40, with hosts who had been arranging such gatherings every five years since Everest was first climbed. John Clegg was not well enough to travel, and Neil Mather required much physical support. The years were catching up on us. For the survivors of the older generation the bond was as strong as it had ever been. Enid and I went by train to London and stayed with Roger and Ann Chorley in their Kensington residence. Ann had been the secretary at the RGS for three of the expeditions with which I had connections. Very special was the evening they took us to dine at the heavily guarded House of Lords, where Roger Chorley is a member.

In London the Alpine Club hosted a memorable evening and next night the four who had been on the summit all shared in delivering a lecture, in considerable detail, on the 1955 climb. This was to a full house in the Royal Geographical Society theatre, which seats 730. The introduction was by Sir Richard Attenborough. Finally we parted from the crowds, had a day at the exciting new buildings on the South Bank, and flew to Vienna and Budapest for seven days. We happily absorbed the music, galleries, architecture and good food of older Europe.

On the way home in the plane we decided that I would accept the invitation to Gangtok, especially as George Band was also likely to go. Brcause it would be a smaller version of the Kathmandu events, we decided to see if our daughter Sarah Jane would like to come instead of Enid, which of course she accepted.

Sarah's available time was limited, so we had to fit everything into 10 days. At Kuala Lumpur airport, after waiting many hours, we were told at 1 a.m. that our flight had been cancelled. This upset our onward passages, including the helicopter coming to Bagdogra to meet us. Messages were sent ahead and, after a brief sleep, we went on to Kolkata and the remote airfield of Bagdogra, one day behind schedule. The helicopter arrived and we were the only passengers as we wound up a steep forested gorge, viewing the incredibly awkward places where Sikkimese build houses and eke out a living. The higher summits were hidden by clouds. An impressive welcoming committee met us, putting best-quality silk scarves over our shoulders. The very tall, silver-headed George Band had arrived the previous day. Regrettably, Tony Streather had withdrawn.

A comfortable, modern four-wheel-drive vehicle, a guide and driver were supplied for our whole stay in Gangtok. On one day we visited three monasteries along narrow dusty one-way roads. These buildings were in quite good repair, and we were told the costs had been met by American donors and much of the construction had been done by Chinese artisans. Although we were at altitudes between about 1,500 and 2,000 metres, the temperatures were surprisingly high. We had brought some warm clothing, which remained packed until the last day.

Gangtok is on a steep ridge on an old trade route to nearby Tibet. It was where yak transport changed over to Indian mules or porters. Now it has grown rapidly as a tourist resort, a site for select high schools and a very large Indian army base. There are shops that sell Indian and Tibetan goods. Most of the buildings are new and of not great architectural merit. Although on a hill like Darjeeling, Gangtok has none of the old dignified British hotels schools and churches of that town. It also has none of the great old Buddhist temples that are so important for Kathmandu.

The seminar began and we gave our lectures. The open sessions did not go far into the past activities that George and I had described. The audience was very critical of the poor sewerage systems of the country, the absence of an airfield, the delays and restrictions on travel in valleys near Tibet, and the absence of building quality controls, especially in an earthquake-vulnerable land. These matters were of great interest to me. The general information about the seminar had made much of the sacred status of the final summit of Kangchenjunga, or Kangchendzonga as it is spelled in Gangtok. The fact that we had stopped a few metres short of the true summit received much favourable comment. In our lecture people could see photographs of the small terrace near the top, with no footprints going above it.

On most evenings we were invited to eat with the senior organisers in one of their houses. It was interesting to see the quality of the better dwellings and to participate in the relaxed conversations. However, the participants were virtually all male, and the only food was hotly flavoured Indian. Bottled water and a good local beer were served and these suited me in the hot climate.

On our second-to-last day our guide said we could look at more monasteries the next day. We declined and said we wanted to go up towards the Tibetan frontier to get a view of Kangchenjunga. Neelam, our guide, asked for our passports and Indian visas to make the application for access to the road. In the morning Colonel Kumar said he would like to go up the same road.

Neelam said we should go ahead as it would take hours for the colonel to obtain permission. This amazed me. Kumar had retired from the army but he had been the leader of the second ascent of Kangchenjunga, in an Indian army party that climbed it in 1977, 22 years after us. I would have thought an army permit would be no problem for him.

George, Sarah, Neelam and I were driven further up the ridge after our early breakfast. Soon we came to a well-marked viewpoint and there was our mountain, standing clearly above rolling clouds and above its neighbours. All the visible ridges were on the

Sikkim side. Our route in Nepal was totally obscured. Sarah was delighted that she had even this view and was able to grasp the scale of the mountain.

Soon after we left we encountered the first army checkpost, where our documents were inspected and copied. We were driven up a precarious narrow road, past many army establishments with notices forbidding photography. The only other vehicles in view had army insignia. There had been many slips, and dozens of gangs were making repairs by hand. Sarah commented that women seemed to be doing most of the work. At just over 3,650 metres we were above the forest line and in more open glaciated terrain, feeling much cooler and happy to be away from the heat of Gangtok. There were some untidy shops beside a small lake and the third (and last) army checkpost. A track went partway around the opposite side of the lake and a notice at the end forbade access because of landmines.

Ever since the squabbles with Chinese troops in the mid-1960s, when I had my call-up, the Indians have been most sensitive about their frontiers. Sikkim had been an independent state with Tibet on its ill-defined northern boundary. But it had no army, virtually no roads and limited contact with the outside world, and the Indian army moved in and has stayed there. India also took over some of the government departments, and Sikkimese who talked with me were not totally clear how much independence they had. In Kolkata and Mombai eight months previously we were usually introduced as the men who first climbed the highest peak in India. My printed invitation to Gangtok was on the paper of 'Tourist Department Government of Sikkim'.

In the early afternoon we drove down the ridge and stopped at a good viewpoint for a late lunch. While we were there Colonel Kumar and his wife arrived on their way up. They had just obtained their permits. Until such red tape is reduced there will not be many keen trekkers going to Sikkim. Even the high frontier to Nepal has restrictions on it, forbidding trekkers from travelling from one country to another.

We returned to our comfortable hotel, said our farewells and were helicoptered back to the sweltering heat of Bagdogra. There were no plane breakdowns on the flights home to Christchurch.

During the long flight there was much time for reflection. The re-unions provided the opportunity to see many old friends and also to meet younger people who will face the problems associated with conservation, tourism and an overcrowded world. In a long life I have had many high points, not just mountain summits and I appreciated the chance to share the Sherpas' way of living. I have added a small contribution to the knowledge of mountaineering history. During my many years I have had countless rewarding friendships and loyal support. To all who have enriched my life I owe a deep sense of gratitude.

BIBLIOGRAPHY

Astill, Tony, *Mount Everest: The reconnaissance 1935. The forgotten adventure*, published by the author, 2005
Bowie, Nan, *Mick Bowie: The Hermitage years*, Reed, 1969
Evans, Charles, *A Doctor in the XIV Army*, Leo Cooper, 1998
Evans, Charles, *Kangchenjunga: The untrodden peak*, Hodder & Stoughton, 1956
Franco, Jean, *Makalu*, trans. Denise Evans, Jonathan Cape, 1957
Gill, Michael, *Midsummer Madness*, Hodder & Stoughton, 1969
Hardie, Jack, *From Timaru to Stalag VIII B*, Macpherson, 1991
Hardie, Norman, *In Highest Nepal*, Allen & Unwin, 1957
Herzog, Maurice, *Annapurna*, trans. Nea Morin, Jonathan Cape, 1952
Himalayan Journal, various
Hooker, Joseph, *Himalayan Journals*, Murray, 1854
Hunt, John, *The Ascent of Everest*, Hodder & Stoughton, 1953
Jackson, John, *More than Mountains*, Harrap, 1957
Johnston, Alexa, *Sir Edmund Hillary: An extraordinary life*, Penguin, 2005
Mahoney, Michael, *Harry Ayres*, Whitcoulls, 1982
Mulgrew, Peter, *No Place for Men*, Reed, 1964
New Zealand Alpine Journal, various
Patterson, Robin, *A Sock in my Stew*, R. Patterson, 1990
Smythe, Frank, *The Kangchenjunga Adventure*, Gollancz, 1931
Steele, Peter, *Eric Shipton*, Constable, 1998
Temple, Philip, *The World at their Feet*, Whitcombe & Tombs, 1969
Tilman, H. W., *Mischief in Patagonia*, Cambridge University Press, 1957
Tuckey, Harriet, 'Dr G. Pugh', manuscript, 2006
Ward, Michael, *Everest: A thousand years of exploration*, Ernest Press, 2005
Wilson, Jim, *Aorangi*, Whitcombe & Tombs, 1968

INDEX

Abbott, Rear Admiral 253
Adams, Ernest 59
Adams, Ruth 49, 51, 54, 56, 59, 65
Adare, Cape 256, 260
Akaroa 291, 296
Alack, Frank 39
Alpine Club (Japan) 206
Alpine Club (NZ) 42, 102, 190, 238
Alpine Club (UK) 86, 93, 96, 103–4, 126, 141, 184, 300, 308
Alpine Express 266
Allen & Unwin 177, 211
Ama Dablam 115, 199, 202, 213–14, 238, 284
Ama Dablam Col 200, 204
Ambu Lapcha 115, 182, 189
American Embassy 193
Amin, Idi 130
Anderson, Peter 267
Andrews & Beaven 40
Ang Temba 247
Ang Tsering 306
Annallu 175
Annapurna 86, 126, 157, 297–98
Antarctic Division of DSIR 267
Antarctic Treaty 253
Arbroath 84
Armidale 252
Arthur's Pass 23, 34–37, 41, 94, 209, 212, 229, 241, 244, 267
Arun Khola 106, 168
Arundel 84
Ashurst, Harry 58
Astill, Tony 29, 301
Attenborough, Sir David 308

Aufschnaiter, Peter 127
Avalanche Peak 41
Ayres, Harry 39–40, 49–73, 95–96, 184

Badian, Ernst 37
Bagdogra 309, 311
Balfour Glacier 56, 64
Ball Glacier 62
Ball, Mike 104, 108
Baker, Philip 32
Ballantynes 44–45
Band, George 130, 138, 141, 147, 149, 152, 154, 156, 298, 301, 304, 306, 309
Banfield, Ambrose 37
Banfield, Bruce 35–37
Barcham, Pat 203
Barun 105, 106, 108, 109, 112, 113, 114, 123, 172, 214
Baruntse 115, 130
Bavaria 300
Beardmore Glacier 225
Bealey 28
Beaths 45
Beattie, Mt 49
Beattie, Sir David 282, 294
Beattie, Lady 294
Beaven, Bill 38–40, 42–46, 50, 58, 64, 72–73, 82, 92, 102, 112, 115–16, 130, 181, 228
Beaven, Don 38, 296
Ben Lomond 30
Bennecke, Udo 249, 254
Berlin 301

Bhote Kosi 120
Bickley 85, 90, 92, 98–99
Bismarck 87
Bloomfield, Nicholas 305
Bohney, Hans 232–33
Bolton, Melvin 241–42
Bombay (Mombai) 85, 104–05, 113, 123, 129, 135, 178, 304, 311
Bonnington, Sir Christopher 298
Bourdillon, Tom 92, 97, 103, 127–28, 133, 145, 159
Bowie, Mick 51–61, 64, 71
Boyd, Lance 21
Boyd Neal Orchestra 42
Boyle Base 15, 18, 20
Bradshaw, Margaret 277, 288
Brewster, Mt 228
Bridge, Alf 128
Bridge, Bill 219
Bristol 88
Brodrick Pass 39
Brown, Joe 130, 139, 143, 147–49, 152–54, 304
Brunner, Mt 38
Bryant, Dan 29, 103
Budapest 308
Burns, Mt 47
Byles, Marie 39

Calcutta (Kolkata) 135, 141, 178, 192, 202, 304, 309, 311
Callander, Bob 25, 30
Canada 239, 251, 293
Canberra 100
Canterbury Opera 36
Canterbury University Council 231
Cape Royds 164
Captur Gun 195
Carnegie 31
Cashmere High School 293
Cass River 29
Cawley, Bob 41
Chamlang, Mt 107, 172–73, 181
Chamonix 148, 157, 297–98
Changmitang 203

Chepua 169, 171
Chief 253, 257, 259
Choba Bomare 122
Cho Oyu 71, 92, 94, 108, 176
Cho Polu 114
Chorley, Lord 98, 307
Choyang 106
Christchurch 20, 27, 32, 34, 49, 50, 52, 59, 68, 183, 186, 189, 205, 211 218, 228, 234, 254, 264, 268, 271, 293, 305, 312
Christian, John 78
Chukhung 115
Clark, Margaret 212
Clegg, John 130, 145, 153, 162, 308
Climbers' Club 96
Coast to Coast 266
Cobb River 72
Coberger, Oscar 94
College House 32, 36
Colon 79
Conquest of Everest, The 102
Cook, Derek 228
Cook River 34, 56, 64
Cook, Mt 13, 29, 35, 49, 50, 66, 71, 81, 190, 207, 209, 212, 219
Cookson, Allan 296
Coombs, Dora (née Hardie) 31
Coombs, Jack 31, 63
Copland Pass 60–61, 65–66, 68
Cora Lynn 28, 264, 295
Coronation 100
Cotter, Ed 73, 83
Court Theatre 36
Crash, Mt 260
Crawford Range 23
Croll, Wynne 219, 221–22, 226, 229, 233
Cromwell 224
Crowley, Aleister 141
Crown Prince of Nepal 307

Daily Mail 130, 165
Dalai Lama 201
Dampier, Mt 65

Index

Darjeeling 113, 124, 136, 148, 159, 174, 237, 301, 302, 309
Dart River 30
Davie, Frank 246
Debenham, Ann (Lady Chorley) 18, 134, 308
Debenham, Frank 98
Dechen, Mt 39
Delhi 127
Department of Conservation 26
Dick, Doug 54–55
Dienhardt, John 193, 198, 202, 204
Dingboche 116, 177, 182
Director, Antarctic Division 268, 276
Doctor in 14th Army, A 125
dogs in Antarctica 219, 222–24, 226, 281, 283
Doidge FV 72
Doig, Desmond 192, 203
Donaldson, Ivan 296
Doole, Phil 71
Douglas Pass 41, 68
Douglas Rock Hut 68
Dowdie, Miss 102
Drake, Mt 51
Dry Valleys 290
Dudh Kosi 172, 196, 198
Dumji 116, 173
Dunedin 31, 43
Dun Fiunary, Mt 63
Dyrenfurth, Norman 173, 177, 182
Dyrenfurth Oscar 173

Edgar Jones, Marjorie 39
Edinburgh 84
Edwards River 34
Eiger 185
Elcho Col 64
Electricity Corp (ECNZ) 299
Elie de Beaumont, Mt 64, 73
Elliott, Mt 39
Ellis, Murray 184, 238, 253, 256, 261
Ellis, Roly 91
Erebus, Mt 246, 249, 269, 284
Ernest Adams Ltd 59

Eskdale 102
Esk Head Station 24, 25
Evans, Sir Charles 86, 94–97, 101–20, 126, 134, 138, 142–146, 150–59, 161, 174, 181, 300
Evans, Lady Denise 126
Evans, Lloyd 85, 99
Everest expeditions *1921* 107
 1935 29, 107
 1951 91
 1953 94, 95, 100, 123, 131, 148, 166, 180, 308
Everest, Mt 71, 107, 156, 184, 202, 235
Explorers' Club 252

Fettes College 40
Fettes, Mt 40
Field-Dodgson, Robert 32
Field Enterprises Corp 188
Findlater, Jock 20–26
Footstool, Mt 46
Forest Service (NZ) 91, 241
Forsyth, Jim 58
Fox Glacier 56, 58, 65
Frame, Janet 31
Franco, Jean 126
French Pass 295
Fuchs, Sir Vivian 186
Fuji, Mt 190, 206–9
Fyfe Pass 38, 46

Gair, Harry 222, 224
Galway, Professor 31,
Gangtok 138, 309–10
Gardiner Hut 50
Gardiner, Ian 232
Gangway 153
Garhwal 72, 161
Georgia 306
Ghat 180
Ghunza 138, 160, 162–64
Gill, Mike 194, 203, 205, 238, 253 257, 303
Gillies, Bruce 57, 66–68

Gladiator, Mt 38
Gokyo 176, 249
Gold Coast 129
Goodfellow, Basil 95
Goodman, Benny 42
Government House (Wgtn) 293
Graham, Peter 68
Graham, Stephen 57
Green Hut 199, 203
Greenland 57
Gulch Creek 54–59, 65
Guyler, Jack 74, 80
Gyalgen 166, 169

Hall, Rob 284
Hallett Cape 185, 252, 254, 261
Hamilton, Neil 56, 59
Hardie, Anne (Harvey) 31
Hardie, Carol (Halvorsen) 14
Hardie, Dora See Coombs, Dora
Hardie, Enid (née Hurst) 37, 42–44, 60, 65, 73, 80–84, 90, 99–104, 116, 127, 134, 141, 159, 162, 178, 180–81, 188–89, 196, 212, 228–29, 234, 246, 264, 267, 285, 294, 297, 301, 304–5, 309
Hardie, Gladys (Revie) 13, 31
Hardie, Jack 13, 14, 30–31, 33
Hardie, Jim 12
Hardie, Sarah Jane 185, 229, 246–47, 266, 309, 311
Hardie, Ruth (Wells) 121, 185, 229, 246–47, 266
Harper Pass 23
Harrington, Larry 252, 257
Harris, Sir Percy Wyn 184
Harrison, John 184, 190, 213–15, 228, 230, 233–34, 264
Harrison, Annie 264
Harrer, Heinrich 127, 184, 230
Harrow, Geoff 104, 111, 115, 181
Hawksley's 89–94, 98, 104
Hawley, Elizabeth 240
Hearfield, Brian 41, 233, 291
Henderson, Jill 137

Hercules 252, 273, 276, 283, 285
Hermitage 38, 44, 46, 50, 56
Herschel, Mt 252, 256–57, 264
Herzog, Maurice 126, 298
Heyerdahl, Thor 78
Hillary, Sir Edmund 49–62, 73, 83, 92–95, 100–5, 108–9, 123, 145, 183, 187–88, 192, 197–98, 200, 204, 213–15, 236, 239, 248–49, 252, 261, 298–99
Hillary, Lady Louise 248, 252
Hillary, Belinda 248
Hillary, Rex 240, 245
Himalayan Club 127, 304
Himalayan Mountaineering Inst. 137, 216, 303, 303–04
Himalayan Trust 173, 216, 240, 245, 248, 251, 267, 305
Hitchings, Terry 296
Hobart 275
Hodder, Ross 241
Hodder & Stoughton 135
Hokitika 36
Holland, Sid 72
Hong Kong 189
Hongu Kola 115, 180, 214
Hooker Glacier 50
Hooker Hut 67
Hooker, Mt 40, 164
Hooker, Sir Joseph 161, 164
Hope family 229
Hopkins, Mt 39
Horder, Lord 97
House of Lords 308
Houston, Charles 131, 148, 298
Hum 120
Hughes, David 37, 39, 84, 93, 246
Hunt, Lord (Colonel John) 86, 95–98, 102, 123, 127–28, 136, 149, 184, 298
Hurst, Colonel H. C. 85
Hurst, Enid see Hardie, Enid
Hurst, Vonnie 44, 45, 85, 90–91
Hurunui River 18
Hurunui South 20–26

Index

Huxley, Mt 228
Hyatt Hotel 307

Iceland 87
Iles, Bett (Godfrey) 60
Indian Army 187, 309
Indian checkposts 129, 150, 165–66, 169, 171, 214
Indian Air Force 150
Indian High Commission (Wgtn) 237
Inglis, Mark 71
In Highest Nepal 177
Institution of Civil Engineers 130
Institute of Architects 206
Invercargill 185, 233
Irishman Creek 62
Ironside Glacier 256
Irvine, Andrew 43
Island Peak 115
Isobel, Mt 35
Iswa Kola 107, 111, 172

Jackson, David 29–30, 68, 103
Jackson, John 130, 139–40, 142, 151, 158, 161, 165, 304
Jannu, Mt 153
Japan Society 212
Jellicoe, Mt 49, 53
Jenkinson, Bruce 253, 257
Jogbani 105
Joint Committee 95–96, 123, 128, 184
Johnson, Elizabeth 98
Jones, Emlyn 97
Jubing 173, 178, 196
Junbesi 178, 196
Junbo Tubei 298

K2 124, 139, 298
Kala Patar 182
Kalaugher, Eddie 49, 52, 62, 64, 69
Kami Doma 178, 181
Kangchenjunga Adventure, The 140
Kangchenjunga 86, 122–23, 131, 134, 139, 163, 174, 186, 194, 215–16, 231, 298, 301, 314, 310

Kanchenjunga: The Untrodden Peak 135
Kaniere Lake 36
Karangarua River 41
Kathmandu 104, 106, 109, 112, 115, 118, 124, 170, 174, 177, 192, 194, 199, 200, 213, 239–40, 243, 246, 306–7, 310
Keen Vic 15, 18–19
Kempe, John 104, 123, 140
Kempe's Buttress 140, 142
Khumbu 112, 161
Khumjung 116–18, 174–75, 180, 236, 241
Khunde 174, 240–41, 248
Kirk, Norman 241, 244
Kiwi Saddle 18
Kodari 122
Koktang 139
Kolkata *see* Calcutta
Kon-Tiki Expedition, The 78
Kraus, Lili 42
Kuala Lumpur 309
Kumar, Colonel 310–11

Lahari, Larry 203
Lake Station 31
Lamabager 120
Lambert, Raymond 94
Lambie, Miss 102
Landsborough River 14, 30, 37–40, 44–47, 62
La Perouse 49–54, 65–66
Lewis, David 54
Lewis Pass 15, 23
Lewisham 84
Lhasa 122, 302
Lhotse 107, 113, 157, 174, 177, 205
Lincoln University 100, 245, 306
Liverpool 104, 127, 134–35
Logan, Hugh 264, 268
Long, Bill 108
Loveridge, Cyril 70
Low, Mt 49–50
Low R. S. 49

Lowe, George 73, 83, 92, 94, 101–15, 194
Lucas, Bing 241–44
Lucknow 126
Lukla 173, 180, 246, 250
Luney 45
Lyminster 84

Macbeth, Marion 229, 246
Macbeth, Norman 229, 246
McCormack, Peter 57
Macdonald, Doug 212
Macdonald, Joe 134, 162, 178, 182
Mace, Snow 66–68
McFarlane, Jim 34, 37, 39, 41–46, 64–66, 71, 82, 104–16, 124, 217, 228, 299
McKay, Isabel (Tocker) 53
Mackinnon, Tom 130, 136, 148, 151, 159
McKinnon, John 240–41, 248
McLeod, David 264, 266
McMurdo Base 185, 218–19, 224–26, 252, 262, 268, 274–75, 277, 279
McNair, Jack 15–19, 33
Magellan 49, 126
Mahon, Peter 246
Mahon, Sam 246
Mahoney, Mike 39, 68
Makalu, Mt 105–06, 156, 168, 172, 184, 187, 194, 213
Makalu 126
Mallory, George 43
Manaslu 207, 210, 298
Marlborough Sounds 228
Marshall, Keith 191, 206, 210, 267
Masherbrum 213
Mason Lake 21–24
Mather, Neil 130, 138, 148, 151, 301, 308
Mead, Jack 20–28
Menlungtse 119
Mera 180
Mesopotamia Station 28
Messner, Reinhold 157

Milford Sound 30
Milledge, Jim 195, 213–16, 302
Minto, Mt 261
Mirgin La 162
Mischief in Patagonia 103
Mishra, Hementa 241, 243
Mombai See Bombay
Mont Blanc 298
Montana Group 296
Monteath, Colin 267–68
Montgomery, Jock 228
Morin, Denise *see* Evans, Lady
Morris, Dick 20–23, 27
Morris, James 100, 170
Morris, John 212
Motueka 31
Motwani, Captain 203
Moubray Glacier 257
Mukut Parbat 91
Muldoon, Robert 294
Muldoon, Thea 245, 294
Mulgrew, Peter 184, 201, 213–17, 238, 249
Munich 301
Murchison Glacier 38
Murray, Lyn 29

Namche Bazar 118, 170, 173, 175, 201, 214, 243
Nanda Devi 43
Nanga Parbat 126
Nangpa La 176
Nango La 164
National Gallery 90, 99
National Geographic Society 195, 202
Natusch, Gilbert 72
Nau Lekh 116
Neelam 310
Nelson 293, 295
Nepal, Government of 92, 170, 238, 240
Nevison, Tom 188, 213–15
New Zealand High Commision in New Delhi 245
New Zealand Listener 64

Index

Normalair 128, 131
Norman, Bob 263, 291
North Esk 25
Norway 87
Norwich 101
Noyce, Wilfred 127

Odell, Noel 43, 82
Ohara, Katsuro 210
Ortenburger, Leigh 213–15
Otago University 31, 43
Outlook 12
Oxford 85–86

Pache, Lieutenant 141
Pache's Grave 142
Packard, Bill 42, 47, 84, 85, 91–93 97, 103, 113 301–02
Pakistan 131
Panama 76–79
Paphlu 248
Paris 297, 306
Pasang Dawa 113
Patterson, Robin 27
Pearl, Max 240, 248
Peel, Mt 27
Pegasus Bay 296
Pemba Dorji 151, 158, 174–75
'Perishable, the' 33
Perkins, Marlin 204
Pethangtse 113
Planters' Club 136
Pole Station 225
Pollux, Mt 228
Porter, H. E. L. 67, 93
Porters Pass 28
Powell, Guy 183
Priestly, Sir Raymond 260
Prince Charles 88
Press (Christchurch) 20, 27, 36
Pugh, Griffith 92, 94, 97, 108, 128, 133, 165, 186–87, 202, 205, 214–17, 303
Pukaki, Lake 45–48, 50, 60, 61, 68 88, 299

Qatar 129
Queen Mary 100

Rakaia 37, 227
Rangitata Diversion 37
Rangitata River 28, 38
Rawlinson, Tony 97
Raxaul 125, 179
Reagan, Ronald 281
Rees Valley 30
Riddiford, Earle 30, 38–46, 57, 58, 64, 72, 73, 82, 91–92, 96, 228
Roberts, Jim 180
Robertson Bay 260
Rolleston, Mt 35, 41, 184, 228 229, 234, 253, 264
Rongbuk Monastery 201
Romanes, Wally 195, 200, 204–5, 213, 238
Rose, Jim 238
Ross Dependency Research Committee 292
Ross Ice Shelf 225
Ross, J. C. 164
Routeburn Valley 30
Rowling, Bill 245
Royal Geographical Society (RGS) 92–98, 102, 106, 134, 183, 308
Royal Society Range 261
Royds Garden 299
Ruapehu 72
Russell, Scott 93, 96

Sagarmatha Park 248
Salzburg 299
Sandhurst 130
Satow, Tel 207, 211, 297
Savoy Hotel 90
Schneider, Erwin 174
Schumacher, Captain 274–75, 281–82, 294–95
Scott Base 185–86, 222, 263, 269 277, 279–85, 288, 291
Scott, Robert Falcon 185, 225, 260, 281, 289

Sears Roebuck 236, 255, 259
Sedua 106, 112
Sefton, Mt 38, 44–46, 66
Semple, Bob 48, 69
Seppelts 98
Seven Years in Tibet 184
Seville 99
Shackleton, Ernest 225–26, 281, 286
Sherpa Trust 211, 258
Shimizu 206
Shipton, Eric 91–94, 102–3, 112–14, 119, 184, 190, 200
Sienna 91
Sikkim 104, 138, 116, 306
Silberhorn 65
Siliguri 136
Silver Hut 192, 199–216, 302, 308
Singh, Captain 170
Smythe, Frank 140
Southampton 80
Southland 261
South Pole 186, 202, 224, 256, 277 292
Spence, Mt 47
Spenser, Martyn 63
Squires, Peter 234
State Services Commission 261
St Andrews Hut 18
St Christopher's School 101
Steele, Peter 95
Stevenson, Harry 91
Strang, Jim 251
Strang, Lindsay 240
Strang, Peter 234, 253, 258, 260–62
Strong, Dr 125, 240
Sturdee, Mt 49
Sukita 302, 306
Sullivan, Mick 49–50, 58–60
Summerhayes, Sir Christopher 182, 306
Summerhayes, Lady 124, 182
Sumner Lake 20
Swan, Larry 108
Sweden 301
Switzerland 91

Tabai, Junko 298
Tait, Mrs 13
Tasman Glacier 38, 212
Tasman, Mt 49, 56, 65
Tangboche 174, 180, 199, 200, 247, 250
Taylor, Don 42
Tekapo, Lake 29, 62, 271, 282
Tenzing, Aila 149, 166
Tenzing, Dawa 105, 123, 137, 158, 175, 194, 196, 199, 299
Tenzing, Norgay 94, 100–1, 137, 149, 216
Tesi Lapcha 118, 198
Thame 201
Third Eye, The 141
Thompson, Priestly 91
Those 179
Thudam 168
Tilman, Bill 84, 103
Timaru 11, 12, 28, 30, 36, 222
Timaru Boys' High School 13, 14, 25, 30
Times, The 94, 97, 102, 138, 165, 170
Tipta La 164, 167
Tirich Mir 131
Tocker, Ken 35, 53, 229, 246
Tocker, Isabel 53, 229, 246
Todd, Colin 104, 115–16, 130, 181
Tokyo 189
Torres, Mt 49
Townsend, Mt 38
Tozer, Fred 29–30, 40
Trade Aid 239
TranzAlpine Express 266
Trappitt, Constable 52, 61
Trumper, Mrs 25
Tuckett's Col 46, 66
Tunzelmann, Nick von 232
Tweedie, Beverley 212

Ulrich, Geraldine (Packard) 42, 65, 73, 82, 85
University of Wales 125
University Tramping Club 35, 41

Index

Urkien 113, 137, 141, 152, 163, 169, 174, 177–82, 194, 204
US Air Force 188

Vancouver, Mt 49
Vanda, Lake 291
Varcoe, Garth 269
Victoria Station 93
VIP groups 270, 276, 280

Wager, Lawrence 184
Waikato 134
Waimakariri River 35, 37, 264
Waitaki River 45, 72
Wall, Gerry 53, 56
Walungchang Gola 164, 166
Warburton, Ralph 57
Ward, Mike 95, 97, 189, 203, 213
Ward, Mt 47, 64
War and Peace 166
Waring, Marilyn 282
Webber family 229
Webster, Don 29
Welcome Flat 60
Welcome Pass 67
Wellington 73, 182, 189, 206, 245, 245 252, 279, 294, 300
Wells family 229

Wells, Marty 247
Wells, Richard 229
West, John 203, 217, 303
Westmacott, Mike 308
Westmacott, Sally 308
White Col 36–37
White, Mike 253, 258
White Star Hotel 30
Wigley, Harry 52
Wilberforce River 33, 36
Wilkins, Brian 104, 109, 111, 124
Williamson, Billy 69
Wimset, Nathlie (Badian) 37
Wilson, Jim 234, 238
Wilson, John 231, 232
Wilson, Malcolm 231
World Book Encyclopaedia 188, 236
World Wildlife Fund 241
Wylie, Charles 98

Yak & Yeti Hotel 121, 307
Yalung Glacier 137, 139, 143, 159, 170
Yates, Roy 232
Yeovil 128, 131, 186, 198

Zemu Glacier 157
Zermatt 91